A million candles have burned
themselves out.   Still I read on.

—Montresor.

MORGAN'S RAID

BOOKS BY ALLAN KELLER

MADAMI (with Anne Putnam)
GRANDMA'S COOKING
THUNDER AT HARPER'S FERRY
MORGAN'S RAID

Brigadier General John Hunt Morgan

MORGAN'S RAID

. . . . . .

by

Allan Keller

 THE **BOBBS-MERRILL** COMPANY, INC.
A SUBSIDIARY OF HOWARD W. SAMS & CO., INC.
Publishers · INDIANAPOLIS · NEW YORK

To

K.M.E. & I.E.K.

Give me another horse : bind up my wounds.

—SHAKESPEARE

Contents

Illustrations

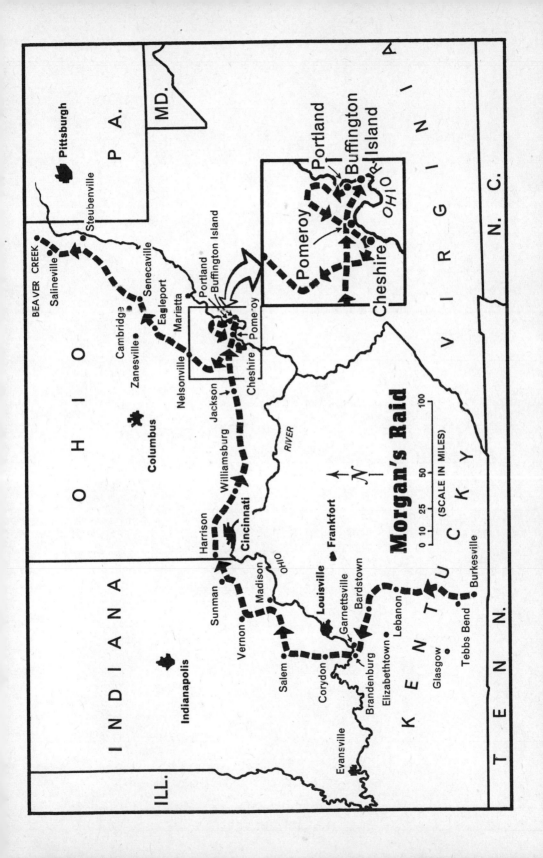

Morgan's Raid

(SCALE IN MILES)

0 10   25   50   100

FOREWORD

JOHN HUNT MORGAN's great raid north of the Ohio had always intrigued me as one of the most exciting events of the Civil War. But what drove me to undertake the writing of this full story of that invasion was an anecdote told me by a little old lady then 102 years old.

She was known as Auntie Waterman and lived two doors away from my wife's childhood home in Pomeroy, Ohio. One afternoon, on just such a scorching July day as the one when Morgan fought his way past Pomeroy on his famous ride, Auntie was reminiscing about the Rebel raider. She described how the Ohio farmers and villagers hid their horses in caves and coal mines to keep them out of the Confederates' hands. Her own father was ready to lead his two mares into a mine when his daughter appeared with a favorite doll under each arm.

"Hide them well," she urged her father. "I don't want Morgan to get them."

From that day on I knew I had to write the story of Morgan's raid, not only as a military movement, but as an event that left its mark on thousands of Northerners for whom it was their only actual brush with war.

Many persons have helped me in assembling the material from which this book was written. Their kindness was unending and I gladly list their names herewith, making it clear the while that what faults and sins exist are not theirs, but mine alone.

Miss Elizabeth Babcock, *The World-Telegram and Sun,* New York, N. Y.

Dr. Guy J. Blazier, librarian emeritus, Marietta College, Marietta, O.

Miss Elizabeth O. Cullen, librarian, Association of American Railroads, Washington, D. C.

Wade Doares, librarian, Graduate School of Journalism, Columbia University, New York, N. Y.

Mrs. William B. Downie, Morningstar, O.

15

Richard K. Gardner, librarian, Marietta College, Marietta, O.

Miss Lenore Giles, Middleport, O.

Edison Hobstetter, Pomeroy, O.

Miss Beatrice Kelly, Ferguson Library, Stamford, Conn.

Mrs. Helen Nease, Pomeroy, O.

Dr. James W. Patton, director, Southern Historical Collection, University of North Carolina, Chapel Hill, N. C.

Mrs. Lauretta Ravenna, assistant librarian, The *World-Telegram and Sun,* New York, N. Y.

Charles W. Reamer, managing editor, *The Messenger,* Athens, O.

Matthew Redding, librarian, *The World-Telegram and Sun,* New York, N. Y.

Mrs. Emerson W. Siddall, Marietta, O.

Monroe Stearns, managing editor, The Bobbs-Merrill Company, Inc., New York, N. Y.

Mrs. Pat Thoren, Minersville, O.

Sylvester Vigilante, New York Historical Society, New York, N. Y.

It is almost futile to try to express the devoted assistance and guidance given me by my wife, but I am happy to acknowledge the obligation. Without her support I would not have brought the book to completion.

ALLAN KELLER

Darien, Connecticut

MORGAN'S RAID

CHAPTER 1

Break-out at the Cumberland

THE GENERAL'S TENT was pitched just off the road from Burkesville to Somerset. Up and down this Kentucky road moved infantry, cavalry and artillery, couriers, ambulances and sutlers' wagons as the grim business of war went on in Kentucky and Tennessee. For several hours, however, there had been almost no movement on the highway, and Brigadier General Samuel P. Carter was making good use of the peace and quiet by working on his dispatches.

He became aware of hoofbeats and wondered what foolish cavalryman was punishing good Federal horseflesh when there was obviously no need for haste. Then the horse was reined to a halt in front of the tent. The General lifted the flap and stepped out into the afternoon sun. Both horse and rider looked utterly spent. The animal was reeking with foam and slobber, heaving with each breath. On its back was a woman, her habit torn and mud spattered, her veil gone and her black hair cascading down her back almost to the saddle.

"Will you alight, Madam?" asked the General.

"Not until I see General Carter," said the woman. "I am in haste. Every moment is precious."

"I am Carter," said the officer.

"John Morgan, with two brigades, has crossed the Cumberland near Burkesville and is marching on Columbia," said the rider, her words coming in a rush, as if she were afraid she would faint before she had delivered her message.

"A Union scout, wounded and unable to ride further, came to my home and asked me to inform you," she went on. "I have ridden without stopping, hoping I would be in time."

It was a dramatic moment—almost melodramatic—but it was based on

19

hard fact. Brigadier General John Hunt Morgan, with 2,460 Confederate cavalrymen, had pushed through the feeble perimeter of scouts and mounted patrols the Federals had posted along the Cumberland River and was on his way north through the heart of Kentucky.

As it turned out it really wouldn't have mattered whether the lady had brought the news or not. By the time hostlers had rubbed down her mount and walked him until he was cool, other riders had brought word to substantiate hers. By nightfall the telegraph wires were hot with orders passing back and forth, setting a pursuit in action.

There was a bit of wry humor in it all. General Carter, in command of Union troops at Somerset, was going to have almost nothing at all to do with the chase after Morgan. If things had gone differently the year before he might have been the one ordered to ride hell-for-leather after the elusive Rebel raider. But Andrew Johnson had written Abraham Lincoln disapproving Carter's promotion to major general, suggesting instead that the former navy lieutenant be sent back to sea. Other men would lead the hounds already baying at the hare's heels.

When he set out on his longest and most famous ride Morgan was already one of the South's great heroes. A *beau sabreur* in the old tradition, with a plume on his hat and a laugh on his lips, he had bedeviled Union forces from the Alabama border to the Ohio River. Cutting in behind Federal lines, bypassing heavy troop concentrations, he had burned bridges, wrecked railroads, sacked supply trains and disrupted military timetables throughout Tennessee and Kentucky.

His exploits resembled some of Robin Hood's and some of Francis Marion's. He had captured Union officers in their beds, whipped forces twice as strong as his own by using tricks and ruses, and had a strange way of turning up far inside the enemy lines where least expected. He loved to ride and fight. A very devout man, he once halted his column in the midst of a cross-country chase with the Federals not too far behind and attended divine services in a small country church.

He had carried guerilla warfare to the enemy, fomenting disorder and delays wherever he struck. His tactics were far ahead of his time. He had no use for the picture-book cavalry charge against massed infantry or parked guns, sabres glinting in the sun. He thought of his men as mounted infantry. They did most of their fighting with rifles and pistols, on the ground, after their thoroughbred Kentucky horses had taken them where they wanted to go.

In the Confederacy he was as beloved as Jeb Stuart. He was likened to

20

Robin Hood—and was just as elusive. Southern women vied for the honor of sewing the colors and guidons he carried into battle, and many songs had been composed about his exploits.

In this last war where chivalry and courtliness could still be found amid the smoke and grime and blood of conflict, John Hunt Morgan was to the South one of the fairest and bravest of knights. One of his men wrote of him:

"General Morgan was a magnetic man, of pleasing personality, very handsome, his manner genial and gracious, his face an open book. A dark moustache drooped over his laughing mouth. His face [was] lighted by a pleasant, perennial smile. I never saw him other than neatly dressed. His extreme sociability won the hearts of his men and their undying affections . . . Riding along the column he would talk in a jovial, free and easy way, putting his cavaliers in the best of spirits. He was the Marion of the Civil War."

His two brigades were recruited from both classes of Southern patriots. Some were sons of planters, merchants, professional men and regular army officers, but most were farmers and poor men.

"Some were in what had been spotless white linen, now badly worn, some in blue homespun," wrote a contemporary observer. "Some wore jackets. Some had long coats, some frock coats and many no coats at all. Side by side with the 'clay-eater' rode the handsome and finely mounted lord of the soil."

These were the sort of men who made the Confederate cavalry, in the first years of the conflict, perhaps the finest mounted arm in the history of war. But in 1863 the prestige that had been won in the early battles had begun to slip away. The odds against the Rebel cavalry were growing. Union horsemen were learning from their opponents, and their advantage of greater numbers was becoming an unbeatable burden for the Southerners. It was difficult to find good remounts, harder yet to find forage for them, and always the Union regiments could make good their losses faster and easier than they could in Dixie. At least half of Morgan's men had joined up riding their own horses, carrying old muskets, squirrel guns or only sidearms. They had had to whip the Yankees to get hold of modern carbines.

Regardless of these disadvantages, they were a superb group of fighting men. Riding light, they found their provisions, not in their own commissary depots, but in the supply trains of the enemy. They had uncanny success in taking what they needed.

21

Now they were on the attack again; 2,460 men against the thousands the northern colossus could throw in their path.

The raid was John Morgan's own idea. It was born of military necessity, but a sort of derring-do and extremism, like twin midwives, sat at the bedside.

As summer reached its halfway mark that year, Braxton Bragg and his army lay at Tullahoma, far down in Tennessee. This was the army the Confederate high command hoped would prevent the Federals from cutting the South in two. Opposing Bragg was a superior, stronger Northern army under General William S. Rosecrans. The only other force the South could count on was the wholly inadequate one led by General Simon Bolivar Buckner in East Tennessee. Against this small force the Union was mustering better than 25,000 men under General Ambrose Burnside. In Washington Henry W. Halleck, Lincoln's general-in-chief, was bombarding Burnside with telegrams ordering him to attack and wipe out Buckner so that Rosecrans could get on with his major thrust through the mid-South.

Wherever the Confederates looked between the Alleghenies and the Mississippi, the skies were dark and ominous.

Morgan went to Bragg with a proposal that he detach two of his three brigades from scouting duty in front of Tullahoma and make a swift raid into Kentucky. If there was anything Morgan hated, it was being tied to the infantry. "Freedom and movement, together with every kind of action are the life and soul of that arm," wrote a great cavalry tactician in World War I. "[It] is bound to decay if it does not succeed in adapting itself." Morgan felt the same way in 1863, for he was far ahead of his times in his concept of cavalry warfare. He wanted to cut his forces adrift, to penetrate the enemy homeland and to subsist it on enemy country.

Braxton Bragg was a good general, but often so cautious he bordered on timidity. He conferred with his cavalry chief, General Joe Wheeler, about Morgan's proposal and finally gave grudging consent to a raid limited to Kentucky, with a secondary purpose of bringing back supplies for his men and fodder for his horses.

To the ebullient, hard-riding Morgan this was only half a loaf. He told his first lieutenant and brother-in-law, Colonel Basil W. Duke, who commanded the First Brigade in Morgan's cavalry division, that Bragg had given him carte blanche to raid anywhere in Kentucky, to gather up badly needed supplies and to keep the Union cavalry under General

22

Henry M. Judah busy and off balance. But he also told Duke what was really in his mind.

He said he intended to cross Kentucky, lead his men into Indiana and Ohio, and strike terror in the hearts of Northerners who deemed themselves safe and secure from war across the broad Ohio. The Rev. Mr. T. D. Moore, a Methodist chaplain who served with Morgan's division, said the raid was planned as retaliation for Benjamin Grierson's invasion of Mississippi, but there was more behind Morgan's planning than mere revenge. With perceptive awareness, the cavalry leader realized the clamor and fear he could scare up by such an invasion would draw off more troops from in front of Bragg than localized forays into the Blue Grass.

Duke did nothing to dissuade his brother-in-law. He wholeheartedly approved of the invasion and said so after the war on many occasions. Together they made their plans, keeping them secret until a few weeks before the raid started, then taking into their confidence only Colonel Adam R. Johnson, commander of the Second Brigade, and the various regimental leaders. To the men in the ranks this was to be another raid into Kentucky—the state that was home to four out of five of the soldiers in the division.

Morgan rendezvoused his forces at Sparta, Tennessee, in early June. At the last minute, however, Bragg ordered him to intercept a Federal column then moving into eastern Tennessee. Several weeks were lost. The significance of those lost weeks was not to be realized to the full until near the end of the long ride North.

When his men returned from their patrol the Rebel partisan leader ordered them forward to the banks of the Cumberland, a few miles over the line into Kentucky. For several days they scouted the area, looking for places to ford, and confusing the patrols sent out by Judah to prevent that very movement.

All through the last days of June it rained heavily and the Cumberland became a swollen, fast-moving stream, its muddy waters cluttered with logs, fence rails and other debris. As so often happens with war's fickle ledger, this had its debit and its credit sides. While it represented a troublesome barrier for Morgan's division, which had no handy means of crossing, it also served to lull the Union forces into a feeling of false security. Surely, the Yankees thought, no one would be foolhardy enough to try to cross the Cumberland until the freshets were over and the crest had passed downriver.

23

To Morgan, the consummate bluffer, the situation was made to order. He called in his supply wagons, had the axles greased, set the blacksmiths to work shoeing the horses, issued leather for repairs to saddles and harness and waited impatiently for the opportune moment to attempt the crossing.

In the middle of the activities Captain Samuel Taylor rode into camp. Earlier that summer Morgan had sent him north to study the roads and particularly the locations of the best fords on the upper Ohio. Taylor had scouted into Indiana and Ohio and had come back at just the right time with the needed information.

Taylor told his chief that the Ohio, too, was high, much higher than it had been in the memory of many rivermen, but he thought it would be much lower by the time the raiders reached that part of Ohio opposite Virginia. The captain used the word "Virginia" from habit. Only a few days before, on June 20, the western portion of that state had broken away from the Old Dominion and set up its own government as the state of West Virginia.

Taylor had seen nothing of Captain Thomas Hines who had gone into Indiana on a similar mission, but no one took this amiss. Tom Hines was an able scout and there was no reason to assume he would have any trouble. He had extricated himself from many a tight spot in two years of war.

Work went forward at a fast pace in the camp. Men who had been home on furlough or sick leave rejoined their companies. A new addition to the division, the 5th Kentucky Cavalry, under Colonel D. Howard Smith, arrived just before Morgan himself returned from a last-minute conference with Bragg at Tullahoma.

All through the encampment men joked and spread rumors as to their destination. They said farewell to wives and sweethearts, putting on a great show as if they knew the General's plans down to the last detail. They polished their guns, curried their horses, oiled their saddles and boots, then waited impatiently, knowing the strange sensation that comes to fighting men as excitement and fear gnaw at raw nerve ends on the eve of battle.

Morgan gave them something to do on the first day of July, something that tired their muscles but steadied their spirits. He had them dismantle the supply wagons and field artillery so that they could be ferried across the Cumberland in the few flatboats and canoes the scouts had acquired for that purpose.

24

That night the wagons were taken across the swollen river and re-assembled in a thicket. But the guns had to wait; Morgan didn't want his artillery on one side of the river and his troops on the other.

Early on the morning of July 2 the division began the crossing. The First Brigade under Duke went over in the area between Irish Bottom and Scott's Ferry opposite Burkesville. Colonel Johnson led the Second Brigade across at Turkey Neck Bend, several miles downstream. Duke had a larger number of men, but he had the responsibility of the four guns—his own section of two 3-inch Parrotts, and Johnson's section of two 12-pounder howitzers.

The Cumberland, muddy and full of floating debris, was better than a half mile wide and out of its banks on both sides. Treacherous eddies swirled in the backwaters and the current in midstream ran swift and ugly. Men lashed canoes and rowboats together, rolled the heavy guns on the unstable rafts, and managed to get them to the northern bank without having the craft swamped. Mules and horses were driven into the river and forced across while the cavalrymen, some in boats and some swimming, got across the best way they could.

If Judah had posted vedettes along the river, instead of keeping them close to his encampment at Marrowbone, the crossing might have become a bloody business. As it was, the 6th Kentucky and 9th Tennessee were over the river with the two Parrotts before any real resistance developed. Then a few Northern patrols gathered on a road below Burkesville to fight a delaying action while couriers went for help.

Downstream, at Turkey Neck Bend, Johnson's Second Brigade ran into serious trouble. There were only a few frail canoes. All the men had to swim, using the canoes, fastened together with fence rails, as rafts on which they piled their arms and saddles. The current was swifter around the bend, and driftwood menaced the swimmers, some of whom seized the tails of the nearest horses to keep from drowning.

Sergeant Henry Lane Stone, who had grown up in Greencastle, Indiana, but who had made his way through the Federal forces to join Morgan, was one of the first to cross the Cumberland.

"Twelve of us crossed with our saddles in one canoe," he said. "The surging waters lapped within inches of the edge and once in a while it came over."

There were scattered enemy patrols on the far bank, and enemy pressure built up more rapidly against Johnson. His men found themselves forced to fight as soon as they moved inland from the river. The sound of firing brought more Federals, and soon the Second Brigade was engaged in a sharp fire fight deep in the woods.

Duke's men at Irish Bottom, several thousand yards down from Burkesville, ran into patrols sent out by Colonel Frank Wolford, of the 1st Kentucky (Union) Cavalry. Captain Tom Quirk and a detachment of Morgan's scouts were fired on while still in the water.

To Bennett H. Young the scene was one of excitement and glamor. As the flatboat in which he crossed bumped against the bank, bullets flicked through the willow branches just over his head. Quirk called for a charge, and the men still in the boats fired as fast as they could pull the triggers and reload, to cover the advance of their friends scrambling up the slippery bank.

"Those who had clothing on rushed ashore and into line," recounted Young. "Those who swam with horses, unwilling to be laggard, not halting to dress, seized their cartridge boxes and guns and dashed upon the enemy. The strange sight of naked men engaging in combat amazed the enemy. The Union pickets didn't know what to think of soldiers fighting as naked as jaybirds."

The Rebels' superiority in numbers was the vital factor, but the psychological shock of the naked warriors must have exerted some effect on the Union troopers, who fell back, leaving the balance of the First Brigade unmolested as they crossed.

When this sharp skirmish ended, the sound of firing at Turkey Neck Bend grew loud enough for Duke to know Johnson's men could use some help. He sent Quirk and the scouts forward to reconnoiter with the 2nd Kentucky close behind. As the van of the little force neared Marrowbone Creek they encountered a hundred or more Yankees. Firing erupted and Tom Quirk fell from his horse, his left arm badly shattered.

Kelion Peddicord was riding with the scouts that day. All through the long ride with Morgan, young Peddicord kept a diary and before he turned in that first night he wrote in his notebook, "Only one man received a wound, but it was Captain Tom, whose rein arm was broken."

Under Duke's urging the advance kept up its pressure, driving pickets and small patrols before it until the Rebels reached a crossroads beyond Burkesville. By late afternoon the Southerners had 600 men and two of the four guns in position at the road junction. It was none too soon. Colonel Wolford was no man to wait for orders. The scattered reports he had been receiving made it clear that Morgan was moving all of his division across the Cumberland. Realizing that Johnson's brigade was the

26

more exposed, the Union leader sent men to drive it back into the river. However, the road to Turkey Neck Bend from Marrowbone was one of those forming the crossroads where Duke had placed his two guns, and as the Federals galloped to the attack they were stopped in their tracks by two volleys from the Parrotts. Before they could rally, Quirk's scouts, who were angry over their leader's misfortune, joined by a detachment from the 9th Tennessee, struck the Federals in the flank, completing the rout. Like those who had tangled with Quirk's men earlier, the Union troops fled back to Marrowbone Creek.

While the main skirmishing was going on in the vicinity of Burkesville, Lieutenant A. T. Keen led Company I of the 1st Kentucky (Union) Cavalry from Jamestown to Creelsboro, about eight miles upriver from where Morgan's main force had crossed. On the way he joined forces with a detachment of the 45th Ohio Mounted Infantry and started a sweep westward along the stream. Around mid-afternoon he encountered a regiment of Southern cavalry and there ensued a hot running battle for ten or fifteen minutes. The Rebels had all the better of it.

"This was how we learned the Rebels had crossed the Cumberland and broken through our line," wrote Keen.

It was a scout from Keen's force who, though wounded and weak from loss of blood, rode to the home of the woman who put him to bed and galloped off to break the news to General Carter at Somerset.

As the day ended, the Confederates had won most of the scattered skirmishes. Almost all of Morgan's division was safely across the Cumberland—a few men killed, a few wounded and a few drowned. In front of him had been a vastly superior force, but one so confused by his sudden movements, and so convinced he would not try to cross a stream in flood, that the isolated components had been unable to do more than offer scattered, ineffectual resistance.

Looking back at this day, long afterward, George Mosgrove forgot the fatigue, the danger and the disorder. He described Morgan riding on his favorite horse, "Glencoe," and sitting tall and erect in the saddle with Duke just behind him, a flowing plume in his hat. Time and distance inevitably bring about these changes in a soldier's memories.

"In high feather and full song," Mosgrove reminisced, "Morgan's gallant cavalrymen formed in columns, looking toward Kentucky."

It hadn't been at all like that, as any one of the wounded men could have told him. Duke wasn't with Morgan until the shooting had ended for the day. Most of the men had been dismounted, fighting like Indians

27

in the deep underbrush. But it was the end result that counted. Morgan's men were now on their way to the Ohio.

The Rebel guerillas' sally out of Tennessee into Kentucky was made easier by a general lack of co-ordination among Union forces. A week or more before the raiders moved out of Sparta toward the state line, General Edward Hobson and the Second Brigade of Judah's second division had been encamped at Columbia, astride the very road Morgan intended to follow toward the Ohio. Judah ordered Hobson to move west to Glasgow, but when Hobson was almost there Judah changed his mind and told his subordinate to turn toward Tompkinsville. Judah meanwhile marched through Scottsville to mount an attack on Morgan at Carthage, Tennessee, assuming for some reason not clear to his staff that Morgan would stand still to await his thrust. The effect of all this marching and countermarching was to shift most of the Union forces completely out of the Southerners' path.

On July 1 Judah had joined forces with Hobson at Tompkinsville. Hobson's scouts had brought him word that Morgan had started to move and would probably cross the Cumberland at or near Burkesville. Hobson passed this intelligence on to his superior, insisting that Judah give him orders to move immediately on that town to prevent it. Judah instructed him to go instead to Marrowbone, ten miles to the west of Burkesville, hold that town at all hazards and await further orders.

All through these crucial days there seems to have been almost no liaison between Judah and Carter, who was far to the east at Somerset, with a few advance units stationed at Jamestown. One other component of the Union 23rd Corps, the command of Brigadier General James M. Shackleford, then bivouacked at Ray's Crossroads, was near enough to have been used to stop Morgan at the Cumberland, but it received no orders to move until it was too late.

The day before the crossing, as Morgan's raiders were approaching the river, Hobson proposed to Judah that he be allowed to attack the Southerners somewhere near Cloyd's Ferry, nine miles downriver from Burkesville. This infuriated Judah. In a pet at the thought his subordinate was spelling out tactics to him, Judah sent a courier to Hobson with orders to "suspend all military operations" and to countermand all orders for the movement of troops. Judah, a West Pointer, outranked Hobson, a lawyer-turned-soldier, and there was nothing for the latter to do but obey—reluctantly.

28

While the Union leaders were quarreling among themselves the Rebels began crossing the Cumberland. Electrified at last by news of Morgan's breakthrough, Judah, having delayed one brigade for twelve hours and another for twenty-four hours, finally adopted Hobson's second plan calling for an end run to get around and ahead of Morgan. One Union brigade was to be pushed through Columbia and the other sent cross-country through Greensburg. Then they were to unite at Campbellsville and proceed to Lebanon.

As if divine justice were punishing him for his wooden-headed obstinacy, Judah, at this most critical moment, found himself trapped south of the Green River when that stream went out of its banks.

Therefore Morgan crossed the Cumberland with almost no opposition, moved through Burkesville and camped for the night on the Columbia road. His first big hurdle was behind him. His deep satisfaction was communicated to his men and as they sat about their fires they sang "My Old Kentucky Home," ending each chorus with a cheer for John Morgan.

If the soldiers were elated over this early success, the men in the commissary department found it less to their liking. They and their wagons had been dispatched at Bragg's insistence to round up supplies for the army at Tullahoma. They well realized that Morgan had stirred up a swarm of bees and knew they would be the ones badly stung if they tried to escape through the gathering Yankee forces. Seeing no safe alternative, they stayed with the raiders.

Accompanying these men was an old Tennessee farmer who lived on Calf Killer Creek near Sparta. He had taken advantage of the opportunity to get a barrel of salt, which he needed badly for his family and his cattle. He got his salt at Burkesville but learned with dismay that Morgan's division was going on north. The old man wanted to go home, but he knew the way led through a no man's land where a band of bushwhackers under "Tinker Dave" Beattie liked to operate. Beattie waylaid couriers, robbed supply wagons and murdered both Union and Confederate soldiers for their arms and ammunition. His men were the villainous outcasts of both armies.

The old farmer knew, Colonel Duke wrote, "that if he fell into their hands they would pickle him in his own salt," so he, too, elected to follow Morgan's fortunes.

Before dawn of July 3 the raiders, with Colonel Dick Morgan's regiment in the lead, moved toward Columbia. By another road, coming in

29

from the east, some of Wolford's Yankee cavalry was heading for the same town. They were composed of men from the 2nd and 7th Ohio Cavalry, and the 45th Ohio Mounted Infantry.

The opposing forces met on the outskirts of Columbia. Each side, surprised, skirmished to test the other's strength. Some riders fought in the saddle, others dismounted to take cover in buildings at the edge of town. But Morgan's men outnumbered the Ohio companies, and the Ohioans had to retreat.

"We thought it might be a small force we could crush," reported one of the Buckeye cavalrymen. "But when we fired musketry we were answered with grape and cannister; when we fired a few rifle shots we were answered with whole volleys of musketry. We speedily beat a hasty retreat, going as fast as our horses would carry us to Jamestown."

By noon Columbia was in Morgan's hands. All afternoon the Confederate column rode through the village, the rear elements not arriving until after midnight. Men slept in the streets, in the yards and in the orchards behind the houses, feeling secure with Colonel Morgan's regiment on guard several miles to the north. Morgan's men, however, did not feel at all secure. All through the night they could hear the sound of axes ringing in the woods ahead of them and the crash of falling trees. As the scouts patrolled the lonely roads they could visualize the reception the Union forces were preparing for their attempt to cross the Green River.

Back in the village, supply wagons rumbled up from the Cumberland, protected by the last of the cavalry units from Tennessee. These men had spurred their mounts in response to a summons from Morgan as he put his raid in motion. With their arrival at Columbia his force was now complete; there would be losses, but no more reinforcements.

The composition of Morgan's division is shown by a table of organization drawn up by Bragg on June 31, 1863, just a few hours before the raid started. It possessed two brigades, the First, led by Duke, and the Second, to which Johnson had been assigned a few weeks before on his return from a trip to Texas.

Duke's brigade consisted of the 2nd Kentucky, Major T. C. Webber; 5th Kentucky, Colonel D. Howard Smith; 6th Kentucky, Colonel J. W. Grigsby; 9th Kentucky, Colonel W. C. P. Breckinridge, and the 9th Tennessee, Colonel W. W. Ward.

Adam Johnson's brigade was smaller. It was made up of the 7th Kentucky, Lieutenant Colonel J. M. Huffman; 8th Kentucky, Colonel R. S. Cluke; 10th Kentucky, Colonel Johnson's own; and the 11th Kentucky,

Colonel D. W. Chenault. After Bragg's chart was published, Morgan organized one more small regiment, the 14th Kentucky, which he put in command of his brother, Colonel Richard C. Morgan. This unit was attached to Johnson's brigade.

Together with the four artillery pieces commanded by Captain Edward Byrnes, these were the men on whom John Morgan relied to put the fear of God into all of Kentucky, Indiana and Ohio.

CHAPTER 2

"A Bad Day for Surrenders"

THE FOURTH OF JULY was a black day for the Confederacy. On the banks of the Mississippi Pemberton and his men walked out of the defenses of Vicksburg, colors furled and drums muffled, to surrender to Grant's victorious army of the West.

Far away in Pennsylvania, Robert E. Lee led his defeated army away from Gettysburg in a rainstorm so heavy his weary, butternut-clad soldiers claimed the heavens were weeping for the uncounted dead.

On this day, too, John Hunt Morgan, in a serious lapse from sound military judgment, suffered a bad defeat.

Early that morning he had ordered his column into motion with Johnson's brigade in the van. His men had been on the road for only an hour when they learned the reason for the sound of axes the night before. Captain Franks, a Mississippian, rode forward with a patrol from Dick Morgan's regiment and discovered the enemy entrenched at Tebb's Bend on the Green River. In command of the Union force of 400 men was Colonel Orlando H. Moore of the 25th Michigan Infantry.

Moore had selected an ideal location for his defense of the crossing. His camp lay within a horseshoe bend of the stream, in a stand of heavy woods and thick underbrush. There was a trench extending across most of the neck of the peninsula, rifle pits scattered at strategic points, and in front of these positions an abatis of tree trunks and heavy timbers. A ravine zigzagged across the neck of the bend roughly parallel to the abatis, and the Michigan infantrymen had disturbed as little underbrush as possible while erecting the rough stockade.

Colonel Duke considered it the strongest natural defensive position he had ever seen. Flanking movements were out of the question because of the river and the cliff-like banks rising sheer from the water.

The 25th Michigan Infantry had been organized in Kalamazoo. When it went to war there was a ceremony at which officials gave Colonel Moore a silken flag on which loyal Union ladies had embroidered these words: "This flag is given in faith that it will be carried where honor and duty lead." The Michigan soldiers had carried it on their marches but had never unfurled it in battle until this anniversary of Independence Day. The Confederates could see it waving in the slight breeze that blew across the river.

Colonel Johnson sent Cluke with the 8th and 10th Kentucky regiments, across the river to cut off the enemy's retreat and to prevent reinforcements from the north. Next he sent Major Elliott forward with a flag of truce. Elliott entered the Union lines and made a formal demand for surrender. If Colonel Moore had uneasy feelings about the size of Morgan's force he showed no sign of awe to the flag bearer.

"The Fourth of July is a bad day for surrenders," said the Michigan officer, "and I must therefore decline."

As Major Elliott turned to rejoin his companions he heard Moore tell his men what to do when the battle was joined.

"Rise up, men," said the Yankee commander, "take good aim and pick off those gunners."

At Colonel Johnson's command Captain Byrnes opened fire on the stockade with one of his Parrotts. As the round shot tore through the outer revetments, the Confederates dashed forward in a frontal attack— the only way they could get at the enemy. The initial rush carried them to the abatis, but they got no further. A murderous rain of small arms fire cut them down as they scrambled through the dense underbrush.

The 11th Kentucky, in the van of the assault, suffered the heaviest casualties. Chenault stormed the earthwork, firing his pistol and calling on his men to follow, but a Minié ball tore through his brain and he toppled into the abatis, dead. Pinned down by the galling fire from behind the earthen redoubt, the men of the 11th sought what shelter they could find behind trees. After thirty minutes of this, their ammunition was nearly exhausted. General Morgan asked Duke to send Johnson assistance, and the 5th Kentucky charged into the woods—only to be pinned down in its turn.

Byrnes and his four guns were of no use. He would have had to level the entire forest before being able to lay his fire on the Michigan men in their trenches. This was a battle where men on the ground fired, ran forward a few feet and then sought cover to reload. There was enough heroism on both sides to have done credit to a truly critical engagement. For the Confederates it was little more than useless slaughter.

Morgan's men found themselves crowded into a bottleneck. Each group of men thrown into the battle charged forward bravely only to find itself jammed into the narrow corridor where men had to scramble through felled trees, dense underbrush and honeysuckle that tripped them as they labored down one side of the ravine and up the other.

Everything about the battle, from the Rebel point of view, was wrong. It was not the sort of conflict for which cavalrymen are trained, not even Morgan's raiders. Even veteran infantrymen backed by artillery would have found the odds too heavy. After Chenault was killed, a major, two captains, three lieutenants and several noncommissioned officers fell in attempting to rally their men. Before Morgan realized that his effort was being wasted, thirty-six Confederates had been killed and nearly half a hundred wounded. Nor did the Michiganders escape unscathed; nine were killed and twenty-six were wounded, although everything was in their favor.

By noon Morgan knew he had made a grievous mistake. Calling off the attack, he forded the Green River a mile upstream, leaving the Michigan infantry where he should have left it from the beginning—inside its impregnable stockade. Moore and his four hundred men had never presented a threat to two thousand well-mounted horsemen. If they had attacked the raiders, the latter could have avoided them. By-passed, the 25th Michigan would have been no more menace than a regiment a thousand miles away.

Before he quit the field, Morgan sent a courier under a flag of truce asking permission to bury his dead. Colonel Moore gallantly consented and the thirty-six who had ridden so gaily out of Sparta a few days before were interred where they died, under the frowning abatis. The wounded were left with a surgeon who was given bandages and morphine by the Northerners.

Major James McCreary, another Rebel officer who kept a diary, was saddened by the useless bravery of his fallen comrades.

"The commencement of this raid is ominous," he wrote that evening. "Many of our best men were killed and wounded. It was a sad, sorrowful day."

If it was a tragic day for the Confederates, it was the same for the men who had beaten them. It was also a day of rare shock.

A burial party went about its unhappy chores as surgeons bound the wounds of the injured. One of the wounded, who appeared to be a boy still in school, was carried into a tent where a surgeon was working and laid on a field cot. When he cut away the bloodied uniform jacket, the surgeon found what no one should find on a battlefield—his hand detected the beautiful contours of a woman's breast, which neither the tunic nor a tightly-bound linen band could disguise. Hurriedly, the doctor probed for the Minié ball that had ripped into the girl's shoulder. He removed it and bound up the wound; then he called for the chaplain.

Several hours later the girl regained consciousness and told her story. Her name was Lizzie Compton. She was sixteen years old and had left her home in London, Ontario, more than a year before, and made her way from Canada into Virginia, where she enlisted with a group of other volunteers in a Union infantry regiment.

At the bloody battle of Fredericksburg she had been wounded and, because of her sex, dismissed from the service. She recovered and re-enlisted. Once again her sex was revealed, so she crossed the mountains into Kentucky and joined the Michigan regiment as a battlefield replacement.

Lizzie did not tell all the details, but Colonel Moore and his officers could fill in the gaps, for they knew the conditions that existed at most recruiting centers at that time.

There were 200,000 soldiers in the Union army under sixteen years of age. Of these 2,000 were fourteen years old and 300 were only thirteen. States were eager to fill their enlistment quotas, and recruiting officers accepted the word of any volunteer. With so many youthful, beardless patriots joining up, it was no wonder that a girl could fool careless officials. There were no physical requirements to be met, no medical examinations and no documents checked. If a boy wanted to fight and looked big enough to carry a gun, he was accepted.

It was not until the next to the last year of the war that all volunteers had to strip to the waist for a rather cursory medical examination. But this halted the feminine enlistments. Brave they were, these shapely amazons—as they proved on many a battlefield—but immodest, never.

Lizzie Compton's smooth cheeks had been no give away and no one guessed she had used tight corsets and linen bandages to hide her feminine curves. Only when she fell unconscious from a wound was her sex discovered.

When the girl recovered sufficiently to be moved with safety, Colonel Moore sent her under escort to Bardstown, where her convalescence was completed and she was once again mustered out of the Union army. If she fought again she must have gone unscathed. Her name never reappeared in wartime records.

Morgan and his men, never dreaming of the consternation caused by one of their bullets, rode north, passed through Campbellsville without seeing enemy patrols and camped west of Lebanon.

But the chase was on. Behind them the Federal cavalry ceased its game of blindman's buff and started in pursuit. Judah was delayed for thirty-six hours in getting his command across the Green River at Vaughan's Ferry, but he was at last on the move. Hobson and his troops turned north, too, but too far to the west to intercept the raiders. Wolford's small force, roughly handled at Columbia, harnessed up its four mounted howitzers and quit Jamestown at the very hour the quarry was eating its evening meal five miles from Lebanon.

"The night was fine, clear and cool," one of Wolford's blue-coated cavalrymen noted in his journal. "The moon, although occasionally obscured by light, fleecy clouds, gave sufficient light to enable us to see well and clearly all around us so that we were free of apprehension of a sudden attack from any hidden foe."

The hounds seemed more worried than the hares. Morgan's men had been whipped at Tebb's Bend, but it was the infantry that had done it. As they ate their suppers around the campfires on that Fourth of July evening, there was neither criticism of their leader for his bad judgment nor evidence of fear about the powerful force of Union cavalry building up in their rear.

Seldom had warfare seen better horsemen than those who followed Morgan's banner. Most of them were Kentuckians, who had chosen the South when their home state was riven by the debate whether to secede or stay in the Union. Many took their own mounts from the Bluegrass country. They were a strangely democratic body of fighters. Some were wealthy planters, or business and professional men who went to war with their own servants and clad in well-tailored uniforms. Others were farmers in denims and calico shirts or the cheap uniforms which were all the Confederate clothing depots had to offer.

But they all knew horses and rode like circus riders. They had little use for the infantry—the "web-feet." The worst fate that could befall a Morgan raider was to be dismounted. For two years these men had followed their chief with absolute devotion. Even the most ignorant country boy in the division sensed he was a member of an elite corps. Not given to spit and polish, what little discipline and military training they possessed had been instilled by Colonel George St. Leger Grenfell, a British soldier of fortune, who had offered his services to Robert E. Lee, been sent to General P. T. Beauregard's army and then transferred to Morgan's division when he expressed a desire for duty with the cavalry.

Grenfell was no stranger to the art—and the drudgery—of war. He had served with the French cavalry in Africa, as a private in the Turkish Sultan's army; with Garibaldi in South America, and with the Arabs in Algiers and Morocco. When England went to war, Grenfell went to war. He helped crush the Sepoy rebellion in India and took part in the Crimean war against the Russians.

But like most British professional soldiers, he was enough of a martinet to want to see all camps well policed, uniforms clean, guns spotless and the men mannerly and disciplined. Colonel Grenfell served as chief of staff to Morgan for a time, and the latter picked up valuable advice from him on guerilla warfare and operations behind enemy lines. The hard-riding, hell-raising Confederate troopers absorbed much less.

"I never encountered such men who would fight like the devil, but would do as they pleased, like these damned Rebel cavalrymen," said Grenfell. Other foreigners, in other wars, have wondered similarly at the ebullient spirits inherent in American fighting men.

Southerners didn't see eye-to-eye with Grenfell. They thought Morgan's men romantic and most of them would have fought gladly beside "these damned Rebel cavalrymen." While Morgan was on his great Ohio raid, Jefferson Davis raised the conscription age from forty to forty-five because manpower was depleting in the Confederacy, although Morgan had never suffered from any want of recruits. His fame was known throughout the South and hundreds begged for permission to serve under him. Major C. T. Goode, commanding officer of the 2nd Georgia Battalion of Partisan Rangers, wrote an appeal that was typical of others sent to Morgan.

"I write to say that I have a battalion of mounted partisan rangers consisting of five companies now in camp in this city (Macon). The authority for the formation of my battalion was issued under the recommendation of General Joseph Johnston, but the field of operation has not been assigned me. It is the unanimous wish of the battalion to be attached to your command. The record of your chivalry and daring has fired them with enthusiasm and awakened a most anxious desire to share the perils and the glory of 'Morgan's Men' and I now tender you my command with the hope that you may be inclined to accept it. Should you signify your willingness, I imagine that the War Department will readily consent to the arrangement. We are Georgians anxious to be led by you to the banks of the Ohio."

That last line made it look as though Major Goode possessed the power of divination. The Ohio was where Morgan and his men were headed, and a long, long way beyond.

Lolling about the campfires on that warm summer evening near Lebanon, the raiders were depressed by the loss of well-loved comrades. As they had done so often in the past, they called on the General's young brother Tom to sing. Tom Morgan, although only eighteen years old, was a lieutenant and a stout fighter, whose friends admired his rich tenor voice as much as his bravery.

Always gay, he sang several sprightly airs but as the fires died to embers his selections became more sober. He sang *Lorena,* and another with this chorus

> "When this here war is over,
> She's going to be my wife.
> I'll settle down in Alabam'
> And lead a quiet life."

One of Tom Morgan's brother officers was Leeland Hathaway, a boy of nineteen from Mt. Sterling, Kentucky, who had risen in one year to become adjutant in Colonel Dick Morgan's regiment. He was another diarist who never seemed too tired at day's end to jot down his feelings about the events of the preceding twenty-four hours.

"Tom sang 'We Sat by the River, You and I,'" recalled Hathaway. "It could have been a requiem for the dead. He was killed the next day and I always thought that event cast its shadow before . . . and that he felt he was singing his own death chant."

Now it seems that Hathaway must have gone back and added to his comments, or altered them at a later date. At no other time did he call the turn of events so accurately.

Early the next morning Hathaway was ordered to capture several pickets who had been discovered near the camp. He took ten men, passed around the pickets' post, then attacked from the rear. As it was not yet daybreak, the Yankees were all asleep.

"They were surprised and chagrined by their rude awakening," said the young officer. "Then there was nothing between Lebanon and us."

Scouts went forward while Colonel Duke questioned the prisoners. From them he learned that Lebanon was held by the 20th Kentucky (Union) Cavalry under Lieutenant Colonel Charles Hanson. After breakfast the scouts returned and told of encountering outposts from the 8th and 9th Michigan Cavalry which were in bivouac with the 11th Michigan Battery, well out on the Harrodsburg road.

When General Morgan was told who held the town he decided to try to avoid a battle. He knew the 20th Kentucky well. Like most of his own regiments, it was largely made up of men from around Lexington. Many of the Federals were former friends and a few were blood brothers of some of the raiders. They were all good soldiers.

Thinking to win his way by a show of force, the Confederate commander formed his leading regiments in a long double line with the men deployed so they extended a mile out from each side of the Columbia-Lebanon pike. In the dead center Morgan placed his four guns, and at the sound of bugles the whole line advanced until it came within sight of crude breastworks erected at the edge of town. Captain Byrnes loaded his two Parrotts and the two howitzers with round shot and shelled the outlying works. The defenders scurried back into town. Then Morgan sent his adjutant, Lieutenant Colonel Robert Alston, under a white flag to demand the surrender of the Union force and the town itself. Nervous Federals fired at Alston, and some of his own men returned the fire, partly to protect the flag-bearer and partly to show their ardor. Alston walked on into town and to the red brick depot of the Louisville & Nashville Railroad where Hanson and his staff had set up headquarters.

Hanson liked the idea of yielding no better than Moore had at Tebb's Bend. He declined Alston's proposal, whereupon the latter warned that women and children should be removed from the town because Morgan intended to shell it.

Half an hour later Byrnes opened up with all four guns. Because of the position of the depot in the center of the city, most of the shells landed in the upper structure of the building, causing little damage to the command post on the ground floor. One of the Parrotts was moved forward and its barrel depressed, but before it got off half a dozen shots, Yankee sharp-shooters posted in the upper floors of buildings at the edge of town made it too hot for the gunners.

Colonels Grigsby and Ward led the 6th Kentucky and 9th Tennessee in a sweep to the right, to flank the town. Colonel Cluke with the 8th Kentucky and Lieutenant Colonel Tucker, now commanding the 11th

39

Kentucky in place of the dead Chenault, moved out to the left with the same objective in mind.

Just then, Southern videttes rode up to Morgan with news that the Michigan cavalry on the Harrodsburg road was marching to the sound of the guns. The Rebel leader sent a force to interdict this movement and decided the time had come to carry the town by direct assault.

The 2nd Kentucky under Major Webber was given the assignment of taking the depot. Captain Franks led an advance party with the specific chore of capturing a battery of guns located near the station. Hathaway thought there was something strange about Franks' behavior this morning. Normally a brave and gallant officer, the Mississippian seemed to be behaving irritably. Clearly he was not himself. Several of the officers, Hathaway among them, told Franks that the battery he intended to storm consisted only of dismounted guns that were not effective and that to charge them point-blank would bring the men directly under close fire from the depot.

Captain Franks took the objections to his plan as a sign of trepidation and replied very offensively that anyone who did not fancy the job could stay behind. This was a challenge Kentuckians would not take.

In column of companies they charged the battery, yelling and swearing. When they were about seventy-five yards from the depot, the men of the 2nd encountered a withering fire from 200 massed rifles inside the building.

Horses screamed and fell; men tumbled from their saddles—some to seek refuge in the plowed furrows of the field, others to lie forever still. At least fifty cavalrymen were down, and the balance spurred their mounts to get away from the leaden hail pouring from the depot.

Hathaway looked about and saw he was practically alone on horseback. He heard Franks, who was wounded, cry to him that he should try to get the remnants of the advance guard out of its predicament.

"I am killed," groaned the Mississippian.

Bleeding from two wounds himself, Hathaway saw that Captain Gardner and Dick Washam of Quirk's scouts, with whom he had ridden and frolicked for a year, lay dead on either side of him. He turned his mare around and asked for all the speed she could give to take him out of danger, rallying his men as he went. Only a dozen of the men rode out of the field with him.

Hathaway reported directly to General Morgan.

"Where is your guard?" asked Morgan.

40

"This is what is left of us," replied the adjutant.

Hathaway had seven bullet holes in his uniform. The top of his hat was entirely shot away, and he was bleeding from wounds in the left side and the left knee.

As he went to the rear to seek medical aid, Morgan sent Cluke and the 8th Kentucky forward to protect the wounded in the field by the unmanned battery. The sun was now high and the mercury registered in the nineties. The rebels moved forward, dismounted now, seeking what protection they could in plow ruts, fence corners and stands of weeds and brush. For more than an hour the men of the 8th Kentucky inched ahead, squirming on their bellies, choking in the dust, hardly daring to raise their heads because of the deadly shooting from the depot.

Morgan was in a dilemma and knew it. He knew the Michigan regiments were coming up from the northeast, eager to relieve Hanson. There was no time for the artillery to reduce the Federal stronghold and it was clear to everyone that Cluke and his men were in serious trouble.

The solution seemed clear to Basil Duke. He went to Morgan and proposed the execution of a pincers movement. He was aware that the 2nd Kentucky had gained valuable experience in street fighting when Duke essayed a small raid across the Ohio the year before. Duke had reached Augusta, Kentucky, on the bank of the river, only to find it defended by home guards and militia. Trying to reach the landing to seize ferry boats, the 2nd became embroiled in a bitter house-to-house battle. Those who came out of it alive learned a great deal about this dangerous, dirty sort of in-fighting. Duke outlined his scheme to his chief. It called for the 5th under Smith to launch a surprise charge on horseback from one side of the town and an assault by the 2nd, dismounted, under cover of the excitement stirred up by Smith's charge.

General Morgan agreed. Couriers had been bringing news of Cluke's straits. The 8th was running out of both ammunition and water, and the temperature in the open field was at least 100°. The battle had lasted more than four hours from the time Byrnes had lobbed his first round shot into the depot attic.

The raiders executed Duke's maneuver with precision and great spirit. As the 5th rushed into town, the Rebel yell silencing the sound of hoofbeats and scattered pistol shots, the men in the plowed field arose and added their fire to the attack. At the height of the excitement, Webber sneaked his men through the streets to the other side of the depot, aligned his forces, and sent them against the rear of the railroad station.

41

Cavalrymen broke in the doors with gun butts as others fired through the windows at the Federals crowded inside. Within minutes after the attack was launched, Hanson's men were in a box. Smith's men dismounted, and with Cluke's, glad to be free to move again, swarmed around the depot. The defenders sent out a white flag.

Just as victory came to Morgan, his young brother Tom, who had sung so sentimentally beside the campfire the evening before, fell, shot through the heart. Against the advice of his friends, he had exposed himself to lead a group of raiders, firing his revolver and urging the men on. He dashed toward one of the depot windows and fell when a rifle inside spat almost in his face. Another Morgan brother, Calvin, caught him as he fell.

"Brother Cally," whispered Tom, "they have killed me."

Kelion Peddicord, who made the charge with Webber's regiment, evinced surprise that victory had been won so swiftly.

"A street fight," he said, "is one of the most desperate modes of warfare known to the soldier. The advantage is strongly against the storming party."

To S. P. Cunningham, acting Assistant Adjutant General of Morgan's division, the victory was equally surprising and most pleasing.

"We had found it fortified," he said of Lebanon. "We attacked and after five hours of hard fighting, captured it, together with a vast amount of stores, 483 prisoners, one 24-pounder and many fine horses."

News of Tom Morgan's death was not so pleasing. General Morgan had to move swiftly to restrain some of the men of the 2nd Kentucky who sought to take vengeance. Fortunately, the men obeyed his orders, and when the Union soldiers laid down their arms and marched out of the depot not one was harmed. But even Morgan could not hide his personal anguish.

When Colonel Hanson surrendered formally, the Rebel commander nodded gravely and a bit absent-mindedly. He had known Hanson well in Lexington before the war.

"Charles," he said finally, "when you go home, if it is any source of gratification to you, tell Mother you killed brother Tom."

The General turned away to arrange for his brother's body to be buried, and the surrender formalities went on without him.

Bennett Young, who fought with Cluke that day, took no part in the scene at the railroad station. He was busy tending the wound of a companion, Private Vincent Eastham, shot down in the early charge across the plowed field.

Eastham was a strange, taciturn mountaineer from east Tennessee who had never told his own tragic story to anyone but Young. One night around a campfire at which the two were eating he had revealed that he had been a cattle drover on the Wilderness Road, a lonely man, without family or known kinfolk.

While driving a herd of cattle over the mountains, he told his comrade, he had been overtaken by nightfall and had stopped at a house and asked for lodging. There he found a pretty girl and straightway fell in love with her. Tall, gangling and ill-at-ease, Eastham had never mustered the courage to propose to her, but he showed her how he felt by giving her gifts whenever his drover's duties took him past her cabin home. He gave her a pocket mirror, a ring, a garnet breastpin and an occasional pretty dress purchased in the city where he sold his cattle.

Then one day, after a long hike in the dust cloud behind his stock, Eastham stopped at the girl's home and learned from her father that she had married another, less reticent, man. He uttered no complaint, but soon after, riding on a spavined nag he called "Bob-tail," a sad creature compared to the fine Blue Grass mounts in Morgan's division, he appeared in the raiders' encampment and volunteered.

He had been a good soldier; he had not sought death out, but had not tried to avoid it. During the fight for the Lebanon depot, a slug from a Union musket inflicted a mortal wound. Young could do little to aid him as they lay in the broiling heat, pinned down by the heavy firing. After the battle was over his friend carried the wounded man into a nearby house, dressed his wound, and left him there when the cavalry mounted up to ride on. Years later Bennett Young visited the military cemetery at Lebanon and found his friend's tombstone. The regiment was incorrectly given and Young had a stonemason correct it so it read "Vincent Eastham. Co. B., 8th Ky. Cav."

While Captain William Davis and Adjutant Alston rounded up the prisoners so they could be paroled, Hathaway and an advance detachment were pushed through town on the road to Springfield. It looked as if the Michiganders were at last convinced they ought to leave their guns behind and make a dash to Hanson's side. Morgan's men saw no point in fighting them, too, although Duke said they could have been whipped easily in the open. Therefore the regiments were put in motion on the

43

way north without further delay. Those Federals who had not been paroled were taken along. By three o'clock in the afternoon the rear elements had quit Lebanon.

Marching along the dusty road in the scorching afternoon sun was a torment to the prisoners, and some of their captors did not make their plight any easier. Negro servants loyal to their Southern masters behaved the worst of all. "Old Box," Morgan's own body servant, was especially rude. As he rode along on a fine horse belonging to the General he called out to Captain H. S. Parrish, of the 20th Kentucky, "Yank, don't you want to ride?" Finally, one of the Rebel officers reprimanded the Negro and the teasing stopped.

Hathaway wrote in his journal that with two fresh Yankee regiments in pursuit, the raiders had to push the prisoners who suffered intensely from heat and fatigue. Halfway along on the nine-mile march to Springfield, the clouds that had been gathering since the battle ended opened up and a summer cloudburst soaked victors and vanquished alike. It was worse on the Yankees who were tired and stumbled through the mire that quickly replaced the earlier dust and dirt. At Springfield their troubles ended.

Alston and Davis set up a temporary paroling office in a house, and one by one the prisoners signed and swore to documents agreeing not to bear arms against the South again until they were formally exchanged.

As the night wore on, Alston and Davis became aware that their host's daughters, Frances and Belle Cunningham, were showing a surprisingly deep interest in the parole formalities. The girls served tea and cakes to the two Southern officers, and when the last of the Yankees had signed and the house had quieted down, Captain Davis made an excuse to talk privately with Frances. They sat on the porch in the warm summer darkness, speaking of the things young men and women find most interesting, even in time of war. Before the girl retired, Captain Davis told her he had fallen in love with her and begged her to allow him to write to her.

Meanwhile, Alston received reports indicating that there were enemy patrols in the vicinity. He knew that Duke had recently named Davis Acting Assistant Adjutant General of the First Brigade and so he ordered his junior to get out of town fast and to rejoin his outfit. Davis, smitten by the lovely Frances, would have much preferred to stay on at the Cunninghams, but he was a good soldier and obeyed orders. It was a lucky break; a few hours after he left Springfield, advance units of Michigan cavalry dashed into town and captured Alston, who had fallen fast asleep in a chair on the porch of the Cunningham home.

Morgan's main column ate cold rations and marched toward Bardstown, riding all night in the clear weather that had followed the summer thunderstorm. Company H of the 2nd Kentucky was sent to Harrodsburg to scare off enemy patrols, and Company C of the same regiment moved ahead at a fast pace to scout the way into the town where Stephen Foster wrote "My Old Kentucky Home."

Captain Ralph Sheldon skirmished all the way into town with local home guards. He captured a train on the Louisville & Nashville, shot up several patrols and finally drove the militia who were guarding the town into a large stable. In an effort to avoid undue bloodshed, Sheldon sent Lieutenant Thomas W. Bullitt under a flag of truce to demand the militia company's surrender. Bullitt tied a handkerchief to a ramrod and held it over his head as he walked forward, but in the early morning light the home guards mistook it for a musket. One of the defenders raised his rifle but Captain W. O. Watts, militia commander, struck it down. When Watts refused to surrender, Sheldon surrounded the barn and there was sporadic firing until Watts and his men heard the sound of the main column approaching from Springfield—they then surrendered meekly.

Then, for the first time in two days, the First Brigade enjoyed a rest; they slept and ate in a stand of trees on the far side of Bardstown while Adam Johnson and his men passed through and took up the advance. After the fight at Lebanon, the long night march, and the skirmishing at Bardstown even an hour's sleep was a gift straight from Heaven.

CHAPTER 3

Lightning on the Telegraph Wires

AT BARDSTOWN John Morgan learned just how big a storm he had
caused by cutting between Rosecrans' and Burnside's armies. The word
came by telegraph, through the intervention of a man who, next to Duke
himself, probably did more to make Morgan the peer of Stuart, Forrest
and Hampton than a full company of men could have done. He was
George A. Ellsworth, a Canadian whose itching foot and dislike for putting down roots had brought him by a circuitous route into the South,
where he volunteered for service with Morgan's division.

The infantry would have been too dull for Ellsworth, whose friends all
called him "Lightning." Some said this was because he could send so fast
with the telegraph instrument; others claimed it was because he moved
so slowly when there was no need for haste; still others thought it had
something to do with a brand of corn liquor distilled in the mountains of
eastern Kentucky, for which he had an abiding fondness.

Ellsworth carried his "bug" and a coil of wire everywhere. By cutting
into a line, grounding one wire, and attaching his instrument to the other,
he could receive and send messages.

On this occasion Ellsworth cut into an overhead wire on the Bardstown branch of the Louisville & Nashville Railroad and heard operators
in several different communities excitedly discussing Morgan's movements and plans. Most of the messages were merely gossip between railroad operators, but he heard several messages from military headquarters
in Louisville to scattered units throughout Kentucky. He reported to
Morgan that Louisville was convinced the raiders were headed that way.
The victories at Columbia and Lebanon were being exaggerated and the
defeat on the Green River ignored. Some of the official messages were

46

concerned with the question of Judah's and Hobson's whereabouts. It seemed to Ellsworth that the size of Morgan's column was growing larger with each intercepted telegram.

After he listened to the army telegraphers, Lightning decided to participate. He had an uncanny ability to imitate the peculiarities of other operators. In the trade it was called a good "fist." After he had listened to a sender for a few minutes he could transmit in the same manner, with the little differences and eccentricities firmly remembered. Even friends and close associates were deceived by this skill. Using this knack, Ellsworth started sending spurious alarms of his own, grossly increasing the number of Rebel effectives, the number of guns they had with them and spreading rumors that other Confederate columns were even now on the march to a rendezvous near Louisville.

There was ample cause for the people of that city to be frightened. Morgan was actually less than thirty-five miles away while his court jester was using so effectively Samuel Morse's recent invention. This was close enough to worry any city whose fighting men were, for the most part, far away in southern Tennessee or over on the Mississippi River.

They were in no actual danger however. Morgan was too wise to attack a city as large as Louisville and had long ago determined to give it a wide berth. But the chance to strike terror in the town, and immobilize as many troops there as possible, was too great to miss. So, as the column rode through Shepherdsville, the General ordered Captain Davis to take Company D of the 2nd Kentucky and Company A of the 8th Kentucky on a sweep close to the southern outskirts of the city. The instructions were explicit; Davis was to demonstrate as if his detachment were the main column. He was to cut the telegraph lines, burn railroad trestles and bridges, and make his way through Shelbyville, Smithfield and Sligo, thus reaching the Ohio above Sligo.

Meanwhile, Morgan and the main column would move swiftly westward from Shepherdsville and Bardstown Junction, and arrive at the river at Brandenburg.

Captain Davis and his men departed on their dangerous rampage, the lovesick officer determined to spread fear and confusion among the Yankees. Several days later, he reached the Ohio and somehow found time to pen his first promised letter to Frances Cunningham, back in Springfield.

"When within ten miles of Shepherdsville," wrote Captain Davis, "General Morgan explained to me his intention of crossing the Ohio at

Brandenburg, and ordered my detachment from the division with eighty men to create a diversion by operating between Louisville and Frankfort. Rapidly pushing forward ahead of the column, I crossed the Salt River at an almost impracticable ford three miles above Shepherdsville and directed my course toward the railroad some thirty miles above Louisville. It and the telegraph lines I destroyed.

"On the 11th I endeavored to cross the Ohio at Twelve Mile Island above Louisville but when about thirty-five of us had crossed a heavily-armed gunboat came steaming up the river . . . and what resistance could rifles offer to its iron sides and heavy guns?"

Poor Frances! Except for renewed protestations of the writer's love, the letter ended there. The girl was left like the heroine in a cliff-hanging melodrama, forced to wait many weeks to learn how her suitor had met the crisis.

With the main column things were going more smoothly. After the rough handling they had suffered at Tebb's Bend, and the bitter fighting at Lebanon, the raiders were happy to learn that events now seemed to be in their favor. They joked among themselves as they thought about the frenetic preparations going on in Louisville. Most of the soldiers had slept briefly, their horses were still fresh, and many sang as the column moved westward at a steady pace adjusted to the speed of the four guns and the supply wagons.

General Morgan called Captains Clay Merriwether and Sam Taylor to his side, and the three rode at the head of the division as the leader explained the task he had set for the two. He said he wanted them to take their companies out of the ranks of the 10th Kentucky, to travel light and fast without any encumbrances, and to reach Brandenburg on the bank of the Ohio before any enemy forces gathered there. Most of all, he said, he desired them to seize any suitable craft to ferry the column across the river to Indiana.

Sam Taylor was a relative of Zachary Taylor and the "Old Rough and Ready" strain was a strong one. This job was the sort of job he liked. He and Merriwether led their men out of the marching ranks and moved ahead at a fast trot—but not before word of the plan was bruited about up and down the column.

Morgan's secret was now revealed. Men cheered the news that they were invading the enemy's own homeland. For more than two years they had been fighting in Kentucky and Tennessee. Now they would give the Yankees a sample of war in their home territory.

48

With the Second Brigade leading the way, Colonel Duke had time to question his prisoner, Captain Watts, and tried to learn what other militia units were active in the area between them and the Ohio River. He was getting little information, but it was a pleasant afternoon, and since Watts was a gentlemanly adversary, there was no rancor as they rode along parallel to the tracks of the Bardstown branch of the L. & N. Suddenly Duke saw a handcar moving along the rails a short distance ahead. One of the four men pumping the handles was clad in blue. The cavalryman, thinking him a Union soldier, assumed the men were racing for Lebanon Junction to give an alarm.

Duke and four or five of his men spurred their horses, jumped the fence beside the road and galloped across the meadow to head off the handcar. Their shouts only hurried the sweating men on the tracks. Several raiders fired in the air, but this was no more effective.

At this moment, Duke was amazed to see Captain Watts, the prisoner, dash past on his horse, firing at the handcar, cursing at the men for not stopping. Finally the terrified quartet braked the car to a stop. It developed that they were all civilians. The raiders let them go, admonishing them to stay behind the van of the column. Still amazed, Duke rode up to his prisoner's side.

"It was to be expected that *we* would try to catch those fellows, thinking they were Federals," said Colonel Duke," but why were *you* so anxious to catch them?"

Captain Watts shifted uneasily in the saddle, and looked sheepishly at the pistol his captors had permitted him to keep when he was paroled.

"Well, Colonel," he muttered, "I wish I may be shot, if I did not forget which side I was on."

Near the outskirts of the junction, Ellsworth again cut into the telegraph wire and succeeded in deceiving E. W. Atwater, the operator there, into believing that he was the Lebanon telegrapher, a man named Bennett. Within minutes Ellsworth learned that Bennett had invited Atwater to join him at Lebanon that evening. Atwater had just bought a new uniform and was so proud of it he talked about it over the wire. Ellsworth promised "to set something up" for him and signed off, assuring him that all was quiet in Lebanon.

Several hours later a train from Louisville pulled into the junction with about thirty passengers, five of whom were women. The conductor asked Atwater if he had heard of any guerillas in the vicinity. Remembering Ellsworth's words to the contrary, the telegrapher relayed the spurious

49

information to the trainman. He then locked his office and boarded the train for Lebanon.

At New Hope thirteen Union soldiers boarded the train to act as armed guards. But the Rebels, who knew what Ellsworth had done, were ready, and at St. Mary's the train was derailed at a wrecked culvert. The Union soldiers poured from the train, guns spouting, but they had no chance. One was killed, and the others threw down their arms. Morgan's men avoided firing toward the train and the passengers were unharmed.

Most disconsolate of the riders was poor Atwater, the telegrapher, who looked very handsome in his new uniform. He could scarcely believe it when Ellsworth, who was with the Rebel detachment, told him how he had been tricked.

The soldiers and Atwater were paroled. There was not anything else the Rebels could do. To have taken them along would have impeded their progress, required men for guards, and been of no avail. Until the time that Grant was shifted to command of the Union armies in the East, both sides paroled their prisoners. Most of the parolees lived up to their pledges, and waited for formal exchange before re-entering combat. With Morgan covering ground as he was, there was no alternative. He could afford no further losses from attrition. Counting the men who had left with Davis, the two small units detached even earlier, and the killed and injured, Duke estimated that the original 2,460 effectives had been reduced by 400 before they marched into Brandenburg.

By late afternoon of July 6, Morgan was on the move again, headed for the Ohio and well to the west of Louisville. Half of Kentucky was alarmed, each town fearing that at any hour the Rebel column would attack.

A newspaper correspondent in Lexington wired his editor that everything was confusion, with orders being issued and countermanded almost immediately, and the streets noisy with the sounds of the military tramping and weary mules braying as wagons were loaded with valuables.

"Everything that cannot be removed swiftly will be sent to Fort Clay," he wired. "Orders have been received from General Hartsuff for all noncombatants to leave immediately. Your correspondent will stay to the last and when Fort Clay goes under he will attempt a skedaddle like the rest. The excitement is intense. The mail is ready to go and so am I."

Rumor fed on rumor until the entire populace of central Kentucky was seeing raiders behind every tree and around every corner.

A train left Nashville bound for Louisville after Morgan had broken

50

through the Union cavalry screen between the Cumberland and the Green. As it approached Elizabethtown, Conductor Sweeny and the passengers worried about the reports received at each station. At one time the train backtracked for fifteen miles, but a family known to have strong secessionist sympathies boarded it with half a dozen large trunks, and the other passengers took courage from this. They assumed with typically faulty reasoning that southern sympathizers would know more about Morgan's plans than they, and would not risk so much luggage if there was danger of a train robbery.

On the train, which had two well-filled coaches, a baggage car and an express car, was E. D. Westfall, a war correspondent covering the pursuit for the New York *Herald*.

At Gaither's, nine miles below Elizabethtown, he noted that "the breeze blew stronger and the little bird sang louder about the rebels in front of us." He hid his paper money in his boot. At the station in Elizabethtown the conductor conferred with the telegrapher, who showed him a message that had just arrived from Louisville. "Come on in," it instructed the trainman, "there are no *Rebs* here." How were they to know this was more of Lightning Ellsworth's work?

Near Shepherdsville, where the tracks crossed the road Morgan was following, the train ground to a stop, sparks showering as brakeshoes pressed against iron rims. In front of it was a pile of ties stacked on the tracks, with what Westfall assumed was a 12-pounder "looking directly into the face of the engine driver." Gray-clad troopers dashed out of hiding on both sides of the tracks, shooting in the air and shouting.

The mail car was rifled, the baggage van was searched, and some of the passengers were relieved of their money. Westfall had to surrender the revolver he had purchased in New York City prior to leaving for the front lines. When Colonel Cluke learned of his identity he was spared from being searched, so his money went untouched. The reporter declined Cluke's offer of a bite of plug tobacco which the officer laughingly called "mule harness." He also declined an invitation to accompany the Rebels on their raid, even though Cluke promised him "lots of items."

After the Yankee soldiers in the coaches had been paroled, this train, too, was allowed to proceed. As it pulled away from the barrier and gained speed, the passengers heard the Rebels jeering. The nineteen- and twenty-year-old soldiers in Morgan's division considered the capture of trains, the rounding up of small bodies of militia, and the tricks Ellsworth was playing as great fun. After the winter of inactivity in Tennessee

51

and the drilling enforced by the old campaigner, St. Leger Grenfell, the raid to them had some of the aspects of a picnic. A few of their companions had fallen in battle, but youth is resilient, and these boys were good soldiers.

They looked at Morgan, sitting jaunty and erect on the beautiful Glencoe, his mustache and imperial neatly trimmed, his eyes warm and friendly—and they were afraid of nothing. Most of them had ridden on his earlier raids when he had extricated them from gathering Yankee forces with astonishing success. They were never reticent about telling their families and their sweethearts about his uncanny ability to outwit his enemies. They worshiped him and would have ridden against Satan and all his minions with John Morgan leading the way.

When the train had disappeared, the buglers called the men to horse and the column started for Garnettsville. As they rode along the dirt road winding between the verdant, tilled fields and occasional patches of woods, the troopers opened the letters taken from the mail car and searched them for currency. Behind them the pieces of paper littered the highway for miles.

At the head of the column Morgan discussed his next moves with Basil Duke and Adam Johnson; he was eager to reach the Ohio River. He was content to have the boys skylarking, knowing their youth, but he also knew that somewhere over the hills behind, Federal cavalry was straining to overtake them. He knew from his experience on other raids behind enemy lines that, by now, the Union detachments would have effected concentration. The initial surprise and demoralization would be over. He sensed that all over Kentucky blue-coated regiments were on the move. The pressure was building up.

Morgan was not overly concerned. He was confident at this stage of the raid. He knew Bragg was in trouble or he would not have asked him to create a diversion in Kentucky. If a diversion was what Bragg needed, then he would damned well supply one. It would be one that would tie up all the Union cavalry in central Kentucky and a lot more besides. But in the meantime, he would keep on the move.

Years later, Basil Duke recorded some of the reasoning of the three officers as they trotted along side-by-side on the road to Garnettsville.

"It has been surmised in the North that Morgan crossed the Ohio River to escape Hobson," wrote Duke. "Of all the many wild and utterly absurd ideas which have prevailed about the late war this is perhaps the most preposterous. Hobson was from twenty-four to thirty-six hours behind us. He was at any rate a good fifty miles in our rear and could learn our track only by following it closely.

"General Morgan, if anxious to escape Hobson, and actuated by no other motive, would have turned at Bardstown and gone out of Kentucky through the western part of the state where he would have encountered no hostile force that he could not have easily repulsed. It was not too late to have done the same thing at Garnettsville. To rush across the Ohio River as a means of escape would have been the choice of an idiot."

A young war correspondent named Whitelaw Reid was winning his literary spurs in the same years that Morgan was making his own name famous as a cavalry genius. Years later, he wrote of the great Indiana-Ohio raid, and his words show he knew Morgan was no "idiot."

"Here then," the correspondent said of the Rebel guerilla, "was a man who knew precisely what he wanted to do. He arranged a plan, far-reaching, comprehensive, and perhaps the boldest that the cavalry service of the war disclosed; and before the immensely superior forces which he had evaded could comprehend what he was about, he had half executed it."

As a matter of simple logic, no commander who harbored a desire to escape pursuers fifty miles to his rear would have persisted in crossing the Ohio, entering territory where he could hope for no aid, when every additional mile removed him that much farther from safety. If escape from Hobson had been his only objective, he would not have sent Davis to Louisville, or Merriwether and Taylor to secure boats at Brandenburg.

He was doing what he had intended to do from the start. He was disobeying Bragg's order because he was convinced beyond all doubt that a raid over the river would do the Confederacy great good. Now as he approached the Ohio, his dream was coming true; he was carrying the war deep into the North. Behind him was an impoverished land, denuded after more than two years of war. It was so barren his fellow cavalry leaders were sending deep into Georgia for their forage. But ahead of Morgan lay fields untouched by conflict, full granaries and overflowing barns.

Above: General John Hunt Morgan, a somewhat idealized portrait photograph.

Right: Martha Ready Morgan and John Hunt Morgan, probably at the time of their wedding, 1862.

University of Kentucky Library

Colonel Basil W. Duke

Colonel Adam R. Johnson

Captain Thomas Henry Hines

Colonel Frank Wolford

Brigadier General James M. Shackleford

George A. Ellsworth, Morgan's "Lightning"

General Edward H. Hobson

Some of Morgan's Raiders clowning for the photographer:
Lieutenant Leeland Hathaway in the center
Lieutenant Will Hays on the right

CHAPTER 4

Behind Them the Hounds, Baying

AT THE HEADQUARTERS of the Army of the Cumberland, General Rosecrans had spent the last two days in futile efforts to ascertain John Morgan's intentions. He had certainly received enough telegrams—that was not Old Rosy's problem. The messages had come in like dry leaves on an October wind. Judah, ignominiously trapped for thirty-six hours below the Green River, had spent a considerable portion of that time dispatching orders to Hobson, Carter, Shackleford and Wolford. Wires had gone to General Burnside, at his headquarters of the Army of the Ohio at Cincinnati. Action copies seemed to have gone everywhere, and information copies were forwarded to Rosecrans as he gathered his strength to make another attempt to drive Bragg out of Tennessee.

Morgan's raid was not Rosy's responsibility, but he depended heavily for his supplies on the Louisville & Nashville Railroad, his main link with the armories, camps and warehouses of the North. If Morgan was really loose, cutting that rail line, the Army of the Cumberland would soon feel the pinch. By the summer of 1863 there had been so much fighting between the Cumberland and Tullahoma, the land was as bare as a dog's old bone.

Late on the afternoon of July 6, Rosecrans found the missing piece for his puzzle. It was a telegram from Major General Gordon Granger, who commanded the Reserve Corps of the Army of the Cumberland. It read:

"The telegraph operator here reports as follows:

" 'Two of the Louisville lines are out and Ellsworth is on the other. He has his ground wire on now. He has been sending bogus dispatches.'

"Nashville operator reports Fort Henry evacuated by our forces. Ellsworth supposed to be at Elizabethtown."

It was not completely accurate. Ellsworth was not within twenty miles of Elizabethtown. But to Rosecrans, who disregarded the gossip about Fort Henry, it meant that Morgan had sliced through Burnside's forward cavalry screen and was well north into Kentucky. There was little Old Rosy could do until Morgan turned back toward Tennessee. The raider's pursuit was clearly left to Ambrose Burnside.

The latter's troops in the field already knew it was going to be a rough, long chase.

Hobson, freed temporarily from Judah's timorous commands, had joined Shackleford and ridden to Lebanon, arriving one full day too late to render aid to Hanson and the 25th Michigan. One of his first acts was to inform his superior of that unfortunate fact.

"I arrived at Lebanon, Kentucky," he wired Burnside, "with my command, the 9th and 12th Regiments of Kentucky Cavalry, also the command of Brigadier General James M. Shackleford, consisting of the 8th Kentucky Cavalry, and a battalion of the 3rd Kentucky Cavalry and one section of the 22nd Indiana Battery. Soon after my arrival at 1:30 P.M., the 1st Kentucky Cavalry, the 2nd East Tennessee Mounted Infantry, the 2nd Ohio Cavalry, the 45th Ohio Mounted Infantry, and battery of four mountain howitzers under Colonel Frank Wolford entered the place, having marched from Somerset (Jamestown)."

Up in Cincinnati, "Granny" Burnside looked at his maps and things took on a rosier hue. He had to show Morgan. To Hobson he telegraphed:

"You will combine the commands of General Shackleford and Colonel Wolford, and, after ascertaining as nearly as possible the direction of General Morgan's route, you will endeavor to overtake him or cut him off. You are authorized to subsist your command upon the country and impress the necessary horses to replace the broken-down ones. Morgan ought to be broken to pieces before he gets out of the state."

The Union troopers were tired, but Hobson, who was happy over being given command of the chase, gave them no rest. They left Lebanon that evening, reached Bardstown the next morning. One of his men, Colonel James I. David, commanding two Michigan regiments, the 8th and 9th, later reported that the pace was so fast that forty of his horses were killed by the forced march and the intense heat. Most of the inhabitants of this section of Kentucky were strongly pro-Union and gladly showed Hobson the direction Morgan had ridden on the Shepherdstown road. Doggedly, Hobson went after the Rebels.

55

Burnside was furious that Judah had allowed himself to be trapped by an unusual ten foot rise in the Green River. Judah was equally furious as his men crossed in a few boats at Vaughan's Ferry. When all were on the other side and he could take up the pursuit, he was nearly apoplectic with rage over his own mishap. General Hartsuff informed Burnside that Judah was so disturbed that he had sent "an almost unintelligible report" in which he said "he feels dreadfully at his luck."

Even when he got moving, however, Judah was bothered not so much by distance and loss of time as by wrong judgment, and for this he was not entirely to blame. Ellsworth had sent enough bogus dispatches and orders to have convinced any Northern commander that Morgan was heading straight for Louisville. Ellsworth cut the wires behind him, some of Morgan's patrols cut others, and the high water on the Cumberland and Green rivers had so damaged still other lines that messages that should have reached Judah did not, and his own dispatches seemed to disappear into a void.

Colonel C. D. Pennebaker, commanding at Munfordville, asked his superior: "Has not Morgan swung a thief on the wires? Too many inquiries for General Judah."

Judah, at long last received information that the Confederates were moving in a westward direction south of the Ohio. This seemed reliable news. To Judah, eager for a hot scent, this meant one thing. Morgan was starting back toward Tennessee. He had made a similar move in 1862. There were plenty of reasons for Judah to assume he was repeating it. Therefore, instead of following the chord of the arc Morgan's column was actually describing which was the natural maneuver to overtake his quarry, Judah moved far to the west at Leitchfield. There he intended to wait for the supposedly unsuspecting fox when the latter went south. In moving to the west, Judah marched through an area where ruptured telegraph lines dropped a curtain of silence behind him so no one knew his exact location.

Hobson, who was close on Morgan's heels, sent this cryptic message to Burnside from Bardstown:

"I move. Not safe to give particulars. General Judah is in the right place; he could not get up with me. I have advised as to the proper distribution of forces."

This was just gibberish to Burnside, who responded by burning up the wires with orders to Judah to communicate with him. Brigadier General Jeremiah T. Boyle, who was in command of Union forces at Louisville, was prodded by Burnside for information about the missing Judah. He followed time-honored military custom by kicking the inquiry along to someone lower in rank—in this case, Colonel Pennebaker. That officer, who knew a hot potato when he had one in his hand, did everything but ride out, himself, to look for the elusive Judah. He reported to Boyle to show what he was doing:

"I sent your dispatch of yesterday evening to General Judah by special courier, who has not returned. Will send your dispatch, just received, by couriers on every road that can be traveled between here and Leitchfield and Big Spring. Will start six couriers, with orders to find him and report."

Burnside's frenzied messages finally reached Judah, who by then had realized that in his shatter-pated haste he had misjudged Morgan's movements completely. The Rebel leader was not executing a full circle, but was still making his way north. In fact, by this time the raiders were over the river and in Indiana. When Judah sensed the error into which he had fallen by trying to outguess Morgan, he was nearly as furious with himself as he had been when he was trapped below the flooded Green River. Shamefacedly, he marched his troops back to Elizabethtown, put his brigade on the cars and rode the Louisville & Nashville into Louisville. Once there, he put the troops aboard steamboats and started up the Ohio, aware that it would inevitably be many days and many miles later before he could throw his forces in Morgan's way.

The burden of the pursuit through Indiana, as it had been through Kentucky, would be on Hobson's shoulders.

On July 7 Burnside received a wire from Rosecrans that sounded as if Rosy were needling him.

"Information here seems to show that possibly a brigade of Morgan's and all of Johnny Pegram's forces have gone over to raid on you," said the wire from Tullahoma. "I hope you will kill or capture them all, and that Morgan will be no longer the terror of the Kentuckians."

Granny could only swallow his wrath and reply:

"Dispatch received. The whole force seems to be Morgan's cavalry. I think we can attend to it."

In his own determined, bull-dog way, General Edward Hobson was attending to it for Burnside. From John Hunt Morgan's point of view he could not have had a more dangerous pursuer. Hobson was a Kentuckian, but one who never wavered in his devotion to the Union. As a boy he had been sickly and had been told to seek recovery in the warmer climate along the Gulf of Mexico. Lacking money to go in style, young Hobson

57

hired out as a hog driver for six dollars a month. He walked the full 600 miles from his home in Greensburg to Selma, Alabama, most of the way behind a drove of ornery hogs. Then he visited New Orleans, rode up the Mississippi and Ohio rivers to a landing near Paducah and walked home the remaining 250 miles, much of it in a bitter winter snowstorm. It was strong medicine, but he arrived home in perfect health.

First a saddler, then a merchant and banker, Hobson later fought in the Mexican War, and won commendation for bravery at Buena Vista. When Fort Sumter was fired upon, he immediately asked permission to raise a regiment. During most of the war, up to the time he pursued Morgan, he had served in central Kentucky, meanwhile keeping an eye on that troublesome adversary.

It is entirely possible that had Judah not pulled Hobson away from Burkesville, the great Indiana-Ohio raid might never have become more than another in the Confederate bag of shattered dreams. As it turned out, Hobson was given the assignment to catch his old enemy, and he went about it with the eager intensity of a bloodhound on a good scent.

His two chief lieutenants were as different as day from night, but they were alike in their desire to snare John Morgan.

James Shackleford was a lawyer who raised his own cavalry regiment in western Kentucky and developed a natural flair for getting good results from his men. His foot was wounded in a battle early in the war, but, riding in a buggy, he led his men, until it healed sufficiently to again bear his weight in a stirrup. He was driven by one overwhelming desire—to win the war and get home to his four motherless children.

Frank Wolford was another Kentuckian, but one from the foothills—rough, uneducated and ugly as sin. He was barrel-chested, hawk-nosed and full-bearded, and had a way of talking that seemed straight out of Elizabethan England.

Morgan and Wolford knew one another well. The latter had been Morgan's prisoner for a while when he was captured in one of the Rebel guerilla's earlier "slash and cut" raids. Morgan's men respected Frank Wolford more than any other enemy.

The contrast between Morgan and Wolford was even greater than that between Shackleford and Wolford. Wolford rode an oversized roan horse as if he were a farm boy astride a Percheron. Morgan had the graceful seat of the born horseman, his every sinew in tune with the thoroughbreds he bred and trained. The Union colonel was a Cromwellian roundhead.

The Rebel brigadier was one of the last of the cavaliers. After two years of bitter war each leader respected the other for identical virtues.

Aside from Judah, all these men—the blue and the gray—were Kentuckians. Why some were for the Union and others loyal to the Confederacy was as much a mystery to them as it is to history. Families were riven, leaving brother to fight brother. Inhabitants of one county were often predominantly pro-Union and those of a neighboring county overwhelmingly secessionist.

That was why, in this month of July, 1863, as Morgan rode toward the Ohio, many in his ranks knew that brothers, cousins and other kinfolk were riding hard behind them, wearing a differently-colored uniform, carrying another flag.

CHAPTER 5

Terror Comes to Indiana

MOCKINGBIRDS WERE SINGING in the mimosa and magnolia trees as the Confederate raiders rode into the little town of Garnettsville on the evening of July 7. The warm air was sweet with the perfume of flowers and shrubs to which the new-mown hay in the fields around the village added its heady scent. Dogs yapped at the sound of so many hoofs on the hard-packed road, but otherwise a somnolent peace brooded over the small cluster of homes.

Southern soldiers made their camp in the meadows at the edge of town. If there was enemy militia in the vicinity, it kept out of sight. Each regimental commander, being a good soldier, posted vedettes. They did this automatically, sensing all the while that this would be a quiet interlude between days of bitter fighting and hard riding.

After their mounts had been fed, watered and curried, the younger troopers strolled through the streets, spurs jingling, big Colt navy pistols swinging at their hips. The people of Garnettsville remained indoors most of the time, but they left their doors and windows unshuttered, and there was no outward sign of conflict. It might have been a village in Alabama or Georgia, except that no girls walked arm-in-arm with the boys in butternut gray.

One Southern rider expressed the sentiments of many of his companions when he sang a doleful but popular tune called "The Kentucky Exile." It was an obvious favorite with the men who had gone south in '61 to serve with the Confederacy, even though it was saccharine and sentimental. The chorus went like this:

"Yes, we'll march, march, march
To the music of the drums.
We were driven forth in exile
From our Old Kentucky Home."

60

The raiders bedded down early, most of them sleeping under the stars, the embers from a hundred campfires slowly dying out. It was almost as if Morgan and his 2,000 men knew that this would be the last night they would know the benison of utter peace.

Shortly after midnight they were on the march again; by daylight they stood upon the heights above Brandenburg, looking down upon the broad Ohio, running full with muddy, yellow water.

They had fought their way across the Cumberland and forded the Green and the Salt rivers. Now there was one more river to cross. Invasion fever gripped each man as he studied the lush, green Indiana shore. There, across a half-mile stretch of water, lay the heart-land of the North —rich, fertile, unprotected. This was their goal.

Down in the town they found men of the 10th Kentucky proud as punch about the successful completion of their mission. By the wharf-boat lay the *John B. McCombs,* the Louisville, Evansville and Henderson mail boat, and the *Alice Dean,* a packet in the Memphis and Cincinnati run. Black smoke curled from their twin stacks, and the new-comers could see the figures of some of their companions standing guard in the wheelhouses and on the decks.

Captains Taylor and Merriwether happily told Morgan of their easy victory the day before. They had found no enemy force in Brandenburg and had learned that the *McCombs* was due shortly after noon. Forty men were detailed to hide in and near the wharfboat. The balance of the men in the two companies guarded the streets leading to the river bank. Soon after lunch they heard the moaning whistle of a boat coming upstream around the bend west of town. The *McCombs* hove into sight, slowed her engines and coasted in smoothly for a landing. Lines were secured and the gangplank swung out to rest on the splintered deck of the small landing barge.

At a shouted command the forty raiders swarmed over the packet and seized control without firing a single shot. Captain Ballard, the crew and the fifty passengers could not have been more surprised if the attackers had been naked Indians. Swiftly, the passengers were hurried off and into town. Then Merriwether and Taylor waited for the passing of the fast packet, due down river from Louisville. Lookouts on the hill behind the town signaled her approach. The Rebels knew she did not make Brandenburg as a regular stop, so they ordered Captain Ballard to take the *McCombs* out into midstream.

All unsuspecting, the *Alice Dean* rounded the last bend above town to find the *McCombs,* under full steam, approaching on her port beam. The two side-wheelers, riding the breast of the current, raced along side-by-side until Ballard, with Merriwether's prodding, steered his boat so close that timber chafed against timber. The frightened deckhands on the *McCombs* lashed the two craft together with hawsers expertly tossed over the *Alice Dean's* mooring bitts.

Only then did the sailors on the second boat see the rifles pointing their way. Unwilling captor and unwilling captive backed their engines, the great paddle-wheels thrashed the water, and after a bit of jockeying both steamboats tied up at the wharfboat.

The raiders eased the passengers' minds, and assured them that their personal property would not be taken. They even opened the safe in the purser's office and gave the grateful men and women the money they had put there for safekeeping when they boarded the boat. Not one cent of the more than $10,000 was taken by the soldiers. Like the passengers on the *McCombs,* those from the *Alice Dean* were led ashore and ordered to stay there, where they could spread no alarm.

Now Morgan had his ferries.

While the two captains were telling their leader how easily the boats had been seized, they noticed a group of men, clad in travel-stained clothes, lounging indolently near the landing boat. They looked closer and then, yelling and shouting, they ran over to the newcomers, greeting them with slaps on the back and good-natured horseplay. The recipients of this rowdy welcome were Captain Tom Hines and some men of the 9th Kentucky Cavalry, back from their scouting expedition into Indiana.

Weeks before the raid started, Hines had been sent into Clinton County to a "dead horse camp," with horses that had to be rested and fed before they could be used on active duty. He disliked this dull service and asked permission to "recruit" other mounts, by taking them from their Northern owners, and to scout "north of the Cumberland." Morgan gave his permission, and Hines stretched his orders just as Morgan did later with Bragg's. With less than two-score men he rode through enemy country in Kentucky, crossed into Indiana and, until driven out by the militia, raised considerable havoc. As Morgan's men were riding into Brandenburg from the southeast, Hines and his men crossed the Ohio in small boats, swimming their horses alongside, and made their reunion at the wharfboat. Most of the raiders assumed—and with some correctness—that Hines had not so much disobeyed his orders as he had acceded to unspoken wishes Morgan had guessed he would execute.

The raiders took a little time out to relieve a few storekeepers of merchandise. The merchants were pro-Union, and the younger soldiers could not overlook the chance to show them they did not approve of such sentiments. At Weatherspool and Jaekel's some of the clerks remonstrated, but the Southerners brushed them aside, saying they wanted the silks and muslins to present to their Yankee cousins in Indiana.

While the rear elements of the Rebel column marched into town, a mist came up over the Ohio, shrouding the Indiana shore. Out of this low-lying fog came the sound of musketry, followed by the crisp crack of a rifled cannon. Someone on the Indiana side wanted no visitors from Kentucky. They must have aimed their artillery before the fog blanket settled, because one of the very first shells landed on the river bank near the landing, wounding one of the quartermaster officers. Confederates scattered as Captain Byrnes wheeled his Parrotts into position. More shells came over, but they did no further damage. Guessing at the range, since the mist obscured his view, Byrnes sent off several rounds. It halted the enemy firing as if it had been turned off with a key.

A short time later the fog lifted. From his headquarters in a house on a hill, Morgan could see militiamen around the gun on a bluff above the landing in Indiana. Colonel Duke ordered two regiments, the 2nd Kentucky and the 9th Tennessee, to dismount and board the captured steamboats. The packets put out into the stream, soldiers standing by each wheelsman to see that orders were obeyed, and tied up at Morvin Landing, just east of Mauckport, Indiana, where the Southern regiments debarked.

Raiders dashed off the steamers and ran toward the bluff, disregarding a ragged volley that peppered them from above. Colonel Ward and Major Webber urged their men up the escarpment. When they broke out over the top, the militia had disappeared, leaving the gun where it had been emplaced between two haystacks.

The *McCombs* and the *Alice Dean* went back for reinforcements. They had barely moored when a small boat, snub-nosed and armored with iron plating, with three howitzer muzzles clearly visible in embrasures cut through heavy oak timbering, steamed downriver and turned toward the landing at Brandenburg. She was the *Springfield,* a tin-clad, and had been dispatched downriver from New Albany by Lieutenant Commander LeRoy Fitch, USN, commanding Union gunboats on the Ohio, when he learned of the capture of the two packets.

"Suddenly checking her way," wrote Duke later, "she tossed her snub

63

nose defiantly, like any angry beauty of the coal pits, sidled a little toward town and commenced to scold. A blueish-white, funnel-shaped cloud spouted from her left-hand bow, as a shot flew at the town, and then changing front forward, she snapped a shell at the men on the other side."

Duke admitted that he was unfamiliar with nautical terminology, but his description left little doubt of the tin-clad's intention. Her commander saw the packets loading more cavalrymen on the south bank, and also saw the advance party on the other shore. It was a critical moment for Morgan with his unhorsed men in Indiana, his ferryboats as vulnerable as sitting ducks to shellfire, and the rest of his men crowded into the town of Brandenburg with Union cavalry approaching as fast as weary horses could be urged.

Every minute of delay was dangerous. It not only played into Hobson's hands, but permitted the militia and home-guards in Indiana to recover from their first fright and gather additional men with which to block the roads. Officers and men realized their predicament, conjuring up unpleasant visions of what their companions across the Ohio faced if attacked before their mounts could be sent over.

Captain Byrnes, however, was not in the least perturbed. He knew what had to be done; he was artillerist first and cavalryman second. Calmly disregarding the falling shells, he and his men hitched up their four guns, rode upriver to where an eminence rose near the river bank, and set them up again. From there he pelted the Union tin-clad with round shot, the solid balls sending up great geysers or smashing against the armor on the lucky hits. Byrnes could not tell whether he was doing serious damage, but one thing was sure. The *Springfield* could do little harm while dancing around in midstream in an effort to present a moving target to the Confederate gunners. An hour later the gunboat gave up the battle and retreated up the Ohio, acting Ensign James Watson having decided he needed help.

Even before she was out of sight, Morgan began shifting his force from the south to the north side of the river. First, he sent Webber and Ward their horses, then the balance of the First Brigade embarked to reinforce the two regiments in Indiana. With them went the two 12-pound howitzers.

By 5 P.M. the shuttling *McCombs* and *Alice Dean* had put Duke's entire brigade over the river. At that hour, with his force almost evenly divided by the broad Ohio, Morgan suffered the worst fright of the day. The *Springfield,* accompanied by a second craft, reappeared from upstream.

The General commanded the packets to continue their ferrying operations and called on Captain Byrnes to handle the enemy with the two Parrotts which had been emplaced for just this eventuality. The guns barked, and solid shells peppered the tin-clad and her consort. The gunboats tried to aproach the packets, but the Rebel gunnery was too good, and once again Byrnes and his field pieces won the strange duel. Both Federal boats backed away, turned their bows upstream, and churned away into the night.

It was after midnight before the Second Brigade joined the First in Indiana. On the last trip the *Alice Dean* brought the two Parrotts that had saved the day for the raiders.

If John Morgan had had his way, both the *McCombs* and the *Alice Dean* would have been put to the torch. Colonel Duke, however, intervened in Captain Ballard's behalf when the latter promised to steam straight to Louisville to prevent his craft from being similarly employed by the oncoming Federals. Morgan gave in, and the *McCombs,* true to Ballard's word, steamed off upstream.

But the *Alice Dean* was set afire. She was old and had been painted and varnished many times. This volatile material and the light wood of her superstructure seemed to explode when the flames reached the upper decks. In minutes the packet was a great flaming torch. The glare from the burning boat illuminated the river for miles, almost turning night into day. As the Rebel rearguard waited to make sure that the fire could not be extinguished, they heard the nasty whine of bullets about them. Looking across the Ohio, they saw the shadowy forms of Hobson's advance patrols shooting despairingly from the other bank. The 7th Ohio Cavalry was just an hour too late.

It had been a near thing. As a matter of fact, the raiders couldn't guess how very close it had been.

If Hobson had not halted at Garnettsville before dark on July 8, while Morgan was crossing the Ohio and fighting the tin-clads, he could have covered the remaining nine miles to Brandenburg before the raider extricated the Second Brigade. Colonel A. V. Kautz of the 2nd Ohio Cavalry called this the worst blunder by the Union side in the entire chase after Morgan.

At first Hobson had urged his men forward, finding the raiders' track an easy one to follow, particularly after leaving Shepherdsville. All the Union force had to do was to follow the trail of letters the Rebels had tossed aside as they rode west from the L. & N. tracks. For ten to fifteen miles the road was strewn with the abandoned mail. Quite possibly the Federal column was slowed by men stopping to pick up some of the discarded letters and read them.

One Union trooper remembered the ones he read. There was one addressed to the sender's "Dear Wife" telling of the death of a relative, and another intended for a business firm which began, "Enclosed please find $150 which you will please place to my account." But the money was missing. A third letter told in a girl's handwriting of gay balls, dances and party frocks. One other letter the soldier remembered well. It was from a clergyman to a woman telling her it was his "sad duty to inform her that her hubsand is no more." The envelope was missing and there was no way to tell whether the dead soldier had worn blue or gray.

So the Federals marched as if they had lost some of their ardor, and when Hobson reached Garnettsville, instead of pressing on, he halted for orders. It gave Morgan all the time he needed.

Perhaps the peace and quiet of a summer eve in Garnettsville influenced the bluecoats that night, as it had Morgan's men the night before.

This strange slowdown in the pursuit was not the only luck that played into the Rebel's hands there where the Ohio rolled her mustard-colored waters past the Indiana foreshore.

The night after the two packets had been seized by the advance guard under Taylor and Merriwether, the commander of the Indiana militia at Mauckport, Lieutenant Colonel William J. Irvin, sent messengers to Colonel Lewis Jordan at Corydon requesting more troops. He sensed that Morgan was going to try a crossing at Brandenburg. Soon after sending for help he saw the steamer *Lady Pike* coming upriver, bound for Cincinnati. Irvin ordered her to stop, explaining the danger that existed just a few miles beyond, and sent the packet back to Leavenworth for artillery and gunners.

At midnight the *Lady Pike* returned with a six-pounder and thirty men under Captain G. W. Lyon of the Crawford County artillery. To avoid being observed by Merriwether's and Taylor's men in Brandenburg, the steamboat landed two miles below Mauckport and the gun was hauled by hand from there to the bluff opposite the Kentucky town. Gunners and militia jackassed the heavy fieldpiece through the woods and fields and floated it over Buck Creek on an old, rotten boat.

Without limber or caisson, the cannon was carried whenever possible in the bed of a farm wagon, lashed to the sides so it would not roll against the powder and shells. Before dawn it was in place in a farmer's yard, its rifled barrel pointed straight and sure at the captured packet *McCombs*. When its initial shot tore through the upper works of the steamboat and wounded Captain W. W. Wilson, the home guards cheered gleefully, but almost the first shell fired by Byrnes in return killed Lieutenant James H. Current of the Mauckport Rifles and George Nance of Harrison City, who were serving the six-pounder. This was too accurate for the militiamen so they took off like frightened rabbits for the ridges back of the landing.

If that one gun from Leavenworth, dragged into position with so much difficulty, had been handled by veteran gunners, Morgan's transit of the Ohio could have been a bloody affair.

If Hobson had not waited for orders, if better men had served the Mauckport cannon, if the tin-clad had out-gunned Byrnes' Parrotts . . . all these "ifs" meant nothing now. Morgan and his division were over the Ohio. Military obedience had been disregarded, and men had died at Tebb's Bend and Lebanon to get them there, but the dream born in Tennessee had come close to fruition in Indiana. John Morgan, a very human individual, could hardly have been immune to the feeling of pride as he reminisced about the days and obstacles that had been overcome.

Behind him was Hobson with better than 4,000 men, needing only a few boats to resume the pursuit. Before him, militia were gathering by the thousands. The newest recruit in his column knew the odds against them were great. There was the telegraph by which men could be rallied and shifted like pieces on a chessboard, a railroad network intact and undamaged, and everywhere, an aroused populace—choleric with rage at being invaded. And there was always the broad Ohio, so beautiful and so treacherous, a barrier now to Hobson but a greater one to Morgan's safe return to the Confederacy. On it the North could move men and horses without tiring either. It represented what every military commander hates—a flank in the air—a flank that could be turned almost at will by the dogged Union tin-clads.

Yet Morgan held the trump card of surprise. His was the choice where to strike. Like a wolf at the edge of a flock of fat sheep, he possessed mobility, superior power at any given point, and best of all, an awareness of the terror inherent in his very presence.

Not unlike sheep, the home guards had scattered from his front. Most had fallen back on the road leading north from the river to Corydon. Lyon and his gunners, Irvin with his militia—all had skittered away in the night.

67

Terror had come to Indiana.

Morgan's advance patrols pushed on from the river and found the farmhouses abandoned. Men, women and children had fled to the woods, leaving the supper fires still burning on the hearths, the tables set for the evening meal.

Colonel Duke stopped at a house by the side of the road and found the door open, the scene inside almost one of welcome.

"A bright fire was blazing upon the kitchen hearth," he noted, "bread half-made up was in the tray, and many indications convinced us that we had interrupted preparations for supper. The chickens were strolling before the door with a confidence that was touching but misplaced. General Morgan rode up soon after and was induced to 'stop all night.' We completed the preparations, so suddenly abandoned, and made the best show for Indiana hospitality that was possible under the disturbing circumstances."

Their sense of well-being would have been greatly increased had they been privy to the excitement their movements had caused in the Federal high command.

General Burnside's fears for Louisville had not been dispelled by Morgan's successful crossing into Indiana. Old Granny was afraid the enemy column would march in a short circle, re-cross the Ohio, and attack the city. Everyone seemed confident that Morgan was about to perform a sudden about-face. So Burnside sent word of Morgan's activities to Brigadier General Orlando B. Willcox, commanding the District of Indiana and Michigan, asking that the 71st Indiana Regiment be sent to Kentucky. Willcox dispatched it to Louisville and added two companies of the 3rd Indiana Cavalry and Myer's 23rd Indiana Battery. Indianapolis was thereby left unprotected except for two companies of the 63rd Indiana Infantry and a few recruits and exchangees.

On the day the raiders entered Indiana, Burnside received word from Edwin Stanton, the Union Secretary of War, that his beloved Ninth Corps, taken from him to strengthen Grant before Vicksburg, was going to be returned. Burnside, with his access to official dispatches, knew the North had won great victories at Gettysburg and Vicksburg, so he wired Stanton:

"Your dispatch received. I thought I was very happy at the success of General Grant and General Meade, but I am happier to hear of the speedy return of the Ninth Corps."

Ambrose Burnside, an earnest but uninspired commander, had gained enough military lore in four years at West Point to know the value of

68

veterans as compared to green militia and home-guards. He had wanted his old Corps back before he undertook the invasion of east Tennessee which Abraham Lincoln had been urging him to mount. Now, with Morgan loose in his own back yard, old mutton-chops wanted his regulars more than ever before.

General Morgan would have been well pleased had he known of the consternation he was creating, but he knew nothing of Burnside's peevish frame of mind as he finished the home-cooked supper and went to sleep in the well-guarded farm house where Colonel Duke was playing host. Although he slept well, he was not without worries of his own.

Adam Johnson, for example, had expressed a desire to turn left after crossing the Ohio in an attempt to capture Evansville, Henderson and Owensboro, but Morgan had vetoed this suggestion, wanting to keep his column intact.

"I thought the diversionary tactic would be worth more than the loss of the regiment," explained Johnson, "but he pointed to the boats and said, 'I ordered them burned. We must go forward together.' "

CHAPTER 6

"The Ugliest Kind of Music"

PETER LAPP WAS the first civilian north of the Ohio to suffer from the Rebel invasion. He operated a grist mill on Buck Creek, three miles inland from the river. Before dawn on July 9 he was routed out of bed by foragers looking for food for Morgan's 2,000 cavalrymen. The only money the Southerners had consisted of greenbacks issued in Richmond, Virginia, and the miller stubbornly refused to accept them. This showed poor judgment on Lapp's part. He paid for it by having his mill burned to the ground—after a dozen barrels of flour had been carried away by the raiders.

The boy from Greencastle, Indiana—Sergeant Henry Lane Stone, who had walked all the way across Kentucky to join Morgan—approved of this act and wrote to his father to explain his feelings.

"I experienced some peculiar sensations as I set foot on Indiana soil," he wrote. "We intend to live off the Yanks hereafter and let the North feel like the South has felt of some of the horrors of war—horses we expect to take whenever needed, forage and provisions also."

Later that morning when the buglers roused the troopers they made their breakfasts of the captured flour, mixing it with water, salt and eggs taken from the chicken coops behind the farmhouses. This batter they cooked in their skillets over hot embers and found it very tasty.

A few of the soldiers had hangovers. These were the younger men in the 2nd Kentucky and 9th Tennessee who, like soldiers everywhere in wartime, did not let a little thing like a fusillade from the Indiana militia prevent them from looting the *Alice Dean's* wine locker. They had taken several score bottles ashore with them, and after the annoying business of driving off the home guards had been attended to, they enjoyed an

70

impromptu champagne party. Kelion Peddicord recorded the additional fact that various other small delicacies had also "come into their possession" during the crossing.

After breakfast Colonel Dick Morgan and the undersized 14th Kentucky led the way toward Corydon, following a road that went due north between ripening fields of corn and occasional wood lots. The sun was already dispersing the night's coolness and everywhere the raiders looked—

> The bloom was on the alder
> And the tassel on the corn.

On the outskirts of Corydon they encountered mounted patrols and drove them toward the militia waiting behind a barricade of fence rails. More than 500 raw citizen-soldiers, most of them in farm clothes and mechanics' overalls, armed with squirrel guns, old muskets and other ancient weapons, held their fire until Dick Morgan and his men charged the barrier.

It was too high for the horses to jump easily. Some fell, carrying their riders with them in a twisting, threshing melee. Others did better, displacing the top rails as they cleared the hurdle. So for a short while the raiders were exposed to scattered, but fairly effective fire. Men died and others were wounded before Adam Johnson could handle the situation. He then sent one regiment in a flanking movement, peppered the barricade with his two howitzers, and launched a heavier frontal attack. It was too much for the green troops, even with the protection of their fence rail bastion. Jordan's men fled, infecting a detachment of local guards known as the Spencer Guards, who joined the rout despite the pleas of their leader, Captain George Lahue.

"The shells made the ugliest kind of music over our heads," said Edwin Wolfe, editor of the Corydon *Democrat*, after the battle. "This shelling operation, together with the fact our line was about to be flanked on both wings at the same time made it necessary for the safety of our men that they should fall back. This they did, not in the best order, it is true, but with excellent speed. From this time on, the flight was converted into a series of skirmishes. Each man fought on his own hook, after the manner of bushwhackers."

This bushwhacking had its serious as well as its comic aspects.

A few miles out of town, unseen civilians fired at a party of raiders and killed one of them. Thinking the bullet had come from the home of the

71

Rev. Mr. Peter Glenn, the angry troopers fired a volley at the minister's house, killing him and wounding his son. They then set fire to the building and burned it to the ground.

It didn't make any sense, of course, but soldiers have always hated bushwhackers. Years later Basil Duke, while not excusing his men's actions, declared it was the only private dwelling burned by Morgan's raiders on the entire raid.

Another scouting patrol ran into resistance when they attempted to steal a horse from George Lyman, whose house stood not far from Mr. Glenn's. The soldiers, convinced that armed men were lying in wait in this farmhouse, searched it thoroughly. They found no one but Lyman's groom, a colored man who was trying to hide his owner's handsome stallion "Tempest" behind the stable. A young raider tried to mount the animal, but it resented this familiarity and kicked the boy out of the paddock. Two of his companions went to his assistance, but they, too, were put to flight by the nervous horse. When they drew off to plan new strategy, the groom leaped on Tempest's back and raced to safety in the nearby woods.

Corydon itself got off lightly. No buildings were burned and not a single private dwelling was entered. But the Rebels relieved the county treasurer of funds totaling $750. Morgan told the owners of three mills that if they paid a ransom of $1,000 each, he would not put their buildings to the torch. They haggled over the figure, and finally the General accepted a cut-rate payment of $2,100 from the three.

Soldiers went through the department store of Douglass, Denbo & Co. like a swarm of locusts, picking up clothing, shoes, hats and other apparel to replace their own badly-worn garments. Some of the men offered Confederate currency—others operated on the theory that finders are keepers.

Irate, the merchants asked Morgan by what right he made his demand for ransom of the mills and by what right his men took what they liked without offering hard cash in payment. The General swept his arm in a wide arc that encompassed hundreds of his troopers idling in the center of town.

"There," he said bluntly, "is my authority."

Ordinary citizens were relieved when their homes were unmolested by the invaders. A few men who said they were Copperheads and sympathetic to the South had to turn their pockets inside out, for Morgan's men hated these supposed friends more than they did loyal Unionists.

"The Rebs were pretty hard on the Copperheads," said Miss Attia Porter, "but they did not take a thing from us."

Morgan's troops paroled 345 of the home guards. The raiders lost eight men killed and thirty-three wounded, a cause for some concern. They realized, however, they would have to suffer from almost constant attrition as long as they rode behind the enemy lines.

Morgan and Duke, together with several staff aides, ate their lunch at Kintner's Hotel in Corydon. During the meal the innkeeper's daughter informed the General that Vicksburg had fallen to Grant and that Lee was retreating across the Potomac after a serious defeat at Gettysburg. News of the double tragedy shocked Morgan deeply. He could hardly believe it until the girl showed him copies of the local newspaper with the dispatches from the two battlefields.

Vicksburg's fall was serious enough. It mean that Grant's western armies could now join Rosecrans in a push that might rapidly cut the South in half.

To John Morgan the Southern defeat at Gettysburg was even more depressing. In the back of his mind there had always been the realization that his own invasion of the North, which followed Lee's by only a few days, might be a small part of a climactic effort to win peace by striking deep into the enemy's homeland. He knew that Lee, had he been success-ful, would have gone on to threaten Baltimore or Philadelphia.

There are some who claim that Lee and Morgan acted in concert and who believe that Morgan had planned, if he had been prevented from re-turning to Kentucky and Tennessee by the intervention of too many Union troops, to strike into Pennsylvania in an effort to join Lee's Army of Northern Virginia.

This high strategy was probably the vaporings of old soldiers re-fighting the war in later years. No papers have been found indicating a plan on the part of the two Confederate leaders to act in concert at that particular time. Supporters of this thesis point out that such a secret scheme would not have been put down on paper. These men overlook Bragg's refusal to give Morgan more than half a loaf. Had there been a grandiose plan for combined operations, it is extremely unlikely that Bragg would have lim-ited Morgan as he did. Until authentic documents supporting such a scheme are found, it will have to be catalogued in the realm of wild surmise.

Both Northern and Southern witnesses to Morgan's reaction to the news given him by the innkeeper's daughter agreed that he was obviously distraught. It was bitter news to John Hunt Morgan—that they could see. The raid went on.

Leeland Hathaway left the main column with a small detachment to look for fresh horses. After more than a week of hard, fast riding some of the division's mounts were exhausted. Even blooded stock from the Bluegrass faltered at the relentless pace the raiders were maintaining. It was not easy on the men, either, and Hathaway fell sound asleep in a wheat field while allowing his horse to feed. He was aroused by one of his men, who said the lady in a house nearby insisted on seeing the commander of the detail.

"She made complaint that our boys were annoying her about the house," Hathaway later wrote in his diary. "When I asked her how, she said they would go into the kitchen and worry the household for something to eat. I answered that we were driven by our situation to live off the country but that the soldiers were not permitted to be offensive or unnecessarily troublesome. If she desired it I would put a guard at her door. She spoke with much spirit saying 'No, I will not have it said that my father's house had to be protected by a Rebel guard.'

"Plucky, certainly, but perhaps a little indiscreet. I could only reply, 'That is all I can do,' and was asleep again in a minute. I was again aroused and the same complaint made. I gave the same offer and she rejected it as she had before.

"So the matter passed and I suppose the hungry soldiers helped themselves as usual to such as they found to eat. This girl was the stuff that heroines and martyrs are made of. She stood to her guns to the last, cool and plucky as a veteran, and declined what she considered a humiliating offer of protection as haughtily as a duchess in her castle."

This Indiana girl made a deep impression on young Leeland Hathaway—the more so because she was one of very few who stayed to face the raiders, refusing to take flight as did so many.

But the girl's courage was not duplicated in high places.

Indiana's governor, Oliver P. Morton, while Morgan was fighting his way into Corydon, issued an order calling on all able-bodied male citizens south of the National Road to form themselves into companies of sixty men each, elect officers and arm themselves with whatever weapons they could find. They were instructed to drill themselves in the manual of arms and wait further orders.

Troops were begged from Michigan and were put in cars bound for Indianapolis. All cars and locomotives in the shops in the state capital were readied for transporting soldiers. The governor instructed the superintendent of the state arsenal to put all available men to work making ammunition. Within hours Indianapolis was a madhouse. Roads leading to the city were clouded with the dust of thousands marching to take up arms. Every open lot, every vacant building became a camp or a barracks.

Downstate farmers left their crops to rot in the fields, hid their stock in the woods, urged their womenfolk to seek refuge elsewhere, and marched—not toward Morgan and his raiders—but to Indianapolis.

In the southern tier of counties near the Ohio the inhabitants were panic-stricken. On the day the Rebels were crossing the river the news of the victory at Gettysburg and the surrender of Vicksburg electrified everyone. Women took out the flags and bunting they had put away after the Fourth of July and displayed the colors to mark the victories. That night all the Hoosiers except the few who had failed to stop the enemy landing at Morvin Landing went to bed tired from their celebrating, but very happy.

In the middle of the night they were awakened by a great pealing of bells. The men dressed and rushed to the village squares.

"Is it another victory?" asked each newcomer in his turn. "Is the war over? Have we won for sure?"

"God no, man," replied one local official. "Have you a rifle? Governor Morton says everyone south of the National Road's got to arm and form companies. Morgan's come across the Ohio."

Hysteria spread as fast as the telegraph wires could carry it from town to town. Down in Bartholomew County a town official wired the chief executive:

"We have a company of mounted men. Where shall we get horses?"

General Burnside had ordered all shipping between Louisville and Cincinnati suspended until sufficient gunboats could be rounded up to protect it. But first he supervised the movement of one million dollars in specie from Louisville banks to banks in Indianapolis. Then the panic reached Indianapolis, and the banking houses boxed up the Louisville money, added their own, and shipped it by fast trains to Chicago and Cleveland.

Brigadier General Milo Hascall, on his way back to duty with the regular army, was handed orders superseding his earlier ones, and sent to Indianapolis to organize the defense of that city. As the farmers hurried north they were joined by others on the way. Mechanics dropped their tools, merchants abandoned their stores, clerks left their ledgers, profes-

75

sional men their desks, and students their textbooks to join the hordes converging on the capital. In less than forty-eight hours there were 65,000 men waiting for orders, waiting to be told how to capture 2,000 Rebel cavalrymen, already weary with constant riding, and mounted on horses that were beginning to fade in alarming numbers.

As the green, untrained recruits descended in a deluge on Indianapolis, Colonel DeLand's 1st Michigan Sharpshooters and the 12th Michigan Battery detrained in the same city. In response to an order from Governor Morton, 900 Wesson carbines were purchased from B. Kittredge and Co., in Cincinnati, and shipped to Indianapolis. It did not matter that they would have been much more valuable if issued to men many miles nearer the invaders' route.

General Morgan himself fanned the flames that spread across the state. With the clever assistance of Lightning Ellsworth, who rode at his side all through the march from the river, rumors were spread that the invaders were bound for Indianapolis, and intended to burn the state house, sack the city and free 6,000 Confederate prisoners held in Camp Morton on the edge of town.

Along the route the Rebel telegrapher cut into the overhead wire and sent a spurious dispatch saying that General Nathan Bedford Forrest, with another division of Southern cavalry, was hard on Morgan's heels.

This took the starch right out of the Hoosier Governor. He wired to Burnside:

"I ask that the 71st Indiana and 23rd Indiana Battery, recently sent to Kentucky, be immediately ordered back to this state for its protection— the protection of our town from burning and pillage. Indiana has repeatedly sent all her troops to protect Kentucky. I now ask the return of some for our own protection."

Governor Morton did not wait for this plea to produce results. He ordered 17,000 muskets rushed from the United States arsenal at St. Louis. Then, remembering that his old friend General Lew Wallace was chafing for action, after having been ordered from the field after the battle of Shiloh in order to serve on military commissions and courts martial, the Governor asked Washington for his services. Secretary Stanton agreed. Wallace was named commander of all Indiana forces and given the task of defeating or capturing John Morgan and his men.

General Wallace was fishing on the Kankakee River when he received urgent orders to report to Indianapolis. He dropped his tackle, rode hell-bent-for-leather to the nearest railroad, and reported the next day at the state capitol.

In his pocket he carried a frantic message from the Governor.

"Morgan has only to make haste, and nothing can save Indianapolis," it said. "Bad enough that, but it is not all. In camp here we have 6,000 Confederate prisoners, and out in the arsenal a supply of arms and ammunition to make them instantly ready for the field. Add them to the 6,000 veterans now with him and Morgan can demoralize the state."

Nothing revealed the hysteria that gripped the Hoosiers more lucidly than the telegram from their chief. If there were sufficient arms and ammunition to arm the 6,000 Rebel prisoners and turn them into a potent fighting force, why was not it issued to the militia? Who knew for certain that Morgan was heading for the capital anyway?

Most indicative was the terror that had reinforced the raider with 4,000 cavalrymen who existed only in the minds of the panic-stricken officials.

Throughout these fear-drenched hours the little Rebel column was moving along the hot, dusty roads of southern Indiana in what amounted to a news vacuum. By cutting the wires behind them and filling those ahead of him with false dispatches and orders, Morgan fostered such an aura of uncertainty that from the Ohio to Lake Michigan no man felt secure.

CHAPTER 7

Cavalry Needs Horses

LATE ON THE afternoon of July 9 Morgan moved out of Corydon toward Salem. Eleven wounded soldiers were left behind in the care of tender-hearted townspeople, but two of them died before the last supply wagon rumbled away behind the column.

By now the various components of the division were performing their duties as if by clockwork. Patrols rode ahead, looking over the terrain, avoiding ambushes, and occasionally seizing local citizens to act as guides. Flankers moved out four or five miles on each side of the main body, trotting down each country road and farm lane in search of food and horses. It was a scouring process that cleaned the line of march so thoroughly that barely a single healthy mount escaped the round-up. Whenever one of their own horses broke down, the Rebels left it in payment for one appropriated.

In the early days of the raid this exchange favored the farmers. The animal left behind by the invaders might be exhausted, or perhaps lame, but with several weeks of rest it would recover. Then the Hoosier found that he had a beautiful piece of horseflesh to replace the inferior animal he had lost.

Later, however, this changed as the column moved through the stifling heat of July in southern Indiana. The farm horses the rebels seized were of poor stock and usually became lame in a day or two; then the exchange left one poor beast for a fresher, but equally worthless mount. Young soldiers wept unashamedly when they had to leave behind their own Kentucky-bred steeds. Often, these animals had taken them over long stretches of rough road and through many battles, but this was the longest raid of all and the miles were inflicting a heavy toll on the horses.

The route from Corydon to Salem lay along two parallel roads and Morgan sent half of his force along one road and the remainder along the other. Major Webber and the 2nd Regiment led one group and Captain Hines with the remnants of Quirk's scouts rode at the head of the other column.

Apparently the grapevine telegraph had carried word that Morgan's men were not so evil as painted, or the women north of Corydon were made of tougher stock than their sisters to the south. Most of them remained in their homes with their children, and only very aged or infirm men were seen.

Colonel Duke noted that whenever one of his men rode to a farmhouse to seek a cool drink or to impress a horse he was met at the door by a dour, usually buxom dame, surrounded by children clinging fearfully to her skirts. Whenever the soldier asked where the husband was the reply was always the same:

"The men have all gone to the rally. You will see them soon."

Once, however, Duke arrived at a farmhouse to find a dozen of his men staring longingly at some apple pies on the kitchen table. They were still warm, and their aroma was about all the young troopers could stand. Yet not one pie had been cut into.

"I asked, in astonishment, why they were so abstinent," Colonel Duke recalled.

"One of them replied that they feared the pies might be poisoned. I have always been fond of pies . . . so I bade the spokesman to hand me one of the largest, and I proceeded to eat it. The men watched me vigilantly for two or three minutes and then, as I seemed much better off after my repast, they took hold ravenously."

Nightfall found the two columns about sixteen miles south of Salem, so they camped in the open fields where they were. Campfires blazed and horses were watered, fed, curried and tethered. As the soldiers finished their suppers, Ellsworth tossed his wire across a line leading to Salem and Seymour, and learned that Brigadier General Hobson was finally crossing the Ohio. Burnside's telegrams and Fitch's gunboats had rounded up several river packets and the Second Federal Brigade, minus its supply train, was ferried across to Indiana, completing the move at 2 A.M. on the morning of July 10.

Hobson was going to make the rest of the race without rations. Orders were telegraphed to all towns and cities in the southern part of Indiana to the effect that 4,000 Union cavalry would be pursuing Morgan, and that loyal citizens should undertake to feed them. It was hoped that by marching unimpeded by heavy vehicles the pursuers could overcome the advantage Morgan had won when he burned one of his ferries and sent the other to Louisville.

The raiders put out vedettes, but all the other men went to sleep, not greatly worried over the approach of the enemy about twenty-five miles away.

In the morning the force was divided into three sections. Morgan took one section along a road leading almost straight north, through Washington County toward Salem. A detachment on the left struck out for Orange County and one on the right headed for Floyd County.

Fractionalizing of his command seemed highly dangerous to some of his junior officers, but it showed Morgan's mastery of guerilla tactics. He knew that militia was being gathered to oppose him, but he had a low opinion of such troops. Much more of a threat were the hard-riding Hobson and the veteran Union cavalry straining to overtake him from little more than a day's march behind.

By cutting the telegraph wires, spreading false stories of his whereabouts, and cutting his force into sections he could confuse the local forces, making it impossible for them to muster at any one place in strength sufficient to cause the raiders concern. At the same time, it confused the pursuers, who never knew exactly where Morgan was going, or where his main body had been. There was still another benefit accruing to the Rebels from this dispersal of troops. Every horse for miles around that was not hidden in an inaccessible spot was rounded up by the raiders even if they did not need it, and poor Hobson found nothing but jaded and lame animals that were no better than his own weary mounts.

The adjutant general of Indiana admitted that by the second day of Morgan's invasion there were enough Hoosier troops available, had they been used correctly, to have crushed him.

"But," said the Indianan, "it was impossible for any merely human intelligence to divine the truth in the flood of conflicting and befogging reports that poured into the Capital."

Typical of the jumbled reports that had to be winnowed were these that arrived on just one day, July 10:

Hoosier forces had retreated at daylight through Fredericksburg (Orange County), pursued by Morgan's full force of 6,000 men; three thousand Rebels had taken Paoli and were advancing on the Ohio and Mississippi Railroad at Mitchell; three thousand Rebels had encamped the night before at Palmyra and were moving toward Vienna. Salem had been sacked and burned and the enemy was then moving north toward

80

Columbus and Indianapolis; Morgan was, in fact, turning back on his route to strike at Madison on the Ohio and, finally, another Rebel division was striking through Kentucky, headed for a rendezvous with Morgan somewhere near the Indiana capital.

The ability of the Indiana militia scouts to see double or triple the number of raiders at any given time was one of the stranger aspects of the entire raid. Lightning Ellsworth was never guilty of belittling Morgan's force, but if he had not sent a single message, the frightened home guards would still have been convinced that their enemy consisted more nearly of a corps than of an undersized division.

At Palmyra the raiders encountered a group of 350 minutemen but they fled toward Salem without showing even token resistance. Everywhere the Confederate cavalrymen went they saw lone horsemen or small parties of scouts racing away over the hill ahead. And never had the church bells pealed so constantly. It seemed to the raiders as if they were forever on the way to church or marching within the sound of a never-ending carillon concert. If any of them were familiar with John Donne's poetry they did not bother themselves to wonder for whom the bells tolled.

There was danger ahead, and behind, and everywhere—on either flank—but most of the young raiders were more immediately concerned with such pressing matters as obtaining food, forage for the horses and new mounts to replace the weary ones in their column.

For long months there had been little or no coffee in Tennessee or southern Kentucky. Here there was plenty, with a pot boiling on nearly every farmhouse stove. The abundance of good food made a deep impression on Thomas Coombs.

"Every morning the Captains of Companies would appoint a man for each mess to go ahead and furnish provisions," he wrote his family. "They would all go ahead of the command and scatter out to the farmhouses for miles on each side of the road, and by ten or twelve o'clock would overtake us with sacks full of light bread, cheese, butter, preserves, canned peaches, berries, wine cordial, canteens of milk and everything good that the pantrys and closets of the Hoosier ladies could furnish."

Nothing interfered with the steady movement of the invaders—Morgan saw to that. As the authorities at Indianapolis tried to make sense of the messages pouring in on them on July 10, Morgan sent couriers to his divided forces, gathered them together just south of Salem and advanced at a trot. Ahead of him rode Lieutenant A. S. Welch with a party of twelve scouts, followed in turn by Major Webber and the 2nd Kentucky, who had

81

been told to let nothing stop them. On the edge of town Welch spied a detachment of militia numbering more than 150 men; but he signaled his men, spurred his horse, and dashed in upon the raw, disorganized home guard. Without firing a shot the home guards broke and ran for safety in town.

Behind Welch's little group galloped Captain W. J. Jones. The sight of the yelling, dusty cavalrymen he led had the same effect on the main body lined up in the town square. Down went their muskets as they ran to the far side of Salem.

The saddest militiaman of all was a rustic who had hoped to spread carnage with the help of an ancient swivel gun which had been used for years by the young bucks of the town to celebrate the Fourth of July. He propped the 18-inch-long barrel on sticks of firewood and loaded it to the muzzle with nails, slugs and bits of rusty chain. In his hand was a pair of tongs in which he held a red-hot coal to use for firing the relic. Straight toward the mouth of the cannon charged Welch and his scouts. The frightened yokel took one look at the thundering horses and the shouting Rebels and dropped his hot coal in the dirt. The fumbling gunner and gun were soon in Southern hands.

That day fortune rode with Morgan's men. As the militia fled pell-mell into the fields north of Salem and the raiders dispersed to seek food, Captain John Davis, with a full company of the Washington County Legion, marched witlessly into town from the east to pick up arms and ammunition they had been promised in orders from Indianapolis. Mounted Rebels, laughing so hard they almost fell from their saddles, rounded them up like fish in a net.

Morgan sent scouts north on the road to Seymour to burn bridges on the Louisville and Chicago Railroad. Tracks were torn up, and the rails stacked in piles and surrounded with ties and brush. The wood was set afire, and by the time the flames died out hours later, the iron rails were warped and useless.

One of the patrols encountered two farmers riding on decrepit, swaybacked nags. One was a Quaker who insisted that he was not concerned with martial affairs and should be freed at once.

"But are you not hostile to the Confederacy?" he was asked.

"Thee is right," he replied. "I am."

"You voted for Abraham Lincoln, didn't you?"

"Thee is right. I did vote for Abraham."

"Well, what are you?"

"Thee may naturally suppose I am a Union man. Can thee not let me go to my home?"

The troopers let the Quaker go. This angered his companion.

"Why did you let him go?" asked the latter. "He is a black abolitionist. Now I voted for Breckinridge. I've always opposed the war."

"You're what they call a Copperhead, aren't you?" asked one of the raiders.

"Yes, all my neighbors call me that."

"Come here, Dave," called the trooper to a friend. "Look at this Copperhead. Now, old man, where do you live? We want your horses . . . and if you've any greenbacks just shell them out."

Many times while traversing southeastern Indiana Morgan's men ran across Copperheads who pleaded for special consideration. Some Northerners thought Morgan invaded the middle west to stir up dissension. Years later, efforts were made to show there was collusion between the Rebel leader and Copperhead elements. Duke denied it on many occasions in the years after the war. What tricked the proponents of this theory was Captain Hines' habit of getting information from dissident elements when he was on his small trail-blazing foray ahead of Morgan. It was natural for him to operate this way, having insufficient men to use force. But throughout the long raid the Southerners were much more severe on secessionists than on loyal Union adherents, having less respect for the former, who gave only lip-service to the South.

While his scouting parties rode the perimeter to prevent a surprise attack, the bulk of the Rebel guerilla's men had a field day. They burned the depot in the center of town and then ransacked all stores, mills, bakeries and saddle shops.

Something about the appearance of Salem must have triggered this pillage. The sight of so much abundance, after months in the impoverished states below the Ohio, was one of the causes. Another was the militant desire to show the well-fed Hoosiers what it was like to have an enemy force sweep through one's homeland.

William Price Sanders had been a torment to the South while leading his blue-clad cavalry in raids that left eastern Tennessee and Kentucky's mountain counties scorched and hungry. And only a few weeks before Morgan led his division on his great raid Benjamin Grierson struck south from the vicinity of Vicksburg and drove deep into Mississippi and Louisiana. He destroyed more than fifty miles of railroad track, seized 3,000 stands of arms and laid waste a wide swath of countryside.

The thoughts of these incursions into their own territory caused the Rebel soldiers to attempt to even the score. They harmed no civilians and bothered no private dwellings, but they were like locusts in the stores. The provost guard detailed by Colonel Duke was almost powerless.

"The men," said Duke, "seemed activated by a desire to 'pay off' in the 'enemy's country' all scores that the Federal army had chalked up in the South. . . . They did not pillage with any sort of method or reason; it seemed to be a mania, senseless and purposeless."

Soldiers ran from one shop to another, snatching articles and dropping them in favor of others they would see a minute later. Within half an hour every good saddle and stout piece of harness had been appropriated. The men who took this equipment did show some common sense. Others went berserk looking at the loaded counters and shelves. Bolts of calico were a prime favorite, with baby shoes a close second. One man took a Dutch clock and another a green glass decanter with matching goblets—just the things hard-pressed cavalrymen needed when they were fighting their way through enemy country.

At 2 P.M. the column again moved to the north and thence east toward Vienna. There was the natural desire to put more miles between it and the Federals behind, but in addition Morgan, Duke and Johnson decided that it would be better for the men if they left the alluring stores of Salem and resumed the open road.

Throughout the great Ohio raid there was bravery, courage, tenacity and great devotion to the Confederate cause, but on this afternoon of July 10 comedy had its hour. Horsemen rode through the countryside under a broiling sun that parched the earth and turned the pikes to dusty, powdery ribbons. The temperature mounted to the high 90's, and sweat foamed on the horses wherever girth and bridle touched their hides. The plunderers, however, did not mind the cloying heat.

Through the white dust of the summer roads rose the incongruous sound of sleigh bells jingling around the shoulders of the troopers. Full of high animal spirits, some of the men unrolled entire bolts of calico and gingham which fluttered behind them as they dashed, whooping and hollering, along the side of the moving column.

One Rebel soldier, unaware of the heat and equally unaware of the laughable spectacle he made of himself, rode for two days with seven pairs of ice skates slung around his neck. Another trotted along for the next forty-eight hours apparently mesmerized by a bird cage in which fluttered three very unhappy canaries.

84

On the pommel of his saddle still another rider proudly carried a silver chafing dish, which Colonel Duke thought looked more like a small coffin than it did a utensil for serving food.

They rode into Vienna, frequently cutting the dust in their throats with corn whiskey taken from the Salem saloons. After Salem, the appearance of the marching column changed, since many of the troopers donned pilfered white linen dusters in a belated effort to keep the ever-present dust from caking on their sweat-dampened uniforms.

As the division entered Vienna Hobson rode into Corydon, thirty miles behind them, but as far as the enlisted men were concerned he might as well have been marching on the planet Jupiter. John Morgan and his staff officers were not so casual. George Ellsworth had not joined the pilferers of Salem in their rounds of the stores. He had attached his instrument to a wire serving the Louisville and Chicago Railroad and for the first time obtained as accurate a picture of the numbers and location of the enemy as their confused state of preparations permitted. Lightning reported to his leader that Indianapolis was jam-packed with militia, that 10,000 home guards were massed at New Albany and that 3,000 additional troops were mustered at Mitchell. This intelligence led Morgan to change direction due east toward Madison on the Ohio River.

News of the gathering of enemy forces did not cause the raiders any particular concern. They felt certain of their own power to dissipate almost any body of green troops that might be thrown in their path. What concerned Morgan much more deeply was an intercepted message from General Willcox in Indianapolis instructing the militia and noncombatants to fell trees and erect barricades on all roads the invaders might possibly use.

Morgan, who knew more about guerilla tactics than any soldier of his time, knew that barricaded roads and burned bridges could delay more than battles with raw recruits. Up to this point in the long ride North, he had been moving with such speed that he always had the element of surprise on his side. Before any real obstructions could be erected, the column had dashed by and was well on the way beyond the barrier. But with the dogged Hobson following only a day or so behind, each hour lost clearing a barricade or finding a ford near a burned bridge would inevitably play into the Federals' hands.

Therefore Morgan closed up his column, warned the wagoners not to straggle, and rode until nearly midnight under a star-dappled sky.

Behind the fast-moving formation the citizens of Salem totaled their losses and damages, repaired the telegraph line and sent word of Morgan's probable destination. Identical dispatches sent to General Boyle and to General Mahlon D. Manson, a brigade commander in Hartsuff's corps, revealed how badly the nerves of Salem's civil officials were shaken. They read:

"Rebels are pushing for Lexington, Greensborough or Madison and will try to cross river at or near Warsaw. They are pushing with great rapidity, and will cut Jeffersonville Railroad at Vienna tonight, probably by this. For God's sake get up the river, seize all flats and steamboats and guard Warsaw Flats. Morgan's whole division is about 7,000 or 8,000; three 24-pounder Parrotts and two 12-pounder howitzers. I would not be surprised at his reaching Ohio by tomorrow morning."

John Morgan would have been elated had he only known how fear magnified the numbers of his column in the eyes of the enemy. This was just what he wanted.

He called a halt when his forward regiments passed beyond the sleepy little village of Lexington. Without taking time to groom their mounts or to eat, the exhausted cavalrymen dropped to the ground and fell asleep. The General occupied a house in the village and slept in a comfortable bed, protected by his personal escort. In the small hours of the morning, a party of Federal cavalry blundered into town and advanced to the gate of the home where Morgan was sleeping, but the escort drove it off, capturing three soldiers, and did not even bother to inform the General of his danger until he awoke.

At dawn the column was well along the road to Madison. Local units of militia converged on that town in order to protect the landing and prevent Morgan from crossing the Ohio at that point. The Confederates encountered one of these detachments on its way to mustering at Madison. It was a body of 300 home guards under an aged captain who had given his men permission to rest in the shade of a small grove of oaks. Horses were tied to the trees and to a rail fence along the road. The old officer asked one of the raiders:

"What company is this?"

"Wolford's cavalry," replied the Rebel.

"We're glad to see Kentucky boys," said the Hoosier. "Where's Wolford?"

Morgan rode up and was introduced as Wolford.

"What are you going to do with all these men and horses?" asked the general.

86

"Well," said the old man, "that horse-thieving John Hunt Morgan is in this part of the country and if he comes this way we'll give him the best we have in the shop."

"He is hard to catch," said Morgan. "We have been after him for fourteen days."

The militia captain, who recognized veterans when he saw them, asked Morgan to show his men a little military drill. The Rebel leader said his horses were too tired. "Take mine," said the guardsman, and helped switch saddles from tired southern horses to the fresh mounts. The Rebels who did the swapping jumped on the Indiana steeds. Morgan moved into the lead.

"Now I am ready to execute an evolution you've probaby never seen," he said. "Line up on both sides of the road."

The Hoosiers followed his orders. With a whoop Morgan led his troop off, and left the home guard with the worn-out horses.

It looked to the Federal scouts who watched the column from the distant ridges, as though the raiders were going straight toward the banks of the Ohio at Madison. At noon, however, the line pivoted to the left, heading away from the river toward Paris. When the last of the main force made the turn and the wagons rumbled north behind them, Colonel Smith and the 5th Kentucky demonstrated in front of Madison, and thereby tied down the troops who had been sent there to guard the crossing.

The ruse worked. Most of the militia was drawn aside, Morgan slipped away, found no opposing forces in his path, and left more than 2,000 men of the Indiana Legion commanded by Colonel Samuel B. Sering in Madison with nobody to fight. That afternoon the raiders rode through Paris, continued north and went into camp outside Vernon, where Colonel Smith and his regiment rejoined the main formation around midnight.

In Indianapolis there was consternation once again. The slippery Rebel and his column seemed headed for the state capital. Church bells pealed. Men who had been put on trains to go south were taken off and told to guard the State House. Extra troops were sent to Camp Morton to prevent the Confederate prisoners from attempting a mass escape. Governor Morton closeted himself with General Wallace to plan strategy. The Governor, after having convinced himself on the basis of all the false estimates pouring in from the southern counties that Morgan had 6,000 men, envisaged the enemy sweeping into Indianapolis with all these soldiers, and sacking the city with the help of the Rebel prisoners.

Wallace had seen some hard fighting with Grant in western Kentucky and Tennessee and did not scare so easily as Morton. Yet he was not re-assured when he thought about the small number of trained troops he had at his disposal, the lack of cavalry, and the difficulties that were presented when he moved infantry over a network of railroads that never seemed to go to the destination he desired.

Several lines ran south out of the capital toward the Ohio. In the southern tier of counties they crossed the tracks of the Ohio and Mississippi Railroad at three places—Mitchell, Seymour and North Vernon —as well as at other junctions nearer Cincinnati. Theoretically, this put Wallace at the hub of the wheel with troops he could send out on any spoke he desired to use. Although many a campaign has been won by a general with similar interior lines of communication there was a joker in the deck in this game of military poker.

The north and south lines were of one gauge, and the east and west line of a wider gauge. Therefore, cars could not be transferred, and Wallace could scarcely hope that there would be an ample number of cars at each and every junction waiting for him to determine which one to use. Also, the cars were small and the locomotives puny by modern day standards. The network that looked so efficient on paper was less than that in fact.

As the governor and the commander of Indiana's forces conferred, Wallace bluntly asked the chief executive what he wished done with Morgan. Governor Morton was so evasive Wallace came to the conclusion that his superior would be satisfied if all responsibility in the matter could somehow be transferred to other shoulders. Finally, Wallace spoke out sharply.

"I think I understand you, then," he said. "First relieve Love [General John Love, who had gathered about 2,000 militia to defend Vernon], then push Morgan on into Ohio, the faster the better."

This sounded like a shameless piece of expediency, but to General Wallace the governor's silence was an endorsement.

The man who one day would write *Ben Hur* hurried off to "push" Morgan into Ohio.

That gentleman was getting reports of a much more immediate danger. Scouts brought him word that Vernon was defended by a heavy force of infantry, well supported by artillery. General Love had several companies of Union regulars, and the 2,000 militia could be expected to fight bravely, strengthened by the presence of the veterans.

Morgan, Duke and Johnson rode forward until they were near enough to the town to recognize the infantrymen posted on the roads leading toward the center, and what looked like breast-works across the streets. Thoughts of Augusta flashed through the minds of the men in the 2nd Kentucky when the situation was clarified. The recollection of the bloody street fighting in Lebanon was to everyone a wound not yet completely healed.

John Morgan wanted no part of another such battle. He swiftly sketched plans to avoid useless and costly bloodshed, and ordered Colonel Johnson and the Second Brigade to swing right onto a side road leading across Graham Creek toward Dupont. He urged speed on his subordinates, and word was passed down the line of mounted men. They quickly reined their horses in the new direction and cantered down the dirt road.

Morgan then sent a flag of truce into the town, demanding the surrender of all the forces. His demand was declined without hesitation. By this time, however, the Second Brigade was well away, and Duke sent his regiments after it—even the wagons rolling along on the double. As his column slipped away to the southeast a train pulled into Vernon from the north, bringing General Love more reinforcements. Morgan, however, was still dealing trump cards. He bought more time for his fast-disappearing supply train and the bulk of his command by sending in a second demand for surrender.

Now time was working for him. The afternoon sun was almost at the horizon, and in the lengthening shadows cast by trees and hills the Federals could not see that all but one regiment of Rebel cavalry had slipped away.

General Love, who was made braver by the arrival of the new troops, refused the demand for capitulation and sent it back with a curt order that Morgan personally come in and surrender to superior numbers. The reinforcements hurried from the cars and marched forward to man the barricades.

Love's note amused Morgan and his chief lieutenant. Morgan, stalling for more time, waited until it was nearly dark, then renewed his demand, coupling it with a warning that he would allow Love just thirty minutes to remove women, children and other noncombatants from the town before he shelled it.

This was the Southerner's ace. The minute the flag bearer returned from his errand Morgan, Duke and the rear guard spurred their horses and rode after the column.

General Love, who took his enemy's word for gospel, scurried about, shooed the noncombatants into the fields north of Vernon, and then awaited with surprising composure an artillery barrage he presumed would be the prelude to an all-out cavalry charge. Men stood bravely by their posts, listening for fearful sounds that might mean death or injury. All they heard, however, was the chirping of katydids and the occasional booming sound of night hawks. After more than an hour of this nerve-shattering torture, scouts from town discovered that Morgan's entire division had disappeared into the night.

This coup extricated the Southern cavalry from one of its most danger-ous situations, but it cost the men more sleep and further weakened the horses. All night long the column slogged on steadily until dawn found it at Dupont, where a halt was called to eat and permit the horses to feed.

Any soldier who has been fighting but a few weeks knows that war, with its lack of communication between opposing armies, constantly and repeatedly conceals information of great importance that, had it only been known to one side or the other at the time, could have altered the entire course of campaigns or battles. It also keeps opposing sides from knowing of the other force's mistakes, except for those that are immedi-ately translated into action on the battlefield.

Thus, Morgan and his tired raiders knew nothing of General Lew Wallace's gallant, but ineffectual, race to the theater of war.

While the gray-clad troopers had been executing their feint toward Madison and the change of direction away from the river, Wallace led 1,300 infantrymen aboard a train at Indianapolis and started for Vernon. When the troop train reached the last town of consequence north of that place, Wallace commandeered a locomotive from a local train on a siding. He told the engineer he wanted him to run the engine a few miles ahead of the heavily-packed troop train and thus avoid an ambuscade.

"I'll go to Hell if you say so," answered the railroad man, "only tell me how to get there."

"That is too far for one night's journey," laughed Wallace. "Just run your engine ahead of me to Vernon, and if you run into the enemy give three quick whistles, open the throttle and let her sing. My train will keep about a mile behind you."

With the pilot engine ahead of it the troop train rolled into Vernon at about the time that Morgan and his men slept in the meadows just west of Dupont. General Wallace hurried up the track to question the engineer.

"No fight today," said the latter, who had had time to talk to some of Love's riflemen. "He is fifteen miles away."

90

Writing his autobiography years later, Wallace admitted that a great weight rolled off his shoulders.

"Gone, you say?" he asked.

"Yes."

"In what direction?"

"East."

The General wired Governor Morton at once.

"Morgan did not attack Love," said the telegram. "He is now miles away going toward Ohio. I shall wait the arrival of Love and Hughes. Together we can follow safely, pushing as we have opportunity."

It was not the type of message one would receive from Grant, Sherman or Stonewall Jackson.

Wallace and his men were not the only Federals left in a quandary by Morgan's speed on the march.

Most of the Indiana militia that mustered in the state capital was divided into western and eastern divisions and sent south by train. The western division detrained at Mitchell, the eastern at Seymour. As other northern states rallied to Indiana's assistance, additional fighting units moved toward the invaders' route.

The Mattoon, Illinois, Sharpshooters—a company armed with modern Henry rifles—was assigned to join the 103rd Regiment of Minutemen. A company from Charleston, Illinois, together with one from Ashmore under Captain Ferris were assigned to the 109th Regiment of Minutemen. Then the combined force was put on the cars for southern Indiana. Somewhere between home and the front so much time was lost that none of them fired a shot at Morgan's raiders.

General George Schofield, who commanded the Department of Missouri, heeded Ambrose Burnside's frenetic calls for assistance and sent the 10th Regiment of Kansas Volunteers and the 12th Kansas Battery. They arrived at Mitchell two days after Morgan had swung east from Salem, twenty-three miles away—the closest he ever came to the junction where all this manpower was concentrated, their guns stacked and their ardor waning.

A combination of fumbling, stupidity and unwillingness to face the fire of battle-wise veterans changed many of the state forces who were arrayed against the Southerners into little more than meaningless groups of men. Because they mustered too slowly at the wrong places and moved too slowly often to the wrong places, they seldom brought their ponderous weight to bear against the 2,000 butternut gray uniformed men who had been case-hardened by more than two years of war.

John Morgan was not deceived by this. He knew what lay ahead. He knew, too, that to his rear Hobson, Shackleford and Wolford, with more than 4,000 Union regulars, were striving to reduce the intervening miles and do battle. These men were from a different mold. One of their regimental commanders, Colonel A. V. Kautz of the 7th Ohio Cavalry, described the pursuit in these words:

"We made haste slowly by maintaining a steady but persistent and uninterrupted walk. For a continuous march there is no gait that excels the walk. The home guards were rushing about at a gallop and usually broke down the first day, and after recuperating, concluded to return home."

It may have been true, as Colonel Kautz recorded, that the Union cavalry was traveling at a walk, but the men were marching eighteen and twenty hours a day, and all but the fortunate men up front were eating one another's dust. The sun shone without mercy and after a few hours in the saddle each man felt as if he were on a rack. As some compensation, however, the blue-coated troopers had nothing to fear from snipers or lurking home guards.

Wherever Morgan and his men turned, there was the enemy. Basil Duke wrote that after the raiders had crossed the Ohio they averaged twenty-one hours in the saddle out of every twenty-four hours of the day. Fatigue was an enemy as dangerous as the militia. Bone-weary, the men hunched over the pommels of their saddles, more asleep than awake, gave their mounts the rein, and followed the men ahead in a half-trance. Only the immediate danger of battle could rouse them from their lethargy toward the end of each day's march.

At Dupont where they slept for three hours, Morgan and his staff knocked at the door of a large house on the outskirts of the village. The owner, Thomas Stout, who with his wife and children had retired many hours before, answered the summons in his nightshirt. Courteously, but firmly, the farmer was told he was to be the General's host. The children were routed out and sent to a small room in the rear of the house. Into the still warm beds tumbled the odd assortment of officers and aides, but not before Stout had been told to rouse them at 3 A.M.

Mrs. Stout had no more sleep that night. Her guests slept as if they had been pole-axed while she prepared a country breakfast of ham, eggs,

92

hot biscuits, buttermilk, coffee and home-canned fruit. At the stroke of three her husband awakened the officers and they ravenously consumed the victuals.

While they enjoyed a second cup of coffee, they heard an altercation down the street. The windows were open, and as the night was oppressively hot and sultry, the officers heard the sounds of soft Kentucky drawls interspersed by the sharper, strident voice of an angry Hoosier woman. Several of the raiders were demanding that the woman remove two American flags that were flying from staffs attached to the porch roof. Miss Sally Trousdale however, was not intimidated by the soldiers' carbines or by their threats. She had never heard of Barbara Frietchie, but the same strain of courage ran through her veins. Those flags would stay where they were and woe unto the Rebel who tried to tear them down.

Morgan thanked his hostess for the three hours of untroubled sleep and the bountiful repast. Then he left to rescue the young Indiana woman from her tormentors. The General issued an order and put a guard on the porch to enforce it. When the last of the troopers filed past Miss Trousdale's home the two banners were still fluttering in the breeze.

Not all the women in this portion of Indiana were as fearless as Sally Trousdale. While the farm wives in Harrison, Orange and Floyd counties had been openly truculent, most of the ones in the region east of Vernon and Madison regarded the Rebels as so many demons straight out of hell.

Sergeant Peddicord was shocked by the terror he saw in many of the women's eyes.

"The women were crying, begging and imploring us to spare their children," he confided to the pages of his sweat-soiled diary. "The boys heard this with amazement, and asked the women if they thought we were barbarians that they thought we could hurt women and children. The men assured them that not a hair of their heads would be injured, nor would they wound their feelings in any way."

Yankee businessmen were not held in equal esteem by the young chivalry from Dixie.

After assuaging the fears of the ladies, the raiders burned a water tank, twelve freight cars and a freight station on the side of Dupont opposite from where they had had their three-hours cat nap. They then bisected four railroads—one between Dupont and Seymour, one between Dupont and Lawrenceburg, another leading north to Columbus, Indiana, and a fourth running southeast to Madison and the Ohio River.

93

Everywhere, there were burning stations, bridges and cars. Compared with these blazes, the bonfires the Hoosiers were lighting in celebration of the victories at Vicksburg and Gettysburg were insignificant.

Before leaving Dupont the Confederates paid one final visit. It was to the packing house of F. F. Mayfield where, their fatigue of the night before forgotten, the men ransacked the pork house, and plundered it of 2,000 hickory-cured, canvas-wrapped hams that Mayfield had prepared for the Cincinnati market. Then the column rode off on the road to Versailles, a fat ham hanging from each saddle. If the few startled church-goers who watched the horsemen filing by that Sunday morning, July 12, had ever witnessed a stranger scene, they left no record of it.

Morgan's men had no time for sermons or hymn singing. On the road to Versailles they encountered bodies of militia at nearly every road junction. Although the home guards did not succeed in halting the column, they stood to their guns until shown the folly of fighting.

One of the captains in the division was a Presbyterian preacher before he signed up with the cavalry as a chaplain. On this Sabbath morning his thoughts were far removed from the Scriptures. His horse had become lame and he needed a replacement. He followed the practice of all raiders in such circumstances and rode ahead of the column, visiting farms in search of another mount. He had no luck; the farmers had hidden their animals in the deep woods or driven them far from the route the raiders were following.

Around a bend between fields of ripening corn, the chaplain encountered a small group of mounted militiamen. Fortunately for the preacher, all Morgan's men had learned the value of fast thinking in emergencies. Those who did not had been killed or captured long before.

The Churchman boldly advanced and heard the men debating as to which of their number should be elected leader. Taking his cue from this, the parson expatiated upon what a brilliant role he had played with an Indiana regiment at the battle of Shiloh. Entranced by his recital, the Hoosier guards elected him commander of the mounted troop. He at once set them to drilling and executing commands. They became so bemused with the business of playing war that they did not notice the approaching Confederate column. The chaplain ordered his charges not to fire, and before they saw through the ruse they were surrounded and captured. Utterly crestfallen, they were paroled and told to go home and to never again seek such big game. Naturally, their fresh mounts were

94

taken by their captors, and the Hoosiers rode away on weary steeds that were barely capable of carrying them.

That Sunday was unfortunate for many in southern Indiana. A family named Robertson, who never forgot that particular Sabbath, lived in a little crossroads town not far from Dupont. The only member who had a gun was an uncle, Dr. H. D. Gaddy, and he filled his pouch with enough bullets "to send the souls of scores of Morgan's men to purgatory," as he expressed it. He went on foot to a muster of home guards at Vernon.

His nephew, Middleton Robertson, who was eleven years old, stayed at home to guard the farmhouse, while his older brother Philander drove a two-horse team to a mill for some flour. As the wagon neared the crossroads at Pisgah Church, fifty gray-clad horsemen rode up and forced Philander to unharness the horses. They then rode away, and left the boy on foot. He arrived home in time to hear his sister Nancy lose an argument with other raiders, who took her favorite mare.

James Robertson lost one horse, but saved four thanks to his son Melvin who was home from college. When he saw a large body of troopers a mile down the road, Melvin led the four animals into a thicket and tethered them close together, so they would not be lonely and make noise.

James was wearing his new Sunday "go-to-meeting" boots and these attracted the eye of a Confederate, whose own boots were falling apart.

"I guess I'll trade," said the soldier. The Hoosier thought it best, under the circumstances, to agree to the trade. Rebecca Robertson and her stepmother lived half a mile down the road. Two soldiers approached the house seeking food, but were met by the older woman, who brandished a carving knife.

"I'll let you know I'm one of the blue hen's chickens from the state of Virginia," she told them, "and if you try to enter I'll cut your heart out."

"I know those Virginians will fight like the devil," said one of the raiders, "and I don't doubt you mean what you say."

Still hungry, the two troopers rode on. Still smarting at the indignities visited upon them by the Confederates, the Robertson clan awoke next morning to find Federal cavalry riding through, as hungry as their predecessors. By the time the Robertson women had finished cooking breakfasts for their own soldiers, they had stripped their pantries, cellar shelves and chicken coops. Middleton Robertson, a child then, recalled years later that it was "one hell of a Sunday."

95

Although Morgan's troopers were hungry and needed horses in great numbers, they behaved surprisingly well for soldiers in enemy country. The younger men liked a good time and although they were a little crude about it at times, they were often softhearted in the presence of illness or trouble.

One patrol discovered that a Methodist preacher by the name of Reuben Rice who lived in Graham Township, was an ardent abolitionist, so they made him get down on his knees and pray for the success of the Southern cause and Jeff Davis' health.

And yet just across the road lived C. H. McCaslin, a boy in his teens, and his mother, who was ill with a fever. All day long the Rebel column filed past, most of the soldiers stopping for water at a well near the house. The boy went to get water for his mother, but found so many raiders already there that he could not approach the well. An officer talked with the boy, learned his mother was ill, and ordered his men to stand aside while the boy filled his bucket.

Leeland Hathaway spent that Sunday leading a detail in search of fresh mounts. They had located several and had stopped near Versailles to rest.

"Soon after we were dismounted," Hathaway noted in his war diary, "there came to me one of our boys leading a very pretty pony, but followed by a rather good-looking girl of about sixteen years, modest and evidently much afraid if not decidedly frightened. However, her love for her pet gave her courage and she spoke up bravely for herself and for him. She had raised the pony by hand and they had grown up together. He was more than her little horse. He was her companion and friend. The tears that came despite her efforts to be calm were more persuasive than words. I told the boy, a gallant Kentucky trooper, to give her her little horse and seek farther afield for a new mount. She cried her gratitude. Maybe that handsome boy did not have a supper served to him by fair Hoosier hands that evening . . . luscious ham and biscuits, hot coffee, butter and preserves all given freely for a little act of kindness. To have seen the one eating and the other happily serving him with no longer any appearance of fear would have given one no thought of the evil war that was keeping these two souls apart."

Adjutant Hathaway received from General Morgan written orders protecting the girl and her pony. But that did not end the entry in the Rebel's dairy. This was an unsophisticated era and to Leeland Hathaway,

96

still young and impressionable, that scene beside an Indiana road, far from his own Kentucky home, was obviously deeply touching.

"The boy often spoke of the Hoosier girl," the diarist wrote, "and insisted that her bright eyes and sweet voice were more to his liking than the supper. Perhaps it is only fair that I should say I shared in the generous fare of that memorable evening and all the details of that incident linger in my memory as one of the pleasant episodes of the relentless realities of war."

After that tender, but sincere, entry it was no wonder that Hathaway wrote:

"I didn't want to shoot at another Hoosier until a sleepless night march had a little rasped my temper and a day of sultry sun and choking dust had given something of acidity to my sensations."

But that was another day. The adjutant and the boy expressed their gratitude and rode off down the dusty country road. The air about them was soft and warm, their stomachs were full, their minds were at ease, and the moon lighted their way.

CHAPTER 8

Trouble at Twelve Mile Island

FEAR WAS A BLANKET that covered Indiana from the Ohio to far above the National Road as the Confederates rode east. From Governor Morton to the poorest hired hand in the state, all considered John Morgan and his men devils in gray uniforms. Every newspaper in the area reported the number of men who crossed the Ohio as double or triple the actual count. It should have been simple for the military to issue an honest appraisal, but soldiers were as inaccurate as civilians.

One prominent resident of Brandenburg rode upriver to report to General Burnside that he "could swear on my reputation that I counted 5,000 Rebels boarding the *Alice Dean* and the *McCombs*." Militia officers at Vernon, who had not seen a raider closer than a mile away—with the exception of the bearer of the surrender demand—reported to General Wallace that they were outnumbered at least three to one. They judged Morgan had at least 7,000 men under his command.

On the Sunday that the Southerners were riding through Jefferson County with succulent hams hanging from their saddles, Indianapolis became a city populated by fear-crazed civilians, home guards less well behaved than civilians, and officials who had convinced themselves that Morgan had at least 10,000 veteran troopers with him. If church bells had been noisy before, on this day they sounded like the clanging of the very gates of hell to the frantic inhabitants. As evening came and shadows slanted across the grounds in front of the state house, all of the city's fire bells added their strident noise to the mad cacophony from the church steeples. Ringing of the alarm bells in the firehouses brought every home guard into line, carrying his musket, or wishing with every sinew of his body that he had a musket to shoulder.

Five regiments slept in the state Capitol yard. It did not matter that Morgan was more than seventy miles away and headed for Cincinnati. In view of the exaggerations of the newspapers, some of the apprehension among the ranks of the ordinary citizens could be understood. For the leaders, however, who had access to telegrams from the area where the invaders were marching, there was no excuse for panic.

In each of the forty counties south of the National Road the story was the same. For every family that remained at home, willing to face whatever came, there were four or five families that fled to the fields and woods, taking horses, cattle, heirlooms, silver and other cherished belongings with them.

One excitable woman, who lived on the road near Pisgah Church, learned that Morgan's men were approaching and decided she would have enough time to hide only one valuable possession. She took a shovel from the barn, dug a large hole in the back yard, and buried a huge mirror. Yellowed records do not reveal whether she was an ordinarily plain woman, or one of great beauty.

Terror rode the rails, traveled via the telegraph wires, and was carried by word-of-mouth from one self-appointed Paul Revere to another. Similar to fire in buffalo grass, panic raced across the flat prairies of Indiana and across the borders into Ohio and Illinois.

Three hundred miles from where Morgan was riding, a young couple was married in a small Illinois town. That night their friends crept near the girl's home, where the newlyweds were packing to leave on their honeymoon, and celebrated the wedding with a charivari—banging on skillets and pans, blowing horns and blasting the night air with pistol shots.

Only one thought came to the young bridegroom's mind. Morgan and his men had come to Illinois!

In fear that his tearful bride would be torn from his arms, the new husband picked her up, carried her to the open fireplace, and thrust her up into the wide chimney. Joining her, he sat all night with his wife clutched close on the soot-covered shelf. Next morning he learned that he was not the only one who had been deceived by the "shivaree." Most of his neighbors, who knew nothing of the plans for the serenade, had fled their homes in their night clothes and spent the night in the corn fields shivering with fear.

Some unhonored, rustic poet composed some verses about Morgan and his swift-moving cavalry division. They may have been composed during the early days of the Rebel raids that antedated the great invasion, or during the early days of that one, but in any event, the words were known to many Indiana and Ohio residents by the time the invaders swept across the Middle West. Men who marched to muster found themselves reciting the last two lines, and mothers shushed their children by whispering:

> "Morgan, Morgan, the raider, and Morgan's terrible men
> With Bowie knives and pistols are galloping up the glen."

Many a Northerner, however, found the Southerners friendly, human, and not at all unlike their own sons.

Victor Milhaus was "host" to forty or fifty soldiers one evening and seemed surprised that the Rebels treated his family with respect. Only food was demanded of the Hoosiers, and several men proffered payment.

"One of the Rebels very cordially invited me to make a visit at his house, 'when this cruel war is over,' " Milhaus told his neighbors. "I gave it as my opinion that his chances for getting home to receive company were rather slim. He replied, saying he supposed I would be pleased to hear that he and all his comrades were killed or captured. I assured him he was correct in his supposition. 'I like your honesty' was the rebel's reply."

In one of the early skirmishes, a fifteen-year-old boy from east Tennessee was seriously wounded and left in the home of an Indiana farmer. He was tenderly cared for until he died, and the farmer and his wife were saddened by the boy's repeatedly-voiced wish to see his mother.

These young, hard-riding troopers may have seemed like villains from a distance; up close, however there was little to set them apart from boys anywhere. They were as homesick in the North as Hoosier boys were in the South; when they were wounded the pain was the same; but this was war—and who looks with equanimity upon an invader?

If the fearful populace of southeastern Indiana had only known it, the raiders were not at the moment concerned with the impression they were making on their enemy. They were, instead, alarmed about the continued absence of that love-smitten adjutant-general, Captain Davis, who had led a hundred men away from the main column at Shepherdsville, Kentucky. His instructions had been to create such a confusion that everyone in Louisville would assume that Morgan and his entire division were soon to join him.

100

Davis and his men performed the first part of their assignment with great success. They dashed through Jeffersontown to Shelbyville, cut the telegraph wires, burned highway and railroad bridges, and set fire to freight cars. They then turned sharply north to Smithfield and Sligo, and headed for the Ohio River at Twelve Mile Island. Nowhere did they see Union troops. In Louisville, they would have found many gathered there under Burnside's instructions to present Morgan's men from burning Rosecrans' vital supply center.

Davis and his men moved only at night, once past Sligo, to prevent the enemy from knowing where they were going to attempt a crossing of the Ohio. On the night of July 10 they made their bid. No longer attempting to hide, they cantered rapidly out of the back country and headed for Westport. The road ran through the rich river bottom and, because of the nature of the soft ground, the road was of corduroy construction, with peeled logs laid side-by-side on the rich black slit. The sound of the horses' hoofs was like distant drumming to some of the raiders; to others it resembled the booming rush of sound made by dozens of partridges.

The Rebel troopers reached the river bank as the first rays of the morning sun sparkled on the wide Ohio. They had emerged exactly where they had intended, opposite Twelve Mile Island. Men prowled the shore, looking for craft in which to ferry the two companies to Indiana. All they found were two decrepit flatboats with rotted planks and seams badly in need of caulking. There was not time to look for others, or to make repairs, so Davis decided to embark at once. The adjutant led the advance party, using one boat. Within two hours, forty men had reached the Indiana bank, the horses swimming alongside the boat. The second boat operated between the Kentucky shore and the island. Soon after Davis reached the far side, another fifty men and their mounts had gained the island in midstream. Only Lieutenant Josiah B. Gathright of the 8th Kentucky and an eight-man platoon acting as rear-guard were left on the southern bank.

Suddenly Gathright saw three tin-clads steaming around a bend up-river. The gunboats from Commander Fitch's flotilla slowed their engines and coasted in close to the far shore. Gathright surmised they had spotted Davis and his party. His suspicion was confirmed when the Federals opened fire, shelling the northern bank. The men in the rear guard could see the puffs of white smoke and hear the shells hurtling toward the Indiana shore.

Gathright knew the peril the whole party faced. They were split into three units, and the tin-clads would have the men on the island at their mercy if he did not act swiftly. Gathright left and the others shoved their flatboat into the Ohio and rowed for the island.

On the first trip they escaped detection, for the trees on the small island hid them from the Union gunboats.

Gathright crowded as many troopers as he could into the boat, and ferried them to the Kentucky shore. Without hesitation the rear-guard again left, and were on their way to safety with a second load when they were sighted. The tin-clads rounded one end of Twelve Mile Island, black smoke spurting from their stubby stacks. Federal gunners loaded their cannon with solid shot, and thereby probably saved the Rebels in the small flatboat. The troopers could see the round shot skipping along the surface of the water—one a very near miss. If the gunners had used canister or grape, it would have been a turkey shoot. With circumstances as they were, Gathright succeeded in rescuing thirty-four men from the island.

Fourteen or fifteen men, fifty horses, and all the arms and ammunition of the thirty-four who had left in such a hurry were abandoned and soon captured. Meanwhile, Davis and his fifty raiders had ridden inland at top speed, knowing there was nothing they could do for the men in Kentucky or for those on the little bit of land in the river.

Gathright was now in a terrible predicament; he had forty-two men under his command, only eight of them mounted, and only eight of them armed. He knew the gunboats would prevent another attempt at crossing the Ohio. If he stayed on the river bank, more Federal militiamen in Kentucky would learn of the trap he was in. There was no alternative but to strike out for the Southern lines—or be boxed in and captured. If they could move swiftly and secretly, they might succeed. None of the forty-three men however, was optimistic about his chances.

Lieutenant Gathright proceeded with the business of saving his men for the Confederate cause. On the water, the tin-clads could make him cautious, but on dry land he would show the Federals he was still a capable antagonist. First, he moved away from the river into the nearest woods and then waited until darkness, thereby giving his men a chance to rest. As soon as it was dark, he formed his little column in marching order, four mounted men in the van, then the dismounted, unarmed men and, finally, four more mounted troopers at the end of the procession as a rear guard. They marched all night, stopping only to permit some of the walking men to ride for a while. Before dawn crimsoned the skies,

102

they hid in a forest. They spent the day there, safe from enemy eyes, and ate their iron rations.

The next night they resumed their trek, avoiding towns and villages, keeping to the back roads. Farm dogs bayed, but their owners stayed indoors. By the third summer of the war, Kentucky farmers and villagers had learned that it was wiser not to investigate the sounds men moving during the night. Both Northern and Southern scouts roamed the border state, and stragglers from both armies used the roads at night to avoid detection and arrest.

By making night marches, Gathright and his men, were safer than they would have been in any other state with the exception of Missouri, where the same conditions prevailed. But safety was not the only thing that disturbed the forty-three raiders. The men who were on foot disliked slogging along in the dust or rain like infantrymen, so one by one they raided isolated barns and stables. Before they had traveled seventy-five miles, every one of them was mounted. Some had no saddles, and some of the horses were of poor quality, but at least the cavalrymen were riding once again.

Gathright took them through Taylorsville, down toward Somerset, and along the route they had followed, when they were riding north with Morgan, in the other direction. Then he started toward the mountains. Most of the men were still unarmed, since rifles and pistols were scarcer than horses, but the group made good progress. They avoided armed patrols by their strict adherence to Gathright's orders that they should travel only at night. Eventually, they crossed the Kentucky border, forded the Clinch River, and reported for duty—all men present and accounted for—at Knoxville. They had crossed the state of Kentucky from the Ohio to the Tennessee line, only eight of them armed, and suffered no casualties.

Captain Davis and his half-hundred men in Indiana were less fortunate. They had left for safer territory far from the river bank when the gunners on the three Federal tin-clads shifted their sights to the fugitives in Gathright's flatboat. John Morgan had arranged a rendezvous at Salem, so it was for that town that Davis and his party headed, after they had given their horses a rest.

The assistant adjutant-general of the First Brigade had no way of knowing that the main column had crossed the river so swiftly. The column had encountered so little resistance that it had gained a day on its own estimated time of arrival at Salem. Davis rode north and slightly

103

west, straight into the wake of the storm left by Morgan's passing. Armed patrols seeking to overtake the main Confederate division were patrolling nearly every road, it appeared to Davis, and he had several near escapes near the little crossroads hamlets of Memphis and Borden.

On the outskirts of Pekin there was a small creek that crossed the dirt road Davis was following. Trees were close to the stream on both sides. The little band of troopers jogged onto the bridge and into a burst of musket fire from an ambuscade on the far side. Several riders fell, and Davis had difficulty regrouping his men and started to lead them into the nearest woods, where he hoped they could better defend themselves. As he wheeled his horse, it caught a leg in the underbrush, and threw him head first against a log. Davis was knocked unconscious and when he revived, discovered he had been overlooked by the enemy. His men had surrendered in the belief that he had been killed, and were being led away by Hoosier militiamen.

The next morning, still dazed, he started walking back along the way he had ridden the afternoon before—unwilling—he later wrote his sweetheart, even to entertain the thought of surrender.

Morgan's men were like that. Some lacked schooling, some were country boys who could ride like Indians and shoot like demons, but they were devoted to their General and to the Southern cause. If he could, Davis swore to himself, he would make his way back to Tennessee. As it developed, however, the luck that rode everywhere with Lieutenant Gathright deserted his leader.

On the outskirts of Borden, Captain Davis was accosted by a small boy who informed him that an injured Rebel soldier was hiding in a farmhouse down the road. The Rebel officer walked into the house to see if he could help his wounded companion and found himself facing six rifles held by Hoosier militiamen. From his captors he learned that the ambuscade at the creek had been planned by the 73rd Indiana Volunteers, backed by a detachment of the 5th U.S. Regulars—men who did not scare easily at the approach of the enemy. Captain Davis was shipped to a prison camp, where he was held fifteen months while awaiting exchange. For Morgan's adjutant there was only one happy note in this. It gave him time to write to Frances Cunningham, far off in Springfield, Kentucky, and he made good use of the opportunity.

The activities of Davis, Gathright, and their men created excitement out of proportion to their numbers. Northern troops, who might have thrown their weight against the main column, were detained in Louis-

104

ville. Gunboats that could have been used elsewhere were held at Twelve Mile Island. But the small size of the diversionary party did not stop Commander Fitch from claiming credit for a major victory. As soon as he could dock at a town with a telegraph station, he sent a message to the commandant of the Naval Station at Cairo, Illinois—a message based on extremely poor information:

"Intercepted 1,500 of Morgan's reinforcements at Twelve Mile Island; forty-five got across, thirty-nine were captured, also forty horses . . . rest retreated back."

CHAPTER 9

Six Hundred Miles of Fried Chicken

WHILE MORGAN'S intrepid men were riding up the glen, General Edward Hobson was urging his tired troopers to forget their fatigue and press on after their adversary. The Union force had lost valuable time at the Ohio, but had been creeping closer to the raiders with the passing of each day— no mean achievement in that Morgan was taking every worthwhile horse he could find in a swath at least ten miles wide, often much wider, when he split his force into sections and marched on parallel roads.

Hobson had the advantage of being in friendly territory. When wires went out to loyal citizens to supply their troops with food, the residents also brought in whatever horses had escaped the Confederate dragnet. Although the encounters at Corydon, Salem and Vernon had been easy victories for Morgan, they had delayed his progress. And the feint toward Madison had taken him along two sides of a triangle, which Hobson later shortened by marching along the hypotenuse.

The dour reception displayed toward the Rebel column changed to one of enthusiastic welcome when the Federals made their appearance. Some of the Union men considered the welcome a bit too fulsome. They were given so much chicken by their loyal supporters that some of the younger soldiers claimed they were sprouting feathers.

Chicken is the poor farmer's chief source of meat. Throughout Indiana and Ohio the birds that had been hatched in the spring were ready for the table when the invasion swept across those states.

Veteran troopers, who had been accustomed to eating hardtack, salt pork, corn pone, and an occasional ham actually found themselves complaining about the fare served by the Hoosier and Buckeye farm wives.

"Spring chickens were then just ripe," a Union soldier wrote, "and in

106

truth and literally there were 600 miles of fried chicken for us. You may look upon this as an exaggeration, but I trust it will not be so considered. I am surprised at my moderation in thus describing the fried chicken prepared for us on this march, in view of the fact that whichsoever way we turned or whatever road we followed, the women met us promptly with the greatest abundance of fried chicken. I am inclined to think it would be entirely within the bounds of truth if I described the same as six hundred square miles of fried chicken."

Other soldiers remarked on this emphasis paid the familiar barnyard fowl, and also recorded that loyal women north of the Ohio served hot biscuits, blackberry pie, crabapple jelly, fresh bread and plenty of milk and buttermilk.

Few cavalry marches have been longer, and the men had every right to be fatigued, but the sight of more than 3,000 troopers riding through the summer countryside, munching on chicken legs or wedges of pie should have amused even the most saddle-worn.

Despite their repeated protestations that they were running a gauntlet of fried chicken, the Union soldiers were surfeited with their compatriots' ardent patriotism. Everywhere north of the Ohio, people gathered by the fences and in village squares to sing "Rally Round the Flag, Boys." The Hoosiers even sang it while serving the fried chicken.

It became an accompaniment more tiring than the sound of hoofs, more wearing than the dust that got into their eyes and mouths from the pall that hung over the marching column.

A young federal lieutenant passed by his home and was overjoyed to see his wife and two small children standing by the fence. He dropped out of the column to greet them. His wife pressed into his hands some of the ubiquitous chicken and he had to ride on. Before he left his doorstep, the tearful woman led the two children in a chorus of the same song.

General Hobson, at the head of the column, could not escape the melody. By the time the end of the mounted procession came along, the singers had often tired, but this luck never favored those up front. Years after the war, the general said that when he went home on leave, after the pursuit of Morgan, the clock on the wall ticked "Rally Round the Flag, Boys," and the katydids on the doorstep chirped the same refrain.

Young blood is young blood, even when it is flowing through veins of men so tired they can hardly stay awake. One day it so happened that a detail of Federal cavalry rode by an Indiana cabin when a mother and her three small children stood in the door.

"They were watching us, silent, bug-eyed and their jaws slack," one soldier remembered. "One of our boys said he was surprised that they were not singing 'Rally Round,' so another soldier said 'I'll start 'em up.' He rode into the yard, asked them most sweetly to sing, and led them in the tune as his friends rode on."

While the Union regulars plodded on after Morgan, General Lew Wallace was having great difficulty in trying to carry out his mission of driving the Rebels out of Indiana into Ohio. He wired from Vernon to the militia in Lawrenceburg, urging them to gather wagons for the rapid movement of his irregulars and for them to meet him at Osgood. Then he ordered his officers to impress all the horses they could find and form a mounted troop. It resembled something from a comic opera.

In more than twenty four hours they could round up only 146 horses—most of these jaded nags that Morgan had left behind. Wallace sent his "cavalry" off in the direction where he assumed Morgan's column was and then put his infantry on the Ohio and Mississippi cars to follow. Hours later his forces rendezvoused at Osgood, but by the time the farm wagons plodded up from Lawrenceburg, all opportunity to overtake the fast-moving Confederates was lost.

Morgan's men had swept into Versailles, captured and paroled 300 minutemen under Colonel James Craven, and seized $5,000 from the tax collector's office. Then Morgan divided his division into two columns so they could march more swiftly and the Rebel commander struck out for Milan, crossed the Osgood-Lawrenceburg pike well ahead of the lumbering wagon train that Wallace naïvely thought could help him pursue one of the hardest-riding cavalry units in the land.

This all proved that raw, green troops, no matter how brave, are almost useless in such a fast, kaleidoscopic campaign. They just could not be hurried. They were disorganized, led by willing but unseasoned officers, and confused by orders emanating from too many headquarters. Burnside in Cincinnati, Morton in Indianapolis and Wallace in Vernon—each had his own idea of how to stop or catch Morgan. But what seemed easy in a headquarters map room did not materialize when troops waited for provisions or ammunition, when trains were held up for hours by conflicting orders or when the differing track gauges forced time-consuming transfers at junctions.

The 300 men under Colonel Cravens could have held Versailles for several hours. However, before the gray-clad troopers reached the outskirts of the town, Morgan's scouting parties had appeared in so many

108

different places that the home guards found themselves completely confused. When the head of the main column trotted into Versailles, the best the disorganized, fearful militiamen could do was to fire a few scattered shots and then surrender.

Colonel Duke considered the ineffectiveness of the Hoosier home guards cause for amazement.

"I am satisfied," he said in his story of the raid, "that we saw often as many as ten thousand militia in one day, posted at different points. They would frequently fight, if attacked in strong position, but could be dispersed by maneuvering. Had they assailed us as the fierce Kentucky Home Guards would have done, we could not have forced our way through them."

Colonel Grigsby and the 6th Kentucky were detached to ride in a circle around Versailles, to burn bridges and destroy railroad tracks. In the midst of their activities they found a large number of horses that had been collected by a dealer, probably to sell to the union army as remounts. Grigsby relieved the wranglers of further responsiblity by driving the whole remuda back to the main column. The animals were of much better stock than most of the farm horses that had been acquired between the river and Versailles. They were greeted by cheers from the Rebel troopers.

Fresh horses always elated the Confederate raiders. Some of the soldiers and most of the officers had left Tennessee on prized mounts. These animals they babied, and lead them unburdened while they rode the decrepit animals collected along the route. Sometimes, when a battle seemed imminent, the Rebels would change mounts, in order to go into action on their own horses. This practice unquestionably saved the Blue Grass stock on the long, arduous march. It was also one more way of keeping fresh stock from falling into Hobson's hands.

Occasionally the raiders captured carriages and wagons along the road and in the barns and stables behind the farmhouses. Wounded and ill men were transferred to these vehicles. When there were more carriages than there were incapacitated soldiers, some of the healthy young troopers took turns riding at ease. The buggies, rockaways and buckboards trailed along at the rear of the mounted column across southern Indiana, and gave this section of the division a most unmilitary appearance.

Even the double threat of opposition by militia and the approach of the regulars could not keep some of the younger Rebels from having their fun. One of the most common expressions of humor was for the men in the carriages to warn Hoosiers that a much bigger army would be along the next day and would burn every house and barn to the ground. Some of the country people were so gullible that when Hobson and Shackleford came by with their men they found that the natives had fled to the woods.

By the time Morgan's men had finished disrupting communications at Versailles, it was four o'clock in the afternoon of Sunday, July 12. The day was disagreeably sultry, and no thunderstorm came to break the oppressive humidity. Sweat streamed from both riders and horses as the division moved toward the east. Chickens in the farmyards sought the shade, beaks agape. Instead of dashing out to snap at the horses' legs, dogs sprawled on the doorsteps, unwilling to exert themselves in the stifling heat.

General Morgan discussed with Duke, Johnson and several of the regimental commanders the best strategy for Cincinnati, not more than sixty miles ahead. He was sufficienty astute to know that Burnside had had time to shift large numbers of troops from Louisville, now out of danger, to the Ohio metropolis. He surmised, too, that militia from Indiana and Ohio would be converging on the city to protect it, and to be handy for an attack on the Rebel column.

The Confederate cavalryman wanted no part of a pitched battle. He knew how futile it would be to invade Cincinnati with only 2,000 mounted men and four guns. He wanted to keep Burnside and the militia commanders off balance and ignorant of his true intentions. His lieutenants discussed the details and finally rode away to execute his orders. The column was broken into segments a few miles east of Versailles, and the various units dispatched in different directions.

One detachment rode straight for Aurora, a fairly large town on the Ohio. It was five miles downstream from Lawrenceburg, about thirty-five miles from Cincinnati, on the bend of the Ohio near the Indiana-Ohio border.

Another force struck northeast toward Pierceville to prevent militia efforts to flank the raiders from Osgood, where Wallace still fumed over the ineptness of his home guards.

Colonel Duke led the main column on the most direct road to Milan. General Morgan, at the head of a smaller section, moved along a road to the south that paralleled it, and bound for the same town. Throughout the afternoon and evening the four columns trotted through the countryside, moving faster than usual, and sweeping an area about twenty-five miles wide.

110

As the raiders moved through Ripley, Ohio, and Dearborn Counties, they dispersed a few bodies of militia that had been assembled at crossroads and bridges in order to impede their progress. Occasionally Lightning Ellsworth listened to the messages crowding the telegraph wires and dashed off a few false reports and orders of his own. Yankee outposts on the hills watched the various bodies of mounted raiders and hurried off to send in their warnings.

The result of all this intentional confusion on Morgan's part, and the overabundance of misinformation collected by the Northerners, was what the Rebels wanted. Union commanders, who received reports of enemy columns in all directions could not make up their minds where to assemble their fighting men.

Two Rebel raiders were caught in Aurora at almost the same hour that Hoosier militiamen were brushed aside by a hard-riding detachment north of Pierceville. In addition to the turmoil in southeastern Indiana, a false report reached Ambrose Burnside and was forwarded to Governor Morton in Indianapolis. It stated that General Buckner with 10,000 men was somewhere in north Kentucky, headed for the Ohio and a link-up with Morgan's men.

This was too much for Governor Morton. He ordered every soldier in the capital into trains and urged their commander, Brigadier General Henry B. Carrington, to move no later than three P.M. with whatever troops he had amassed by that time. General Orlando Willcox, who discovered that the 12th Michigan Battery of Light Artillery had just disembarked from trains from the north, sent it racing through the city to support the troops supposedly moving south toward Cincinnati.

The Michigan gunners gave their horses the whip, and guns, caissons, and supply wagons went careening around corners and bouncing over the cobbled streets toward the depot. In the middle of town one of the caissons exploded with a great roar. Two of the gunners were killed instantly; the horses fell, dead or injured, in their traces; and two citizens who had been standing on the sidewalk watching the battery thunder by, were mortally wounded by flying fragments of metal.

Teams drawing the guns and caissons behind the explosion became tangled in one another's harness in efforts to avoid the crater in the street. It took a long time to achieve order. Finally, the rest of the Michigan battery went down to the tracks where the Indiana contingents were waiting.

At nine P.M. Carrington had not made a move, and the apoplectic Willcox removed him from command and appointed General Hascall to replace him. Engines were coupled to the coaches, and Hascall's force steamed out of Indianapolis, bound for battle.

The situation was no better downstate.

The Madison Courier published an edition that reported Morgan and his men had ridden four and six abreast through Versailles, and took five hours to pass through the city. The frightened Hoosiers did not realize that such statistics would have meant Morgan had more than 10,000 troopers. They were seeing "butternuts" everywhere they looked. If the paper said they were riding six abreast, that was good enough for them.

A regiment of militia from Columbus came down the railroad as far as New Point, north of Osgood. They left the train at New Point and marched toward Sunman, not aware that Sunman was the place where Morgan intended to reunite all his scattered units for a dash across the line into Ohio. If they had remained there and fought bravely, the story of Morgan's raid might well have been drastically altered. The 300 men, however, encountered a smaller party of militia which had been sent north by rail from Lawrenceburg to interdict Morgan's passage at the same spot. They held a council of war and in the middle of their debate about the best course to take, they saw a half-dozen Rebel outriders on a rise of land to the west. In fear that Morgan would move down Manchester Ridge and find Lawrenceburg undefended, the militia at Sunman boarded the train in the station and hurried back to Lawrenceburg.

Sunman was left unguarded, and Morgan had a straight and unobstructed corridor to the Ohio border.

While Northern troop units frittered away their chances to combine and force the Rebels to fight, the Southerners were riding steadily to the east. Night overtook them as the main column marched through Milan. A short distance from that village, the raiders halted. Sheer physical weariness had accomplished what home guards had been unable to do.

Bennett Young recorded the scene in his notebook. He moved through the halted column and saw his fellow raiders "scattered along the fence corners for four miles." Some were sprawled on the grass by the side of the road; others were sound asleep as they stood against the snake-rail fence, their horses' bridles looped over their shoulders, the faithful steeds also asleep.

Morgan and Duke let them sleep. The stars came out, and whippoorwills sang from the depths of the woods beyond the fields of golden corn. Grigsby's regiment rode in from the north; a little later the detachment

112

that had threatened Aurora jogged in from the south. No one ate. Hunger took second place to the need for sleep, and the late comers dropped from their saddles alongside their companions.

Nearby, the tracks of the Ohio and Mississippi Railroad wound close to the village of Sunman. A long string of box cars, in which 2,500 Hoosier militia were crowded, was on a siding. Some of them slept and others lounged away the dark hours, smoking and talking of Morgan's raiders—never dreaming that their enemy lay asleep just over the ridges to the west. In the morning the train departed for Cincinnati and removed the force from the invaders' path.

Equally unaware of the existence of the foe so close to them, the Rebel raiders slept where they had fallen. A few officers and pickets, who found strength where they thought none was left, mounted guard over their weary friends. Within a score of miles, more than 15,000 Northern soldiers waited for daylight to come so that they could resume the hunt for Morgan and his men, but not one approached to mar the peace and quiet of that last Indiana bivouac by the side of the road.

CHAPTER 10

Thirty-five Hours of Hell

MORGAN'S RAIDERS were in the saddle by the time the sun came up on the morning of Monday, July 13, 1863. They moved in the direction of Harrison on the Ohio line. With less than three hours' rest, the 2,000 troopers faced the longest continuous cavalry march in history. Ahead of them lay Cincinnati, crowded with Union regulars and militia. Around them were scattered forces of home guards and behind them, less than five hours' marching time away, came Hobson, Shackleford and Wolford with more than 4,000 veteran horsemen.

John Morgan knew the odds against him. What he anticipated was an attempt by Burnside to make him fight as he crossed the Cincinnati, Hamilton and Dayton Railroad which ran north from the Ohio River. Colonel Duke later quoted his commander as saying that if he could break through the forces expected along the railroad and thus pass this ordeal, there would be every reason for continued success on the raid and an eventual escape into West Virginia somewhere upstream where the shallows would prevent the gunboats from operating.

Showing no sign of fatigue, the handsome General rode to the head of the column and waved his gauntleted hand at his followers. He had rested no longer than the others, and the heavy weight of responsibility was mainly on his shoulders, but he seemed unconcerned. His eyes were gay, the mouth beneath the mustache full and generous. Six feet tall, he towered above his slight, small-framed brother-in-law and chief lieutenant, Basil Duke. He rode his beautiful mare, Glencoe, with effortless ease, his sinews seeming to merge with those of his mount.

At thirty-eight, he was one of the South's greatest cavalrymen, honored for his daring and uncanny successes. This was the man about whom Mary Boykin Chesnut, the South's most famous diarist, had written so lyrically at the time of his courtship of Mattie Ready, the Murfreesboro beauty who became his second wife.

"Mattie Ready got tired of hearing Federals abusing John Morgan," said Mrs. Chesnut. "One day they were worse than ever in their abuse and she grew restive. By way of putting a mark against the name of so rude a girl, the Yankee officer said, 'What is your name?.' 'Write Mattie Ready now,' [replied the girl] 'but by the grace of God one day I hope to call myself the wife of John Morgan.' She did not know Morgan, but Morgan eventually heard the story; a good joke it was said to be. But he made it a point to find out; and, as she was as pretty as she was patriotic, by the grace of God she is now Mrs. Morgan."

The Christmas before the raid, while Bragg's army was camped near Murfreesboro, Jefferson Davis visited the stanch Rebel town and attended the wedding of John Hunt Morgan and Mattie Ready. It was performed by Lieutenant General Leonidas Polk, a bishop in the Episcopal Church. He was a West Pointer turned churchman soon after graduation, and put his robes over his general's uniform to conduct the ceremony.

It had been a gay week in Dixie, with parties and dances and scores of good friends to wish the newlyweds happiness. Photographers begged the cavalry leader to sit for portraits so that they could sell them to his thousands of admirers. Theater owners and managers offered him choice seats to attend their plays and concerts. When the ceremonies were over, a Confederate officer and friend wrote the new Mrs. Morgan:

"It is certainly the match of the times. 'The Belle of Tennessee' and the dashing leader whose name rings through the civilized world. It has certainly given me a higher opinion of him than I had before, exalted as that was. It is his greatest victory."

Summer had come, ending the winter's stalemate. Union armies were pressing Bragg and his men near the Alabama border. Polk had doffed his churchly robe and was holding a thinned gray army together south of Murfreesboro. Mattie Morgan had fled over the mountains into South Carolina to escape the blue-clad patrols.

Her husband, not one to be downcast, was in the heart of the enemy's homeland leading 2,000 Rebel soldiers in one of the most daring expeditions of the Civil War. Hundreds of miles inside the Northern lines, he put his column into motion and started for Cincinnati.

A few miles from Sunman, the raiders wrecked the tracks of the Indianapolis and Cincinnati Railroad, between Weisburg and Van Weddon's Switch. Continuing northeast, the column passed through New Alsace, a tiny hamlet on Tanner's Creek settled by German immigrants. In that village some of the raiders found a wagon loaded with lager beer.

115

Delighted, they confiscated it. As the horsemen rode along the dirt road toward Dover and Logan, the wagon slowly fell back along the file of mounted men and gave the parched riders a welcomed opportunity to sample the foaming brew.

Colonel Cluke and the 8th Kentucky rode rear guard, "eating the dust" of their companions and prevented the supply wagons from straggling. The land was cut by ridges where the streams ran toward the Ohio to their right, and whenever the 8th topped one of the hills the tall, raw-boned, swarthy-complexioned Cluke reined his horse to one side far enough to escape the cloud of dust and looked back on the road over which they had ridden.

Between Dover and Logan the Colonel saw what he long had been expecting. Far to the west, clearly discernible in the bright morning sunlight, was a low dust cloud, rising above the treetops. Cluke spurred his horse and informed General Morgan. Hobson's 4,000 men were only a few hours behind them, in fact, the gap was so slight that some of the German settlers in New Alsace told the Union leader that Morgan's men had left town only two hours before his entry. The Northern cavalrymen rode on, with no lager beer to slake their thirst.

Maintaining a fast jog trot, the Confederate force rode through Logan down a winding road that descended to the Whitewater River—which crosses out of Indiana into Ohio at the town of Harrison on the Ohio side of the state line. Their thoughts occupied with the Regulars driving hard to overtake them, they knew nothing about an abortive attempt to stop them before they left Indiana.

A Hoosier Methodist preacher, Dr. Johnathan Flood, had organized a home guard company in Dearborn County. Most of the men in the unit were his own parishioners. Lacking orders from higher authority, the clergyman put himself at the head of the little band and rode toward the Sunman-Harrison pike. They had armed themselves with long, muzzle-loading guns into which they had rammed healthy charges of slugs. The muskets were used by most of the volunteer soldiers only to slaughter hogs during the fall butchering season. But they gave the men courage, and as the Indianans rode along on their heavy farm horses, they considered themselves a formidable body of fighting men.

They suddenly encountered Rebel pickets and chased them over the fields until they found themselves confronted by a group of gray-clad cavalrymen prepared for battle. Forgetting their loaded muskets, the home guard gave rein to their horses and galloped away as fast as their

116

mounts could carry them. But two of the volunteers, who had ridden too far in the van, were captured. The Southerners relieved them of their horses and forced the two to accompany them on foot into Harrison.

A fine bridge, of heavy oak timbers, spanned the Whitewater River at Harrison. Without interference, the raiders crossed into the town beyond. Colonel Cluke's men had carried straw and brush onto the span after the wagons, and the rear guard had set it afire. The dry, weather-beaten timbers caught fire and blazed fiercely until the bridge gave way and fell into the stream.

A cloud of steam rose from the riverbed. Through this patch of mist Hobson's advance patrols saw the last of Morgan's column disappearing on the road leading out of Harrison—it had been a narrow escape.

Morgan was out of Indiana, but the shooting was not yet ended in the Hoosier state. Two companies of militia, which had mustered at Lawrenceburg to guard against a Rebel crossing at that point, were sent north on a report that Morgan had reversed his route and was marching back from Harrison.

Colonel James Gavin, in command at Lawrenceburg, sent his own regiment, the 104th Indiana Volunteers, half a mile beyond Hardinton, where they erected a barricade of logs and cut down trees.

Colonel Kline G. Shryock, with the 105th Indiana Volunteers, was ordered to a position a mile to the rear of the 104th. Night approached while the 105th was marching to its post and, without realizing it, the regiment took a road with a sharp curve, caused by a turn in the Miami River. In the darkness, as the road went through a heavy stand of trees, the men in the rear of the file saw the head of the column outlined against the night sky, apparently moving in their direction. Shouldering their rifles, the Hoosiers in the rear fired on the men they assumed to be Morgan's raiders. The latter, uncertain of themselves in the dark, returned the fire.

Men fired at the flashes of guns around the bend in the road, shooting from behind trees as their forefathers had fired at the Indians in this same forest. Bullets whined through the underbrush and made sickening sounds when they struck tree trunks or human flesh. The men of the 104th, hearing the fusillade behind them, moved back in an attempt to discover the reason.

Colonel Shryock sensed what had happened and rode along the road, yelling at his men to cease killing one another. After what seemed an interminably long time the shooting stopped, but not before five men

117

were dead, one was mortally wounded and seventeen others were hurt. One of the wounded was a Private David S. Gooding, who had served as a state senator and circuit court judge before taking up arms.

Morgan's passage from Indiana was not marked by this carnage alone. It was also accompanied by events of much lighter vein.

Among these was the misfortune that befell the two men of Reverend Dr. Flood's home guard company. They had walked disconsolately beside their mounted captors into Harrison and watched as the bridge burned and fell into the Whitewater River. Then they had been released. They knew they had to cross the stream, so they forded it, wading through water up to their necks. When they were only three miles into Indiana, and their clothes were just starting to dry on their backs, they were seized by a patrol from Hobson's advance and forced to march back to Harrison. Again they waded through the chilly Whitewater River. Residents of Harrison who knew the two unfortunate men, convinced the Union soldiers that their drenched captives were loyal Northerners, and they were freed. Once more they started for their homes in Indiana, fording the river for the third time. They had good cause to tell their preacher-commander that their sins had been washed away in the Whitewater River.

They were not alone in their misery. General Hascall's men who had been sent by rail out of Indianapolis with the Michigan battery—minus one gun—to help capture Morgan, reached Hamilton, Ohio a few hours after Morgan left Harrison, twelve miles to the south. He was, he reported to Governor Morton, "just in time to be too late."

His men were not so disconsolate. Some of them were rustics with a love for practical jokes. In one of Hascall's companies there were seven preachers who had taken up arms to rid Indiana of Morgan's demons. The clergymen were the objects of constant jokes and tricks. One parson hastily fell into line on debarking from the train and unwittingly carried a sign on his back that advertised a popular brand of bourbon whiskey.

A Quaker, Sylvan Johnson, of Irvington, Indiana, frankly admitted in a letter written after the futile pursuit that never before or since had he experienced such a pleasant sense of relief as when the home guard company in which he served failed to connect with the fleeing Morgan.

After that failure to find a battle in which to try their valor, the Hoosier defenders went to Cincinnati in order to take trains on the Indianapolis, Cincinnati and Louisville Railroad to their homes. There, in a town disturbed at Morgan's nearness, they were ordered to participate in a dress parade to impress the citizens. When the time came for the parade, only eight men mustered for duty. The rest were drunk in the local taverns or were on the river bank trying to determine if their rifles could fire bullets across the Ohio into Kentucky. One wag wrote that the Indianapolis minutemen went to war "battle-scared" and came home "bottle-scarred."

But for every coward or clown there had been scores of valiant Hoosiers who had taken up their guns and left their homes to seek John Morgan. They had not been able to stop him, but they had slowed him, and only Hobson's trouble in getting his artillery over the hills had prevented his making good use of the delays brought on by the militia.

The raiders were overjoyed to be out of Indiana, where, as Morgan himself said, "Every man, woman and child was an enemy, every hill a telegraph and every bush an ambush." He little knew, as he complimented the Hoosiers, that the people in Ohio would prove to be far more fierce.

The men liked Harrison, and called it the fairest town they had seen since leaving Dixie. Tired as he was, James McCreary found time to record that he had seen a surprising number of beautiful women in the first Ohio community through which they rode.

Morgan let his men rest for three hours outside Harrison. The bugles then sounded "Boots and Saddles," and the column moved on; Adam Johnson's brigade in the van, Duke's bringing up the rear. The General rode with Colonel Johnson for a time and asked him if any of his men were familiar with Cincinnati. Johnson said that two of his troopers had been reared there and that Captain Sam Taylor, who had helped capture the *Alice Dean* and the *J. H. McCombs* back at Brandenburg, had lived there for many years. Morgan asked to talk with them, and so Taylor, Lieutenant John McLain and McLain's cousin joined the officers for a conference.

As a result of the conversation, the three troopers hastily changed into farm clothes acquired in Indiana and rode into the city to get information for Morgan about Burnside's preparations and the disposition of troops. Johnson arranged a meeting-point where the three were to rejoin the raiders after their reconnaissance.

Morgan then determined to do his utmost to confuse Burnside as to where he would by-pass Cincinnati. He sent a detachment northeast toward Hamilton, the largest city inland from the river, then followed with his main column. When he reached farm country, away from too many prying eyes, he ordered his main force to veer sharply to the south-

119

east and gained the main pike leading into Cincinnati. When he made this move, his men cut the telegraph wires, which had intentionally been left undamaged up to that time, in the hope that they would be used to spread word that the entire division was headed toward Hamilton.

Morgan could not have chosen a better night for his dangerous march around Cincinnati. There were a few stars, but they did little to illumine the pitch-black darkness. Lack of wind assured the raiders that noises of the marching column would not be carried far.

Through the Stygian, awesomely silent night, the Southern cavalrymen marched. Every man understood the danger he was in, and each loosened the pistol in his holster, shortened the reins and rode alertly, in an effort to determine the presence of enemy soldiers. The thick dust of the road muffled the sound of hoofs except when an iron horse shoe struck a stone.

Burnside, perturbed in his Cincinnati headquarters, would have given much to know the whereabouts of John Morgan at that hour. He had sufficient worries to have occupied a half-dozen army commanders. He still did not know the truth about the rumor that Buckner was nearing the Ohio. He had no way of knowing that it was not Buckner at all, but Colonel John Scott, on his seven-day raid into Kentucky—and that it represented no menace.

On his desk were telegrams full of details about the draft riots in New York City. He wondered if the killing and the burning that took place there might be duplicated in Cincinnati. Also, there was a wire from Halleck, the General in Chief, in Washington.

"I must again urge upon you," the wire said, "the importance of moving forward into east Tennessee, to cover Rosecrans' left. Telegraph what you are doing toward this object, so that we can have definite information to act upon."

Old Granny would have been even more unhappy had he seen the wire Halleck had dispatched to Rosecrans at the same time. It read:

"General Burnside has been frequently urged to move forward and cover your left, by entering east Tennessee. I do not know what he is doing. He seems tied fast to Cincinnati."

He was certainly tied fast, trying to determine a method of capturing John Morgan, afraid that the raiders would attack the city, and afraid that they would not.

David Tod, Ohio's Governor, had taken a leaf from the book of Governor Morton of Indiana and called all the militia in the southern half of the state to arms. All the men from thirty-two counties were ordered to assemble at four centers, those nearest Cincinnati were to report to General Burnside, those next to the east were to report to Colonel George Washington Neff at Camp Dennison. Those in the central block of the southern tier were to report to Camp Chase at Columbus, and the balance from southeastern Ohio to rally at Camp Marietta in the city of the same name.

Tod instructed the citizen soldiers to form companies, regiments and battalions, to elect officers and to start drilling. By train, by wagon, on horseback and afoot the militiamen from Butler, Clermont and Hamilton counties started on their way to Cincinnati. It was not their fault that they had so little time. Morgan had moved so swiftly that Tod had not issued his mobilization order until the day before the raiders rode into Ohio.

Burnside proclaimed martial law in the sprawling city of a quarter of a million and also in Covington and Newport, Kentucky, across the Ohio. While the citizens of the Ohio metropolis were debating whether to shutter their store windows, Morgan and his men were marching out of Sunman on the start of their ride around the city.

Cincinnati itself was in a frenzy.

General Jacob Cox, Commander of the District of Ohio, did his best to prepare the city for defense. Cox was a strange man, a sort of jack-of-all-trades who was also a master of them all. He was an authority on literature and cathedral architecture, on microscopy and art, on politics and soldiering. Burnside may have been confused, but Jake Cox was not.

He divided the city into four districts, the first under the command of Brigadier General S. D. Sturgis, with headquarters at the Broadway Hotel; the second under Major Malcolm McDowell, with headquarters at the Burnett House; the third under Brigadier General Jacob Ammen, with offices in the Orphan Asylum. The fourth was commanded by Colonel Granville Moody, who set up his command post at the Finley Methodist Episcopal Chapel.

Butchers, bakers and candlestick makers; lawyers, mechanics, and clerks; drapers, millers and draymen mustered at their posts—some with arms, some with none. Wives and sweethearts tearfully kissed their menfolk goodbye and then shuttered their homes, hid valuables and tried to quiet their frightened children.

Louisville had known panic when Morgan's division approached after the battle of Lebanon. It was now Cincinnati's turn. Gunboats moored at the wharfboats and along the river bank trained their guns on the city, as

121

if their commanders believed the shells could hit Confederates only in the labyrinth of twisting streets. Butter went from eighteen and twenty-three cents a pound to seventy cents. Eggs skyrocketed from two dozen for a quarter to a dollar a dozen.

Excitement reached such a level that no one laughed when Gus Copt, a deserter from the German Imperial Army, now a gardener for the rich Mrs. J. Handasyde Perkins, organized his own seriocomic home guard company and drilled in an open field.

General Burnside ordered every packet on the Ohio to tie up in Cincinnati or to moor on the Kentucky bank, for fear that Morgan would seize them to use as ferries.

Everyone was waiting for the militia, but Tod's order to mobilize had come too late. There was a great rushing about and scheduling of extra trains, but not enough men reached Cincinnati to form a company. That city was going to have to face its ordeal unaided.

At the offices of Cincinnati's two newspapers, the *Gazette* and the *Enquirer,* tired printers, setting type by hand, tried valiantly to keep up with events. Special editions were on the streets every few hours. People bought them avidly, eager to learn of Morgan's movements. What they learned was confusing. And it confused Burnside as badly as it did the citizens.

Residents of Hamilton telegraphed that the Rebels were headed for their city, unaware that only a single detachment was demonstrating in that direction and would soon turn away to rejoin the main column. A fire broke out in Miamitown, and pickets were rushed to guard that road. Another flared up in Venice, and home guards rallied on that community.

Two deputy sheriffs wired Burnside that they had been captured by Morgan and paroled, adding that they had conversed freely with the Rebel leader, who had confidentially confided that he was going to invade Hamilton.

In his search for men to join the chase after the raiders or to help protect the city, Burnside remembered a small force in a barracks across the river in Covington. It was headed by Major George W. Rue, a huge Kentuckian in Judah's brigade, who was ill at the time the raiders crossed the Cumberland. His regiment—the 9th Kentucky Cavalry—joined the pursuit at the Green River. A few days later Rue got out of his sickbed and went to the depot in Somerset in order to go to Louisville. The conductor ordered him off the train, saying he was forbidden to carry any men in uniform. Rue changed into civilian clothes at a friend's home,

122

took the next train, and eventually reached Cincinnati. When he reported to Burnside, the General said he did not know where Morgan was at that time, but asked him to take charge of the Covington barracks. Rue found about seventy men of his own regiment who had been sent for ammunition by Shackleford, and about a hundred infantrymen from scattered regiments.

While Morgan was riding around Cincinnati, Burnside sent for the soldiers across the river. Rue mustered all he could find and ferried them over the Ohio. That night Rue stabled his horses in Fountain Square and slept in Burnside's quarters.

As darkness fell the streets of Cincinnati were deserted except for the soldiers and a few thousand townsfolk who crowded into the downtown business district. Horsemen galloped to and from Burnside's headquarters, and municipal officials dashed about on a hundred ineffectual errands. Police were ordered to remain on duty, and they patrolled the streets, not knowing whether to look for Rebel raiders or grab thieves and pickpockets.

The town was a prisoner of its own fearful imaginings, and wild rumors and stories coursed through the streets, embroidered and enlarged upon as they passed from mouth to mouth. There was one so fantastic that no sensible person would have believed it. This night, however, the residents of "Porkopolis" were not sensible persons.

A fantastic, night-blooming flower of a rumor had it that General Morgan, disguised as a civilian, had come into town to attend a gay ball and reception in some rich merchant's mansion. The foolish rumor would not die, and long after the invasion was over, there were those who swore they had seen the Rebel cavalier dancing at the party while Cincinnati trembled.

The timid residents, who refused to be reassured, read the papers under the corner gaslights, trying to follow the raiders' progress from such bulletins as these:

"11:20 P.M. A courier arrived last evening at General Burnside's headquarters having left Cheviot at 8:30 P.M. with information for the General. Cheviot is only seven miles from the city. He states that about 500 of Morgan's men had crossed the river at Miamitown and attacked our pickets. Morgan's main force, said to be 3,000 strong, was then crossing the river. A portion of the Rebel forces had been up to New Haven and another had gone to New Baltimore and partially destroyed both of these places. The light of the burning towns was seen by our men. When

123

the courier left, Morgan was moving up, it was reported, to attack our advance."

"1 A.M. A courier has just arrived from Colerain with dispatches for General Burnside. He reports that the enemy, supposed to be 2,500 strong, with six pieces of artillery, crossed the Colerain Pike at dark at Bevis, going toward New Burlington or to the Cincinnati and Hamilton Pike in the direction of Springdale."

"1:30 A.M. A dispatch from Jones Station states that the enemy are now encamped between Venice and New Baltimore."

"2 A.M. Another dispatch says the enemy are coming in, or a squad of them, from New Baltimore toward Glendale, for the supposed purpose of destroying a bridge over the Cincinnati, Hamilton and Dayton Railroad near Glendale."

"2 A.M. A dispatch from Hamilton says it is believed that the main portion of Morgan's force is moving in that direction going east. At this writing—quarter past two A.M.—it is the impression that Morgan's main force is going east while he has sent squads to burn bridges on the railroad and over the Miami River, but he may turn and come down this way on some of the roads leading through Walnut Hills and Mount Auburn."

The printers labored all night at their type fonts, and Burnside and Cox, almost snowed under by the blizzard of dispatches, sought to get men in front of Morgan. There were already plenty of them to his rear. Every word brought out of the dark night told of where Morgan had been. What the two generals wanted to know was where he was going. The bulletins, confused as they were, however, served to mark the Southerners' route. It finally became clear that the wily Morgan was not bent on attacking the big city.

In the middle of the excitement Colonel Sanders and the 5th Kentucky Federal Cavalry, together with some Michigan cavalry, steamed into Cincinnati aboard river packets. They had ridden from east Tennessee and then taken boats for the last leg of the race to help catch Morgan. Their horses were relatively fresh, and Burnside had hoped to throw them out ahead of the raiders, but Morgan had been too fast. All Sanders could do was join Hobson in the pursuit.

Morgan might have been brought to battle on his ride around the Queen City had luck ridden with Henry Judah. Trapped when the Green River flooded, Judah had lost more than a day in taking up the pursuit. Then, to make matters worse, he had attempted a fancy bit of master-

124

minding to prevent Morgan's return to Tennessee and had marched on a wild-goose chase to Leitchfield. By the time he learned Morgan was not retreating, he had lost another day. He took the cars to Louisville and then, shifting to steamers, he had set out for Cincinnati.

The force, all regulars and veterans of more than two years of war, much of it against Morgan, consisted of the 11th Ohio, 23rd Michigan and 107th Illinois Mounted Infantry; the 14th Illinois, 5th Indiana and 11th Kentucky Cavalry, two sections of artillery and four mountain howitzers.

With their horses rested by the boat trip up the Ohio, Judah's brigade could have been thrown in a wide arc north of the city to trap the raiders. The weary Confederates would have been at a heavy disadvantage against these men mounted on fresh horses.

The day that was lost behind the swollen Green River made just enough difference to save Morgan. Judah was somewhere downriver with 3,000 excellent fighting men—too far away to be of any help—and Burnside could do nothing. Cox rallied his raw militia to protect the city, and home guards milled about the suburbs, unable to make up their minds where the invaders were headed. No one seemed really able to dispute Morgan's passage.

With no regulars in his path, the militia not yet organized, and Hobson delayed twelve hours getting his guns across the Whitewater River, Morgan's worst enemy now was fatigue.

For eleven days the Confederate cavalrymen had been riding and fighting almost continuously. They had averaged more than forty miles a day, most of it through grueling heat, and seldom had they enjoyed more than four hours of rest in twenty-four.

When Stuart made his famous ride around McClellan's army, his men were rested, and his Chambersburg march came when the troopers were relatively well refreshed. Forrest's dash after Streight was initiated after a short but welcome bivouac at Courtland, Alabama.

Morgan, however, started on his great ride with but three hours of sleep, his men weary, his mounts almost exhausted, and with the whole division suffering from the cumulative effect of driving themselves each day to the very edge of collapse.

The General rode in the van with Adam Johnson. Out ahead of the Second Brigade were some of Tom Quirk's scouts and a score or more of men from Lieutenant Colonel John M. Huffman's company of Texas Rangers. Occasionally men from these units rode up to isolated farm-

125

houses, seized the owners and made them serve as guides to point out the route around the city to the south. Long before midnight all of the scattered detachments, sent out to create diversions, had been called in, and the long column wound its way, intact, through the velvet darkness.

At a point near where the road crossed the Miami River, Captain Taylor, Lieutenant McLain and McLain's cousin emerged from the shadows. They had ridden into Cincinnati and out again without incident. The report they made was that the city was torn by confusion, with raw, green troops milling about, fear on every face. Although Taylor urged Morgan to march in and demand the city's surrender, Morgan knew better than to heed this alluring advice. He patiently told those about him that his 2,000 men would be lost in Cincinnati's streets, that it would take twenty-four hours to regroup them if they escaped capture, and that the delay would provide Hobson sufficient time to overtake the column.

The temptation was great. For a day Morgan would have been master of one of the great cities of the North. However, had he been unable to get boats to take his men across the Ohio, he would have been trapped, and his troopers would have been hunted down in the streets and alleys of the business district.

Bennett Young recorded that Taylor estimated Burnside had 30,000 soldiers in the city. They were green and untrained, but against such odds the valiant 2,000 would have met certain defeat. It was not that they feared a fight. Morgan had determined to keep his force in action for as long as possible, to pull all the Northerners he could into the pursuit, and thereby give Bragg more time. He would ride on, fording the Ohio further east, thus maintaining pressure on the Yankees until the last.

When the last wagons rolled off, Duke's rear guard burned the long wooden bridge across the Big Miami. The flames mounted into the night sky and cast shadows that stretched for miles. This sight oppressed some of the troopers, who feared it would pinpoint their whereabouts for the enemy. However, a bridge was a dangerous thing to leave intact between themselves and Hobson's eager horsemen.

The tiring raiders marched on through New Baltimore, Bevis and New Burlington. The terrain was hilly and heavily wooded in spots; the slow crawl of the artillery, the supply wagons and the buggies bearing the sick and wounded impeded the entire column. Men could scarcely see their companions before or behind them, and the sound of hundreds of hoofs shuffling through the loose dirt and dust of the country roads was like a narcotic. A rider would doze, ease up on his reins and his horse would fall back until bumped by the horse following him.

126

The 2,000 raiders, with their vehicles, were strung out over several miles. Officers had to use all their persuasion, horsemanship and patience to keep the march from becoming a disorganized rout.

Duke was in the rear, where Morgan thought the greatest danger lurked. When night had fallen, they had no way of telling how close Wolford, who was leading Hobson's forces, might be. Basil Duke was at his best when danger threatened. He kept the 2nd Kentucky Regiment tightly massed in order to prevent a sudden attack, leaving Morgan free to find the way around Cincinnati.

"In this night march," recalled Duke, "we met the greatest difficulty in keeping the column together." He described the position of the Second Brigade in the van and said it experienced no trouble. "But the First Brigade was embarrassed beyond measure. Cluke's regiment was marching in the rear of the Second Brigade, and if it had kept closed up, the entire column would have been directed by the guides.

"But this regiment, though unsurpassed in fighting qualities, had, from the period of its organization, been under lax and careless discipline. The effect of it was now observable. The rear companies straggled, halted, and delayed the First Brigade, for it was impossible to ascertain immediately whether the halt was that of the brigade in advance or only of these stragglers, and when forced to move on, it would go off at a gallop. A great gap would thus be opened between the rear of one brigade and the advance of the other, and we who were behind were forced to grope our way as we best could."

At first the men talked in an attempt to avert sleep. They discussed their chances of passing around the great sprawling city without being detected, and they wondered if Burnside could manage to create enough order out of the chaos Sam Taylor had witnessed to send a force down upon their flank.

They knew their greatest danger lay almost entirely to the south. More than a score of highways led out of Cincinnati to the northwest, north and northeast, similar to the spokes of a great wheel. Their own route cut across these spokes not far outside the city limits, and at each road junction scouts moved cautiously ahead to determine if the enemy had marched out on that particular spoke and was lying in ambush.

After a short time Duke left the rear guard in the capable hands of Colonel Grigsby and the 6th Kentucky, and rode forward to effect better liaison between the two brigades. It was a Herculean task.

By midnight the column had marched fifty-five miles—out of Sunman, Indiana, through Weisburg, New Alsace, Logan and into Ohio at Har-

127

rison. Thence, on through Miamitown and across the Big Miami, not stopping to eat or let the horses feed, one weary mile after another.

Gone was the excitement of the captured wagon of lager beer, forgotten was the burning of the great bridge over Whitewater and the beautiful women of Harrison. Horses lost their shoes and became lame, forcing their riders to leave them behind or to walk, leading them, until a near-by barn or stable offered them a substitute mount. Men accustomed to the power and strength of the horses from the Blue Grass cursed the "big-bellied, barefooted, grass-fed beasts" they had acquired in Indiana. When these animals cast their shoes, they often broke their hoofs on stones, and soon refused to go farther.

Horses, like men, gave out where they were weakest. The big draft horses, heavy in the belly, were also usually sway-backed. After they had gone their limit, they sank down in the road as if poleaxed, their spines no longer equal to the task of bearing a rider. Those with weak legs went lame and a few, unused to prolonged road travel, dropped out on the hills, completely exhausted.

The riders' weary bodies cried out for sleep, but there could be no rest now—no rest until the column passed well beyond the city to the east. Rein arms grew sore, and the pain in their pelvic bones and at the base of the spine was a torment from which there was no respite.

"At midnight fifty-five miles had been covered by the ceaseless tramp of the wearied steeds," wrote Bennett Young. "They had taken one hundred forty-four thousand steps already and still more than a hundred thousand were to be required before they could rest their tired limbs."

Men whose horses failed walked beside the column or jumped up behind companions, adding to the horses' burdens.

"The exhausted animals," said Young, "sank down in death with their riders astride, still urging them onward, and under the dreadful physical burdens, strong men fell from their beasts as if smitten with sudden death."

Hundreds of soldiers rode fast asleep. Their mounts, aware of the lack of tension on the reins, slowed to a crawl or stopped altogether. The men, awakening, would then gallop to regain their places. Others lashed themselves to their saddles to keep from falling off. The wisest of the veteran troopers took turns riding side by side, one man asleep and the other guiding both horses until it was time for a turnabout.

"As we rode along," Duke later wrote in his memoirs, "Colonel Cluke, tired and weary, rode up and said he would give a thousand dollars for an

128

hour's sleep. I told him I would hold his horse and he could sleep until the scouts came in. He assented and fell immediately asleep in the saddle."

No one in the slow-moving column was sufficiently alert to comment upon the odd sight of the small, wiry, 130-pound Duke leading the huge, bearded, six-foot Cluke, hunched over the pommel of his saddle, sound asleep.

As the early hours of the morning came on, the suffering of both men and horses became almost unbearable. The night was oppressively quiet, broken only by the occasional jingling of harness and the squeaking of leather against leather. Toward the rear of the column guns and wagons creaked and groaned as they traversed the rough, rutted roads. Lulled by these noises, some of the riders left the column and fell asleep in the fields, unnoticed by their friends. Some of them awoke in time to gallop and catch up; others came awake only under the prodding of home guards or militia.

Throughout this night of torture and fatigue, John Hunt Morgan behaved as if no human exertion could tire him. He rode in the van part of the time, staying close to the farmer guides. He changed these men, three times that night, letting one go for another seized farther along the route. He bluntly warned each one that the compasses Johnson and he carried would tell them if the guides were leading the raiders in the wrong direction. Death, he told the frightened farmers, would be the penalty for misdirecting them.

At other times, he rode up and down the long file of groggy, weary troopers, and urged them to remain alert.

"If you love your country's cause," Lieutenant Peddicord heard him say again and again, "keep one another awake."

Back and forth beside the moving column rode Morgan, laughing with some, joking with others, assuming a fierce demeanor with others. He well knew their natures and did his utmost to bolster their morale and maintain some semblance of military order.

Each time the head of the division reached a crossroads, the General managed to be present, prepared for an ambuscade if the enemy had gathered.

The straggling became more aggravated despite his efforts. The gap between the Second Brigade in the lead and the First Brigade in the rear lengthened with each passing mile. As they marched eastward, their route took them closer to the edge of Cincinnati. At one o'clock in the morning they were directly north of the city, less than two miles from the corpora-

129

tion limit. Between Lockland and Duck Creek some of the scouts were so close to the subsurbs that, undetected, they gathered a score of fine riding horses from the stables of wealthy residents.

The roads became more numerous, and each junction increased the chance that the First Brigade would fail to follow the correct route. At each, the lack of cohesion between the leading and the trailing brigades forced Duke and his staff to hunt for the right road. They lighted bundles of paper or slivers of wood to help find the way their companions had passed. Hoof marks were of no value where so many horses had used the roads. Sometimes the slaver from the horses' mouths, still wet on the dry dirt of the highways, gave them their clue.

They often relied upon a device known to cavalrymen since ancient days. On a still, windless night, the dust kicked up by the passing of a number of horses will remain suspended in the air and will drift slowly in the direction taken by the steeds that raised the dust.

At each crossroad, Duke's scouts dismounted, lighted their brands or the candles which a few were foresighted enough to carry, and on their hands and knees studied the earth. It was grueling labor; each time the men felt that they were on an illuminated stage inviting enemy fire.

Although the raiders were passing near or through the suburbs of a city of a quarter of a million, they saw but a handful of Northern pickets and were hardly ever fired upon.

Men who had endured two years of war, and were inured to almost every danger and fatigue, fell from their horses on this terrible march. Officers, as weary as their men, helped them back into their saddles or patrolled the length of the column crying: "By fours, close up, close up. By fours, trot."

When they could, the regimental and company officers called for changes in gait. The horses usually moved at a walk, but the raiders knew that a few minutes at a jogtrot, a fox-trot, or even an occasional slow canter, would serve to rest their mounts. Often, when the utter stillness of the night was unbroken by any sound other than that of shuffling hoofs, the men could half hear, half feel the labored breathing of their mounts. It tore at their hearts, exhausted as they themselves were, to know how grievously their beloved horses were suffering.

Peddicord recorded how, in the brief seconds when flames cut the darkness at the crossroads, he could see "both man and horse nodding together, and at such times the horse staggering as one intoxicated."

Just before two A.M. word was passed down the line from the scouts up front with the guides that they were nearing Glendale on the Reading

130

Pike. This road debouched from Cincinnati's northern-most section and paralleled the Little Miami Railroad tracks in the direction of Middletown and Dayton. It was here that Morgan anticipated his hour of gravest danger. Lightning Ellsworth had been unable to intercept any messages telling where Burnside had deployed his militia. The Rebel chieftain wondered if the feints and countermarching earlier that evening had confused the enemy, or if, as he thought possible, Burnside had decided to put a line of troops along the pike and the railroad to interdict his passing.

Groping their way in the dark as well as they could, the raiders closed ranks. They unslung their rifles from their shoulders, and placed them across the pommels of their saddles where they would be handy; then they loosened their pistols and spurred their exhausted horses into a caricature of a gallop as they passed through Glendale.

The clatter of iron horseshoes on the cobbled streets of the village aroused the inhabitants. Some hurried from their dwellings in their night clothes, and others peered from windows. Realizing that the dusty, heavily-armed column of men was Morgan's raiders, they fled into the darkness, but not before a few troopers, who still had enough strength to enjoy a moment of humor, cheered for Jeff Davis or shouted that Granny Burnside had lost his best chance of capturing them.

A few men, riding out of Glendale on the Milford road, looked south toward Cincinnati and were surprised to discover that they were so close they could see the lighted spires of the city.

The Confederate riders thought of Glendale, situated on the Pike and the railroad, as the deadline. They had passed it without a hostile shot being fired.

The march continued. Reaction after the brief excitement set in and extreme fatigue assailed their tired bodies. Yet Cincinnati was no more than eight or ten miles away, and, as one man said, there were enough troops in the city "to eat them up." They therefore plodded on, the short staggering gallop forgotten—in its stead, a shambling, tortured walk.

Each mile seemed endless. Water was gone from the canteens of those who still carried them, and thirst added its burden to hunger and dust. Their throats were raw, their tongues and mouths thick with powdery grit. Scores of the raiders who had taken veils from the counters of pillaged stores in Salem and Dupont, wound them about their heads to fend off the dust pall, but they were of little avail. Dust caked their eyelids, clogged their nostrils and grated on their teeth. For the horses it was even worse.

On slogged the 2,000 men. Through Sharonville and Montgomery, too tired to cheer or jeer, rode Morgan's "terrible men." The first light of morning on July 14 found them widely scattered. They closed up the column when they could see better, as though ashamed of their disorder. The sun rose, burned off the mist; and a breeze sprang up, fresh and cool, which was like a tonic to the drowsy men.

"I never welcomed the fresh, invigorating air of morning more gratefully," said Colonel Duke.

Scouts routed a few enemy patrols, and Morgan halted the column long enough for the horses to slake their thirst in streams that meandered through the meadows outside Montgomery. The animals were allowed a few minutes to graze, but the men did without breakfast, not daring to rest so near Cincinnati.

A few miles farther, they approached Camp Dennison, a Northern camp for convalescents, which had been alerted by General Burnside. Colonel Neff, the Commandant, sent his wife and servants up the Goshen Pike to a private house where Mrs. Neff had buried the post records, her jewels, and the family silver. He then ordered Captain V. A. Doehm to erect entrenchments on the Madisonville Road. A few of the ambulatory soldiers were issued guns, but there were only enough for a few score.

Duke led the First Brigade in a flanking movement, trading shots with the Union troops but making no attempt to invade the camp. In the middle of the skirmish, the raiders heard the whistle of a distant train and hurriedly stacked ties on the track. When he saw the Rebel cavalry, the engineer opened his throttle and tried to out-race them. Then too late, he saw the barricade.

"The train shot past us like a blazing meteor," wrote Lieutenant Peddicord, "and the next thing we saw was a dense cloud of steam about which flew large timbers. Our next sight startled our nerves, for there lay the monster floundering in the field like a fish out of water, with nothing but the tender attached. Her coupling must have broken, for the passenger carriages and express were still on the track, several yards ahead. Over three hundred raw recruits were on board, bound for Camp Dennison. . . . They came tumbling and rolling out in every way imaginable."

The Southerners paroled the soldiers, burned seventy-five army wagons neatly drawn up in an ordnance park near the camp, and rode away on the Batavia road before a force of regulars could arrive on the next train. One of Duke's patrols, on a search for fresh horses, found Mrs. Neff and other officers' wives huddled in the farmhouse where they had fled with their valuables. When Mrs. Neff later told her husband about it, she said

132

the Rebels had taken all their mounts, but "had offered no insult to the ladies, asking them for water, and conversing with them most politely."

Colonel Neff sent an armed detachment, consisting of militia and a few convalescents, in pursuit of Morgan. Near Batavia the men stopped long enough to fell trees across the road to check Morgan in the event he should decide to return over the route he had just traveled. Such lack of battle strategy seemed typical for the Northern troops. One militia officer wired Governor Tod to tell him Morgan's exact location, although he did not know it, and said in the telegram that the Rebel chieftain had exactly 4,750 men with him. Burnside himself telegraphed that it was now known that Morgan had 4,000 men.

Morgan really had only 2,000 riders who had been in the saddle since five A.M. of the preceding morning—soldiers who had marched in the blazing sun, scarcely knowing what they were doing. The brief respite from the morning breeze was over, the skirmish near Camp Dennison had drained them of their last reserves of strength; now they were caked with dust and sweat, their faces cracked and bleeding.

The road they were traveling was a great scar running through rich fields of corn or meadows lush with summer hay. It passed through Milford and Batavia, empty of fighting men because they had all been called to Cincinnati. Women watched from door stoops, fear on some of their faces, hatred on others. They were not disturbed by the raiders. Morgan's men were too weary to eat, too wretched to want to ride even a few score feet into a farmyard for water.

Beyond Batavia they struck a plank road which magnified the sounds of the passing column. Iron shoes clumped rhythmically on the dry wood, trace chains jangled and axles squealed and groaned. The plank road was a torment to the sick and wounded in the buggies. The washboard effect created a bouncing ride that no springs could soften.

From a sky unmarred by clouds, the brassy sun beat upon the raiders, making them feel, one soldier remembered years later, as if they were being broiled over embers. Frequently a soldier would fall from his horse. His companions would put him back in the saddle and hold him there, riding knee-to-knee throughout the hot July afternoon.

Shortly before four o'clock the column passed through Williamsburg, twenty-eight miles east of Cincinnati. Beyond the town, Morgan led his men into a wide meadow beside a tiny stream. The longest continuous cavalry ride in the history of warfare, by such a large body of men, was ended.

133

From Sunman, Indiana, to Williamsburg, Ohio they had marched ninety-five and one-fourth miles in about thirty-five hours, not stopping to rest and skirmishing and fighting as they went.

No one bothered to eat or build a fire. Some of the raiders dismounted, staggered a few feet onto the clean, fresh grass and sank unconscious to the ground. Some fell asleep while still holding their horse's reins; to others sleep came while they leaned against a split-rail fence that snaked its way along the road.

John Morgan and his lieutenants discussed their chances of being overtaken and decided that Hobson, delayed by the burning of the bridges, would be unable to overtake them for twenty-four hours. They knew that most of the home guards had gone into Cincinnati. Without bothering to post pickets or send out patrols, they, too, lay down in the thick grass and fell asleep.

CHAPTER 11

"Morgan's Coming! Morgan's Coming!"

"WHAT IS BURNSIDE doing?" demanded headlines in Ohio newspapers.

Days were going by. Morgan was moving steadily eastward. Irate, frightened Ohio residents could see no signs that their military leaders knew how to stop him.

The truth was that Old Granny had done about all that was possible with the resources he possessed. Morgan had moved fast—too fast for the regular cavalry on his heels that could not find decent remounts—too fast for the home guards to muster, and too fast for the militia on foot, or even when transported by rail. But the net was tightening. Hobson would never surrender—that was certain. Judah and his brigade had landed at Cincinnati ten hours too late, and Burnside had ordered them back onto the boats. They were to steam upriver, and keep as close to Morgan as possible, using the few scattered reports he could forward to them along the way. An impressive flotilla carried Judah's force in an effort to overtake the Rebel column. Henry Judah rode on the flagboat, the *Bostona,* and behind steamed the *Scioto, Undine, Swallow, Saline, Bostona No. 2, Fisher, Emma No. 2, Wren,* and *Silver Moon.*

Morgan would have to reckon with the men on these boats, at some future hour. What bothered him the most, when he renewed his march, was the fact the Buckeye home guards refused to be intimidated. Burnside and Tod had telegraphed all local commanders and instructed them to have their men barricade the roads they thought the raiders would use. They did with dispatch. Trees started crashing all over Clermont, Brown and Adams counties.

While he marched after the fast-riding Morgan, General Hobson pondered the problem of trying to overtake the enemy long enough to force

135

battle. The arrival of Sanders and his fresh detachment gave him such an opportunity. He decided to detach part of his better-mounted troops and rush them forward to overtake the raiders, even if it meant splitting his force.

"As I faced great difficulty in bringing my artillery forward," he reported, "owing to the horses having broken down and the impossibility of procuring fresh ones on the road, I separated my command, ordering Colonel Kautz to move forward with his brigade, composed of the Second and Seventh Ohio Regiments and to make every effort to overtake Morgan, attack, and compel him to make a stand; and I would support him with Colonel Sanders' brigade, while the balance of my command would follow as fast as their jaded condition would permit."

The plan looked fine as written. Its execution was altogether a different matter.

Kautz broke away from the main Federal column at three A.M. on July 14, while Hobson was grinding his slow way through Springdale. Strangely, the Ohio regiments did not know the route through their own state. On the way through Batavia at two o'clock the next morning the advance party found a Methodist preacher who undertook to guide them. The Buckeyes soon realized that the parson had made them travel fifteen miles, nine of it unnecessarily.

"Whether this was intentional we did not know," one Union trooper stated, "but he semed very anxious to escape after that. If hard swearing on the part of the boys will injure anyone but the swearer, then is that Methodist preacher cursed for all eternity."

With the coming of daylight, the pursuers had an easier time following Morgan's line of march. They occasionally captured raiders who had crawled into the fields during the long night ride and fallen asleep.

"They were not stragglers in the true meaning of the military word," wrote a Northern soldier. "The men held Morgan in such high respect they didn't straggle, but some were so exhausted that they just couldn't go on. When found, these men were always asleep, not in a gentle doze, but in deep sleep, and we would have to roll them about roughly to awaken them. Often we would stand them on their feet, and they would reply to our questions, but in a dazed sort of way, evidently yet asleep."

The long night's sleep in the meadow near Williamsburg greatly refreshed those of Morgan's men who had completed the march. They awoke, ate good breakfasts, and curried their horses in order to make the mounts more comfortable. They then divided their column, the main one pushing east toward Sardinia, Winchester and Locust Grove. A smaller one, under Colonel Dick Morgan, struck out for Ripley on the Ohio, to create the illusion that they were eager to cross the river.

Dick Morgan's party, composed of the 14th Kentucky and some of Quirk's scouts under Captain Hines, felt so refreshed and full of vigor that they sang as they rode. Some of the troopers had found two violins, a guitar and a banjo, and played an accompaniment as the Kentuckians sang *My Old Kentucky Home, Juanita, Arkansas Traveler,* and the *Hills of Tennessee.* But their favorites were *Lorena* or one that had this chorus:

> "Georgia's girls are handsome
> And Tennessee girls are sweet,
> But a girl in Old Kentucky
> Is the one I want to meet."

On this ride the smaller column rode within ten miles of the birthplace of a Northern soldier named U. S. Grant, but there is no record to show that they knew it or thought about it.

Their ebullient spirits had returned; they were young, the day was pleasant. They raided some stores for new boots and leather to replace rotting harness

They continued their practice of not molesting private homes except to demand horses and an occasional meal. In stores and shops, however, they observed the old soldiers' belief that "everything outdoors is mine, everything indoors belongs to my messmate."

The roads were dusty and the sun was hot, so they often stopped to allay their thirst. It was:

> Sometimes water, sometimes milk,
> Sometimes applejack, fine as silk.

As they rode through one small hamlet, they saw a man leaning against a tree, who watched them with apparent interest.

"What do you think of rebels now?" asked a young raider.

"Rather a hard-looking set," replied the man with no sign of fear.

"Well," said the raider, "I haven't seen a good-looking Yankee since I've been north of the river."

The rest of the riders whooped in glee and they rode on, leaving the rustic unharmed.

137

When they reached the Ohio River at Ripley, Dick Morgan's men found the river near flood stage, a most unusual situation for so late in the summer. Again they headed north into Georgetown, the county seat of Brown County, to investigate a rumor that a large sum of gold had been deposited there by Kentucky banks when the raiders first started across the Cumberland. Sentries were posted about the institution, and men went to seek the cashier.

"We located him at his home," Leeland Hathaway wrote in his journal, "and he showed us to our satisfaction that the rumor was groundless. We released the sentries, and the cashier insisted we share his good dinner, and a few of us did."

Late that night the small detachment rejoined the main column at Locust Grove. Some of the younger men in the party told the others how they had amused themselves in the town of Winchester by tying American flags to mules' tails and chasing them through the streets.

The next day events became serious. The word that Morgan had circumvented Cincinnati without being delayed had reached all the small towns in southern Ohio. Local militia units took up axes and saws and started to block the roads ahead of the raiders. It was a case of "axes to the front" time after time as the advance guard of Southerners had to cut their way through the barricades.

Morgan found that the Buckeyes were tougher opponents than the Hoosiers.

"Small fights with the militia were of daily occurrence," said Basil Duke. "They hung around the column, wounding two or three men every day and sometimes killing one. We captured hundreds of them daily, but could only turn them loose again after destroying their guns."

At one point, several hundred home guards took up a very strong position on an eminence that commanded the road the raiders were following. Hathaway was ordered to lead an attack to dislodge the militia.

"We made quick work of it, and soon the enemy was scattered and the way clear," recorded the young adjutant. "General Morgan and Colonel Duke came up just as we went through with the Rebel yell over the works of Yankee troops."

When the General asked who led the assault, the men pointed to Hathaway.

"I salute you, Captain Hathaway," said Morgan, promoting the adjutant on the field, "for such reckless gallantry as could carry such a position."

138

There were other skirmishes at Berlin, Jasper and other small communities. At Jasper, the town's doctors, lawyers, clerks and clergymen joined farmers and laborers and built a barricade, but they could not withstand a charge by determined veterans. Across the Scioto River lay Piketon. When the defenders there saw what had happened at Jasper, they deserted their log barricades and ran into the fields, only a few of them remained long enough to trade shots with Rebel scouts. No one was left to interfere while the raiders burned the bridge across the stream behind them.

Chillicothe officials telegraphed the bad news to Colonel Putnam at Camp Marietta:

"Morgan crossed the Scioto River at Piketon at 3 o'clock this P.M., marching toward Jackson and Gallipolis or Pomeroy. He has a large drove of mules and horses with him. Our scouts were at Piketon, advanced, crossed his route, and were chased two miles this side of Piketon by his advance. He burned bridge at Waverly about 4:30 P.M."

The affluence of the northern towns amazed the Southerners, whose own homeland had been stripped of all that was not essential to the war effort—a result of the Union blockade.

Colonel Duke watched with understanding and pity when one of his men, who had been born and reared on a small Kentucky farm, "broke through the guard posted at a Piketon store, rushed in (trembling with excitement and avarice) and filled his pockets with horn buttons."

They were fine riders and brave fighters—these young men who rode with Morgan—but many of them, reared in backwoods poverty and frugality, behaved like boys in a toy shop, excited at the sight of so many luxuries.

To General Morgan it became increasingly apparent that while his force could overcome the home guards in their rough defensive position, he was being delayed by repeated skirmishes. He called Lightning Ellsworth to his side and prepared several messages for the telegrapher. Ellsworth dispatched them with his ground loop and pocket key the next time he came to a telegraph line. He sent a series of spurious news dispatches supposedly revealing that the Confederates were headed straight for Chillicothe to cut the Marietta and Cincinnati Railroad. This ruse succeeded. The local axmen disappeared from Morgan's front in haste to protect Chillicothe, and the raiders swept into Jackson to the south with no further opposition from home guards.

The Rebels camped at Jackson at 11 P.M., but were astir early the next morning. Their first task was the destruction of the press, type, and office of the Jackson *Standard*, a Republican newspaper. Several stores were then pillaged. Although the veils stolen in Indiana had helped but little to keep out the dust on the long night ride into Ohio, the younger troopers confiscated a large number of the filmy articles. Jackson residents, who watched the raiders cantor out of town, thought they looked like ladies from a Sultan's harem, out for a morning ride.

Near Jackson, Hathaway and a patrol encountered a detachment of militia led by Colonel Benjamin P. Runkle, an aid on Governor Tod's staff. In a brief fire fight a young Irishman named Tom Murphy was wounded. Tom, a great humorist, was a favorite of the division. After the Ohio home guards had been driven away, Hathaway went to Murphy who had been badly wounded in the neck. The newly promoted captain bound the wound and revived the young trooper with a stiff drink of bourbon.

"I think they've got old Tom this time," said the wounded man. "I've tried to be a good soldier and do my duty. I want you to tell my old mother I have done my very best and that I died like a man."

Murphy knew that he could not be carried with the column and did not object when he was left in a nearby farmhouse. Hathaway asked the farmer and his family to do their best for the Rebel cavalryman, pressed his hand and rode away.

"Feeling sure that he would die," wrote Hathaway in his diary, "we went on, pursued by thousands of regulars, opposed in front by thousands of militia. This was the best we could do for our dead or wounded."

More than a year later, after the raid was over, Hathaway was walking down a street in Richmond, Virginia. He turned to answer a hearty slap on his shoulder and a greeting of "How do you do, Adjutant?"

"I stood face-to-face with old Tom Murphy," said the officer. "Old Tom in the flesh, looking sturdy, game, and as jolly as ever. He told me his injury had proved to be only an ugly flesh wound, that he recovered and was exchanged."

Not all were as fortunate as Tom Murphy. Bushwhackers continually harassed the column's flanks. While their aim was bad, not all their shots missed. Every hillside hid its enemy scouts; every ravine and road junction, its blockade.

The Federal troopers tired of "Rally 'Round the Flag, Boys," and the Confederates grew to hate the tiresome call, "Axes to the front."

As one observer said of Morgan, "the country was roused in all directions; the dogs of war were on his track; he could remain in one place

140

hardly an hour, and the only course left him was to keep in motion ahead of his pursuers."

Irrespective of the fact that 50,000 militia had been called to arms; that Hobson with a superior force was only a few hours behind him; that the telegraph and railroad networks all aided the Union commanders in deploying their forces, and that every home guard with a rifle or an axe represented a potential loss of time—the one thing Morgan needed more than anything else—his force was a fearsome thing that struck terror in the hearts of every Ohio inhabitant south of the National Road.

Nowhere did Morgan's approach breed more consternation than in the city of Chillicothe, which once had been Ohio's capital. While the raiders were still in Clermont, Brown, and Adams counties, handbills in large letters appeared in Ross County towns calling men to arms. As the raiders neared Locust Grove, the residents of Chillicothe awoke to find posters nailed to trees and public buildings. They carried this message:

To The People of Ross County:

In accordance with orders of the General Committee, the people of Ross County will, upon the approach of Morgan toward the Scioto, tear up every bridge, and fell trees and in every manner impede the progress of the enemy.

It was signed by Colonel Runkle.

"Farmers, mechanics, laborers, loafers—all were commanded to assemble at the Chillicothe courthouse, and an urgent call was made for arms," a resident wrote later. "From 1,500 to 2,000 men rushed to muster on the courthouse steps. Rifles without ramrods, rifles without locks, flint, percussion and caps; shotguns, rusty old muskets from 1812; they were all there, but not a bullet, a grain of powder, or a pound of shot."

The home guards drilled on a vacant lot on Paint Street, and pickets were posted on the roads leading into town. The Chillicothe Grays, a company of high local repute, had left for war months before; so replacements, for the most part old men, assumed their duties. They were dubbed the "Silver Grays," and they marched off bravely to guard the ford at Kilgour's farm. Another detachment from Zanesville went to guard the Portsmouth and Columbus Turnpike Company bridge over Paint Creek south of town. The Zanesville men tore the planking from the bridge and waited by their guns for the enemy.

141

A scout rode into Chillicothe that afternoon. His horse was covered with foam and he was covered with dust and he yelled at every bound of his steed, "Morgan's coming, Morgan's coming." He had only a rumor heard on the Piketon Pike to prove his words. The next night General J. T. Worthington, an old West Pointer, who was in command at Chillicothe, had the alarm sounded on the courthouse bell. Armed and ready, the whole town rallied at the front steps.

Old Dr. Samuel Dunlap, who had been wakened by the bell's tolling, dressed hastily, tucked his nightshirt into trousers, seized his old Jager rifle, which he had loaded the day before, and rushed into the yard to await the enemy. It was dark and the old doctor could not see well. Not perturbed, he called his daughter to his side. She and the old gentleman stood watch throughout the night—the young woman bravely holding a candle.

As Morgan swept by to the south excitement mounted by the minute. Orders and countermanding orders issued from every headquarters. The least sensible issued from the office of General John H. Taylor, who was second in command at Chillicothe—a military figure known to his neighbors as a "watermelon general." He had won this appellation in the days after the Mexican War, when the militia held its annual musters while the melons ripened.

Tired from lack of sleep, confused by rumors and conflicting orders, the unfortunate guards at the town's approaches began to see Rebel raiders wherever they looked. The inevitable happened. The morning after the general alarm, the Zanesville detachment at the Paint Creek bridge sighted a cloud of dust beyond Cook's Hill on the Piketon road, a mile out of town. Certain that Morgan was approaching, they fired the bridge and burned it down—although there was less than a foot of water running over the near-by ford. They learned too late that the dust was stirred up by a party of Ohio scouts sent by another route to seek the enemy.

Forty miles away the rebel raiders, moving steadily away from Chillicothe, overtook a buggy in which Dr. James Miller was making his rounds. They took his horse out of the shafts and ordered him to pump water for them and their thirsty horses at a well in a near-by farmyard.

As the long, dusty column rode by, the doctor worked the pump handle until he could scarcely lift his arm. When the last raider passed the pump it was discharging sand at every stroke.

142

CHAPTER 12

Women Always Weep

SOUTHERN OHIO's most important railroad was the Marietta & Cincinnati, later incorporated into the vast Baltimore & Ohio system. It ran west from the Ohio River at Marietta through Athens, Chillicothe and Greenfield to Cincinnati. During most of his march through the state, Morgan remained south of the tracks, partly because he was eager to reach the ford at Buffington Island in Meigs County and partly because the militia tried to use the railroad as a sort of *cordon sanitaire* beyond which the raiders would not be allowed to pass.

In this endeavor the military authorties were aided and abetted by W. P. Cutler, vice-president and operating manager of the Marietta & Cincinnati. He would have been a good general, had his efforts to thwart Morgan been considered a criterion. Cutler left his wife and home in Marietta and took charge of an effort to use railroad workers as an engineer corps to transform the right-of-way into an impregnable barrier. In close harmony with General Burnside and Governor Tod, Cutler used his company telegraph in an effort to determine where Morgan would try to cross the tracks.

On the day when the raiders were recovering from the terrible ride around Cincinnati, the agent at Chillicothe wired his superior in Marietta a summary of the preparations at the other end of the line.

"All the bridges west are well guarded," said the agent. "Morgan is supposed to be marching on Hillsboro, and this city. The governor has ordered all the militia at Pickaway, Fayette, Muskingum, and Ross counties to this place. Guns and munitions of war are on their way from Columbus by canal. There will probably be 5,000 troops here tomorrow."

In order to show how well informed he was, he added this postscript: "Port Hudson is taken by Sherman; 17,000 prisoners."

What neither the agent nor most of the military authorities could understand was the speed with which Morgan could move, even through enemy

143

territory. Guns and ammunition moved by canal were too late. John Morgan's movements were based on the technique later to be known as *blitzkrieg*. Nothing comparable had been seen before in Indiana and Ohio. Troops mustered to oppose him were gathered together repeatedly only to discover that the Confederates had escaped before the home guards reached the rallying point.

Cutler sensed that even a blitzkrieg, although he never heard the word, could be slowed down by civilian resistance ahead of the moving column.

The railroad executive moved across the Muskingum River to the end of the railroad at Harmar, Ohio, and sent telegrams up and down his line, instructing agents and stationmasters in this new type of guerilla partisan warfare. Typical of the orders was one to the agent at Athens:

"I wish you to procure axes for all your men and proceed to obstruct the roads leading from the direction of Morgan's forces to our railroad. I wish you would operate southwest of Athens, on the west side of the Hocking River. Press axes and teams for transportation and provisions. By order of Gen. Cox."

Everything was being done to reduce Morgan's twelve-hour lead. In some manner the Federal commanders hoped to hold him at bay, so the Union cavalry could get within rifle shot.

The Yankees were using everything they had in the effort. By the time the Rebels passed south of Chillicothe, Burnside had succeeded in setting five separate forces in motion, not counting the various militia units engaged in erecting barricades.

Hobson's main column, with Kautz's detachment pressing ahead as fast as the worn-out horses could go, trailed the raiders mile by mile, like a great pack of staghounds after a wounded buck. To his right, following the river roads, marched Judah, who had left the steamboats at Portsmouth on the assumption that the enemy was striking for the river there. He learned that once again, instead of being in front of Morgan, he was behind and to one side.

North of Hobson was a nondescript force of more than 2,000 green militia under Colonel Runkle, which had made one abortive attempt to bring the raiders to a stand near Berlin. They had fled, however, when Captain Byrnes fired a few shells into their ranks.

On the Ohio River, Fitch and his gunboats moved upstream, high water permitting him to warp his boats over the shoals, intent on preventing the raiders from crossing into West Virginia.

144

Last of all the units to be marshaled in the mammoth dragnet was a detachment headed by Brigadier General E. Parker Scammon, who commanded the Third Division of the Army Corps in West Virginia. Burnside and the Secretary of War, Edwin M. Stanton, were scraping the bottom of the barrel to find troops with which to confront Morgan.

Scammon and the Kanawha Division were high in the hills of central West Virginia at Fayetteville when the orders reached him. Scammon took the 12th, 23rd and 91st Ohio and 13th Virginia Volunteer regiments of infantry and McMullin's battery of six-pounders, and marched over incredibly poor roads to the banks of the Kanawha, put his men aboard boats and steamed down to the junction with the Ohio near Gallipolis. He accompanied Fitch and the gunboats as they patrolled the upper reaches of the Ohio, keeping his men on the steamers.

These men and at least 50,000 state militia were pursuing Morgan and his 2,000 by July 15 and 16. Even these odds did not satisfy the terrified residents of Ohio.

A newspaper echoed the feelings of thousands of Buckeyes when it asked:

"Where is Burnside that these depredations are permitted?" (It had referred to the burning of bridges and told of the return of the Tuesday westbound train on the Marietta & Cincinnati which had been forced to turn back after going only as far as Chillicothe and finding the tracks torn up).

The paper replied to its own rhetorical question:

"We answer that his troops were sent to Vicksburg and are not available. . . . A large force is in pursuit, but it is impossible for infantry and artillery to overtake the hurried march of well-mounted cavalry."

The answer was only partially correct. Burnside's beloved IX Corps, later described as "a wandering corps, whose dead lie buried in seven states," had been sent in support of Grant before Vicksburg. The newspaper editorial writer erred in his belief that it was only infantry and artillery that pursued the Rebel raiders. Runkle's men although on foot, often found it possible to travel by rail, and Scammon's force was composed of infantry but was able to do most of its traveling in luxury, aboard the river boats.

All of Hobson's and Judah's men were mounted. Morgan's efficiency in acquiring every animal capable of lateral motion, however, left much to be desired in the quality of mounts left for the Federal forces.

These cavalry units, which had begun the chase so long ago on the northern bank of the Cumberland, were making an all-out effort to reduce the space between them and their quarry, "still straining every nerve on his ruin-strewn track" as a newspaper reporter described it.

Confederate cavalrymen complained about the horses they seized to replace some of their own. To the Federals pounding doggedly along behind them, however, the Southern force had all the better of it.

"Morgan's troopers were exceedingly well-mounted," said a member of the 7th Ohio Cavalry, "having many of the best-blooded horses in Kentucky, horses capable of long and rapid marches. In justice to General Morgan and his officers, it must be said that they handled their men and horses with superb skill. It was on this raid that General Morgan established the world's record for moving cavalry."

Certainly the Rebels husbanded the strength of their own mounts as expertly as possible. Many of their Kentucky favorites covered the bulk of the long ride with empty saddles while their owners rode the nondescript plow horses picked up along the way. This practice was copied by a few of their pursuers to a much smaller degree. On both sides, some horses made the entire march, being ridden every day, and never breaking down. So it was with the Union soldier who praised Morgan so warmly.

"On this march," he said later, "I rode a well-seasoned black mare over the entire route and on the return to Kentucky . . . after covering fully 1,000 miles, this mare, Nellie, recognizing her old camp, pranced in sideways, thereby saying to me, in language without words, 'If there is any one thing I like better than another it is these little thousand-mile excursions.' "

Most of the troopers were not so fortunate.

"Hobson's and Judah's men," an Ohio newspaper reported, "were urging their worn-out steeds forward, leading them or driving them, nursing their strength, reassured by the knowledge the militia were out in front blocking roads, catching fresh hope from the still-blazing ruins of mills, bridges and homes."

If Hobson had relied on "still-blazing homes" to point out Morgan's route, he would have lost him at the start in Kentucky, but it sounded good in the Northern papers. A soldier in the 7th Ohio left an account much more trustworthy.

"When we followed Morgan, we often reached diverging roads," he recorded. "We scouted the roads for short distances in all directions until we found the heavy trail of dust which had settled on weeds and bushes of the roadside from the passage of so many horses."

146

The pursuit was a grinding, grueling chore for Hobson's men. They stripped the column of everything that impeded their progress, abandoned supply wagons even before they reached the Ohio at Brandenburg, and retained only the artillery. The 7th Ohio unharnessed the horses from the regimental ambulance, and the medical officers rode the ambulance horses the remainder of the way.

Undaunted, Hobson continued the pursuit, never complaining, except to inform Burnside of the poor condition of his mounts. He urged Kautz and his picked units along, and moved his guns across streams by force wherever the raiders had burned bridges.

The Federals were never hungry—the Ohio folk saw to that. In some of the counties they were crossing, the men passed their own homes. The second lieutenant of one company in the 7th Ohio saw his two small children on his doorstep, stopped to pick them up, and rode on for a mile or more before putting them down and sending them home.

As hard as he could, however, Hobson could not close the gap. At Jackson he rode into town about noon of July 17th and learned that Morgan had ridden out twelve hours earlier. This must have annoyed him greatly, for the wrecked the press and burned down that town's other newspaper, the Jackson *Express,* which was the organ of the so-called Peace Democrats. This was a singularly unmilitary thing for Hobson to do—one of the very few he committed on the entire ride—but his nerves quite understandably were becoming frayed.

August Kautz was also disturbed. He had the best men and the freshest horses, but he was failing in his assignment to bring the raiders to a stand. He vented some of his wrath weeks later when he wrote that despite plenty of propaganda to the contrary, "there is no record of an organized attack on Morgan by militia or temporary volunteers. In every instance they contented themselves with resisting an attack, in some cases unwisely, because unavailing. Some good work was done in obstructing roads, but the only foes Morgan really feared were the regular troops."

In Jackson the Union soldiers took time to enjoy a hearty repast prepared by the loyal women of that town. The food was cooked at home, carried to the central market and served from rough tables that were usually stacked with garden produce.

"Nearly every Federal soldier had a woman or maiden to wait on him," a trooper remembered.

After they had eaten this bountiful meal the Union soldiers became the victims of another of the wily Morgan's ruses. They had ridden only a short distance out of town when several men, dressed in butternut jeans and rough coats, jogged up on unshod farm horses and warned that Morgan's men were in ambush just over the next hill, well entrenched beyond stout barricades.

Bugles blared. Officers dashed about, getting men into position and sending out flanking parties. Reinforcements moved up and scouts went forward to study the lay of the land. In the midst of the excitement, everyone forgot about the yokels who had brought the warning, and they disappeared. When the Union commander was satisfied that all was ready, he ordered an attack, and the Union troopers dashed over the rise of ground, yelling with pleasure at the chance to fight. Within a short distance, they realized they had been tricked. Morgan was nowhere near and neither were the innocent-appearing rustics who had described the ambush so expertly.

The same trick was used several more times. Each time it delayed the pursuit, since the Northerners could never be certain it was another case of "Wolf! Wolf!"

Morgan and his men were making good use of the purloined hours. After leaving Jackson, the division was divided, Duke leading his brigade on a road leading through a town with the strange name of *Roads* and on to Wilkesville. Johnson took his brigade by a more southerly route through Vinton.

Duke halted at Wilkesville. His men rested until three A.M., when the brigade moved out to the east, scouts having brought word that Judah had disembarked from the boats at Portsmouth and had struck out toward Oak Hill at nine P.M. of the previous night.

On this same night, July 17, 250 militiamen from Athens, Ohio, set forth on a venture that proved Colonel Kautz was completely accurate in his appraisal of the home guards' contribution to the effort of halting the raiders.

Together with a few men from Bedford Township in Meigs County, the men from Athens left for Wilkesville in wagons, having heard that Morgan was encamped there. Many of the soldiers were students at Ohio University in Athens.

The night was chilly and, as the wagons rolled past farmhouses on the way to Albany, Major de Steiguer, who lead the van, called on the inhabitants to donate quilts to protect his "college-bred gentlemen" from the night air. These were provided and the men rode on, bundled in the hay. Two miles from Albany, Captain J. C. Stedman's company was ordered from their warm nests and told to march to Wilkesville; the

148

wagons had been moving too slowly in the hilly country and the roads were deeply rutted.

"We set out in dim starlight," recalled one of Stedman's men. "As the night wore on we heard naught but the measured tramp, the low word of command, or the occasional click of bayonets striking against each other; except for the barking of watch dogs startled by the unwonted intrusion. In one place we noted a number of women, pretty excited and wringing their hands in apprehension of a battle so near their own homes.

"An hour before dawn, a wagon arrived bearing the remembrance of our friends, upon which . . . we fed with eagerness and gratitude. At six, we were on the march toward Harrisonville."

They had marched all night, enjoyed a good breakfast, and now waited for scouts to bring word of the enemy's whereabouts. The word was not favorable. Morgan and his main force were approaching Rutland. The militia was afraid to attack the main Confederate body and withdrew to a narrow defile in the road. They prepared to fight there if the raiders came that way. At two P.M., reinforcements failed to put in an appearance and the college boys were ordered to return by the route on which they had come, their officers convinced that it was now their duty to defend Athens.

As the militia neared Morgan, their outlook on the fortunes of war seemed to change. The newspaper in Athens carried valiant words in its columns as the Confederate raiders approached. The editors noted with joy that the order for the militia to go to Marietta for the appointment of officers had been rescinded

"They will meet in their home counties and elect their officers," said an editorial, "and drill at home with whatever arms they may have, with a fair prospect of being ordered toward the invaders, instead of away from them. We would urge them, every man who can carry a musket, to join one of these volunteer companies and strive to obtain the greatest possible proficiency in drill, that we may drive these hordes back upon the forces following them and thus rid the country of its greatest guerilla band."

Handsome words in print, but they must have disgusted the home guards, who had returned from the wars without so much as trading a single shot with the greatest guerilla band in the country.

One editor confided to his readers that the chips were down, and he might have to join the forces arrayed against John Morgan. He explained it thus in an editorial:

"In common with all other kinds of business, the regular issue of the

Athens *Messenger* will probably be interrupted by the call for volunteers of this place to which we, as well as our foreman and compositor, belong. The prospect is that we shall be ordered to Chillicothe or some other point today or tomorrow, but we will get this issue ready for the press and have employed a pressman, not capable of bearing arms, to get it ready for the mails in due time. We are at the orders of the Company and shall go with them, so that if the *Messenger* is not received next week they will understand the cause; and if they do, they may understand that the Morgan raid is over."

No master of grammar, the editor was patriotic. He could scarcely have guessed he would have to write another editorial for his weekly newspaper before Morgan's raid was ended.

Before the editor marched off to battle, he indulged in one last lyrical bit of writing to point an example for his compatriots. His prose dealt with the exploits of a Lieutenant Long of Vinton County, who was active in trying to bar Morgan's progress.

"He [Long] called for axmen and they poured from every farmhouse," wrote the newspaper man. "The fires of '76 were rekindled and the whole land was ablaze. Knowing every ford on the river for which Morgan was aiming, Lieutenant Long hung about his front and whenever the head of his column emerged into a road, the forest came crashing down in a confused and tangled mass barring all progress."

The militia was a nuisance in spite of its bumbling. James McCreary recorded their nuisance value in his dairy:

"The enemy are now pressing us from all sides, and the woods swarm with militia. We capture hundreds of prisoners, but a parole being null, we can only sweep them as chaff out of our way."

The countryside through which the raiders were now passing was beautiful—heavily wooded in spots, broken by low rolling hills, ravines and scores of streams, or "runs," as they were called in southern Ohio. Most of them were beginning to dry up in the hot July sun. With the exception of the largest streams they were fordable, and Morgan's fast-moving men found most of the bridges over the main rivers still intact.

They reached Meigs County before the raiders encountered a burned bridge. The people of Meigs County had found time to plan their delaying tactics as Morgan rode across the state from the west. Stout-hearted folk, some of them were of English ancestry from Connecticut and Massachusetts who had come to Ohio in the years after the Revolutionary War. Some were of German descent who had emigrated from their fatherland

150

in 1848 and found the land along the upper Ohio reminiscent of the Rhineland.

When the news first reached Meigs County that Morgan had crossed into Indiana, there had been a feeling of dismay. Bulletin boards on the county courthouse in Pomeroy, and also the newspaper office were besieged by crowds eager to learn the latest news. At the Governor's call to arms, men of the militia dropped their tools and books, and took whatever firearms they owned, ready to defend their homes.

Two companies of Middleport militia, one of infantry, with Captain R. B. Wilson commanding, and one of artillery, Captain John Schreiner commanding, a total of 120 men, were ordered to rendezvous at Camp Marietta. On the night of their arrival, the telegraph brought news that the raiders were approaching the border of their home county. They immediately demanded orders to return to their home town, so they could join in its defense. They were given their orders, put aboard a steamer, and started down the river. Before morning they docked at Middleport and, without resting, marched toward Rutland. Some of these men went by way of Bradbury Hill, where later that day Morgan was turned away from the Ohio.

Convinced that the invaders were headed for the shoals at Buffington Island, at the eastern border of the county, other militia moved in that direction.

When Morgan and his men encamped at Wilkesville on the night of July 17, they were within a mile or two of the border of Vinton and Meigs counties. No Meigs County homeguard slept that night.

"At last the announcement came on the lightning's wing that they had entered the county," a local historian, still deeply moved by the event, wrote months later.

Rutland's defenders hurried westward on the road toward Salem Center and Wilkesville. At Langsville they burned the bridge across Leading Creek near McMaster's grist mill, urged the residents of the small community to take to the woods, and returned to Rutland. Some of the officers thought it wiser to wait for reinforcements from Athens County, although a few of the soldiers disagreed.

One was seventeen-year-old Joe Pickering, who had enlisted as a ninety-day man, fought at Harper's Ferry during the Antietam campaign, been captured and exchanged. He was at home, waiting orders when Morgan's force swept into Ohio.

Young Pickering oiled an old flintlock pistol, took his father's shotgun,

151

and rode to Rutland with a friend, Major D. H. Moore. About the time they cantered into town from the east, some of the scouts from the 2nd Kentucky entered from the west, their horses still wet from swimming the river at Langsville. Joe and the Major fired a few shots. The Major then rode for help, as he saw still more Southern troopers riding down the hill from Salem Center.

The Pickering boy hid his guns and horse in a creek bottom and went into a deserted farmhouse. He threw aside his coat, donned a denim jumper and put a straw hat on his head. Two Rebel cavalrymen rode into the yard.

"Where's that damned Yankee officer and the man who was with him?" asked one.

Joe said he had seen no one. Disliking the answer, the Rebel soldier lifted his gun, but his companion brushed it aside.

"Don't go shooting a harmless country boy," the second raider said.

After the main body of raiders had left town, Joe Pickering joined a friend, Charley Finsterwald, and pursued the enemy, hoping to find stragglers. Luck was with them, and they captured five, although the Pickering boy was wounded in the thigh. When the two rode in with their prisoners, the militia officers thought so highly of Pickering's deed they permitted him to keep the best saddle and harness belonging to his captives.

Some of the Rutland inhabitants, who watched the raiders ride into their town, thought they looked "more like a motley array of Falstaff's ragamuffins than chivalry gleaming in purple and gold," but they looked from a distance, having quit their homes in a rush.

Basil Duke could not help noticing what he termed the Ohioans' "kind hospitality."

"At every house that we approached," he wrote, "the dwellers thereof themselves absent, perhaps, unable to endure a meeting that would have been painful, had left warm pies, freshly baked, on the tables. This touching attention to our tastes was appreciated. Some individuals were indelicate enough to hint that the pies were intended to propitiate us and prevent the plunder of the houses."

To judge the feelings of the entire community by what they found in the kitchens of some houses was hazardous. Not all inhabitants of the section manifested such friendliness. One woman, in particular, was motivated by altogether different feelings.

Although this matron lived in a village forty miles from the route

152

Morgan was following, she resolved to do her utmost to save the family carriage horse from the raiders. Her husband was absent on some distant battlefield, and she had no intention of having him return to find the horse gone. Knowing no safer expedient, she led the horse from the barn to the house, through the front door and into the parlor. There she tied him securely, locked the door and bolted the shutters at the windows. Throughout the next night, her neighbors later claimed, they heard the animal's hoofs thumping on the puncheon board floor. It sounded like distant artillery and kept half of the town awake until morning.

These humorous incidents subsided as the militia turned to bushwhacking. Raiders fell, killed or wounded, when they came under fire from an enemy well hidden in the woods beside the road. Even when the Rebel division passed through small hamlets and crossroad communities, deserted by all but women and children, the raiders sensed the gathering storm.

Lieutenant Peddicord recorded that whenever they passed homes and saw women weeping, they knew that Northern solders were close at hand.

"Women always weep at the thought of imminent encounters," he said.

On the way through Rutland, the Rebels saw Joseph Giles, a blacksmith, working at his forge. They asked him if he knew the way to Chester. Giles said he did, that Chester had been the former county seat of Meigs, and he had gone there frequently to pay his taxes. At this juncture Colonel Duke rode up and, learning of the conversation, said he was glad Giles knew the route, as they needed a guide.

"I sensed I had got myself into trouble by talking too much," the blacksmith later told his neighbors.

With General Morgan, Duke and the blacksmith leading the way, the Southern cavalry headed east, then turned sharply south toward Middleport, on the bank of the Ohio. The road climbed steeply up Bradbury Hill, and near the top they encountered heavy fire from well-placed militia. Morgan and Duke had no way of knowing whether they faced home guards or some of Judah's regulars. They knew that Judah had been marching by parallel roads between them and the river ever since he disembarked from the boats at Portsmouth. In fact, Judah had not yet arrived on the scene. The enemy consisted of Meigs County militia, in nearly impregnable positions of superior elevation and heavy woods. To have driven them from their positions would have been possible, but the cost would have been heavy. Morgan rejected a frontal attack. He withdrew his forward companies, shifted his route to the east, then headed for Chester on a road that ran two or three miles behind Pomeroy, which was the next large town upstream on the northern bank of the Ohio.

The terrain here was distinctly unfavorable to the invaders. Middleport and Pomeroy are both located at the river's edge. Behind them the land rises sharply to a ridge a mile or two in width, then falls abruptly into a ravine running east and west a few miles north of, and roughly parallel to, the river. Morgan's men followed a road that wound through this ravine. The high ridge was intersected by small streams running into the Ohio, or by defiles along which ran dirt roads. The first of these was traversed by a small stream called Thomas Fork.

Semantha Scott, a nineteen-year-old girl who was attending a wedding breakfast near her home, lived close to Thomas Fork Creek. The table was set, and the food was being served as some of the guests started to arrive. They had decided not to let the presence of invaders in the county prevent their celebration. Up rode a number of Rebels who dismounted, saw the bountiful repast, and sat down at the table. Semantha later told her descendants that the uninvited guests did not harm a soul, but that they ate all the food. Then, to the bridal party's surprise, the raiders took all the pillow cases they could find and pulled them over the heads of some of the worthless horses they had acquired along the route. They could not hope to ride through enemy fire in any other manner.

It was also near Thomas Fork that other young raiders rode into the yard of an old lady, Aunt Zilpha Price. She had a reputation as a fortune teller with cards. Frightened at the appearance of the heavily-armed soldiers, Aunt Zilpha spread out her cards and read good fortunes for all the Rebels, thereby hoping to keep them in good humor.

They would have been in a much better humor had the militia not been so active. The young troopers who had eaten the wedding breakfast, and those who had been assured of rosy futures, rode to join the main column. The Southern cavalry turned up the Thomas Fork road as far as Murray's Ford, where they crossed the run and headed east under the brow of the ridge behind Pomeroy. Immediately, they came under a galling fire from militia under Captain Thomas Smith of that town. They heard the snick-snick of bullets slicing through the leaves of the trees that arched above the dusty road. Sometimes they heard the thud of the balls against flesh. Men plunged from their saddles and sprawled in the dirt. Now and then a horse, badly wounded, screamed and ran blindly into the woods. Its rider either reined it to a halt or it stumbled and fell.

154

Duke's brigade was in the van, and he sent men from several regiments into the woods on foot to rout the militia. Several of the horse-holders were struck. Stray horses galloped through the column, unseating raiders until they were caught, or until they dashed into the forest.

Stiff skirmishing continued all the way to Hiland Bridge, where the ravine narrowed. Duke sent Colonel Grigsby and the 6th Kentucky to take the lead, and ordered him to cut his way through without stopping. Behind Grigsby, the balance of the column bunched up, tightened its reins and prepared to run the gauntlet. The four guns rumbled after the carriages and wagons bearing the wounded, and, bringing up the rear, rode Major Webber and the 2nd Kentucky, as usual assigned to one of the toughest spots.

The division rode under an intermittent, harassing fire for five miles and endured the most opposition they had encountered since they had stormed the depot at Lebanon. Men who fell were left behind. They dared not stop in such a hailstorm of bullets or send out flankers to turn the enemy positions. To some of the raiders, it was like riding through a giant cattle chute with sides so steep they could not be climbed on horseback.

On several occasions, when the militia bunched up ahead of the column, Grigsby dismounted his men and sent them forward on foot to dislodge the enemy. The home guards could not withstand attacks by the veterans and broke for cover. Each time, however, some of the men of the 6th Kentucky failed to rejoin the column.

Webber and the 2nd Kentucky likewise had their hands full. As soon as most of the column had passed, the militia did its best to "bite off some of the tail," and made short dashes out of the woods under the covering fire of their companions. The 2nd Kentucky drove them off repeatedly, but the attrition showed in the number of bodies of gray-garbed men who would never rise from the narrow road.

Near the end of the five-mile gauntlet, the road debouched into an area of open land near the Rock Springs fairground, where a side road followed Kerr's Run to the river above Pomeroy. The opposition grew more fierce at this point, and the raiders saw the blue uniforms of regular troops interspersed with the nondescript costumes of the home guards. These were men of the 23rd Ohio Infantry, part of Scammon's force from up the Kanawha.

Assuming that Judah was closer than he was, Scammon had invested one regiment in an attempt to delay Morgan. Once in the clear with room to maneuver, however, the Southern cavalry charged their new enemy and routed them. Except for occasional bushwhacking by scattered militia-men, the worst was over by eleven A.M., and General Morgan called a halt for a five-minute rest at a small crossroads hamlet. The exhausted Colonel Johnson led the Second Brigade into the village and was astounded to see Morgan calmly sitting on the railed porch of the town's one store. He told his men to dismount and rest the horses and went over to speak with his chief.

"I found him sitting on the gallery of a crossroads store, where there was a fine well," recalled Johnson. "The boys were filling their canteens from the pump. The General greeted me with his bright smile, asking me to get down and rest a little, remarking: 'All our troubles are now over, the river is only twenty-five miles away, and tomorrow we will be on Southern soil.' "

It was such spirit that made his men love Morgan and face heavy odds in his behalf. In later yars, George Dallas Mosgrove, one of his men, wrote of the famous guerilla leader. For a New Orleans newspaper, he began his eulogy with the flowery words, "I rode with John Hunt Morgan, the *beau sabreur.*" As it developed, it was no exaggeration.

"In person, General Morgan was notably graceful and handsome," wrote Mosgrove. "Six feet in height, his form was perfect, a rare combi-nation of grace, activity and strength. . . . When invading a far country . . . he marched swiftly and continuously, much of his success being due to his possesion of a faculty that enabled him to move with as great facility and confidence without maps and guides as with them. When advancing he rarely declined to fight, believing that then a concentration of superior forces against him was more difficult, the vigor of his enemy being some-what paralyzed by the celerity of his own movements and the mystery that involved them."

Morgan was only thirty-eight years old and most of his men were much younger. All were influenced by his great personal magnetism. He was friendly and understanding when young men failed or became exhausted, but at other times a strict disciplinarian, especially with those who should have known better.

Morgan could excuse an eighteen- or nineteen-year-old trooper for fall-ing asleep, but he could not forgive an officer or older man for bad con-duct. At one time one of his officers was found guilty by a court-martial of conduct unbecoming an officer. Morgan wrote the sentence, ordering the officer "to be dismissed from the service, and that the crime, name, place of abode and punishment of the delinquent be published in the newspapers

156

in and about the camp and the state from which he came and where he usually resides, after which it shall be deemed scandalous for an officer to associate with him."

Probably the reason that more than 2,000 Confederate soldiers could cross Indiana and Ohio and inflict so little damage on private homes was their deep-rooted understanding of Morgan's distaste of thievery. Earlier in the war, when one of his soldiers was found guilty of this crime, Morgan sentenced him "to have the right side of his head shaved in the presence of his command on evening parade; that he be made to walk around a ring 20 feet in diameter from sunrise to sunset—allowing one hour's respite at noon—during the space of 15 days successively (Sundays excepted), at the expiration of which he shall be put on every detail for fatigue duty in his company for two months without being relieved from other duties."

While on leave from camp another man stole a horse and a shirt and was sentenced "to be marched at the point of a bayonet in the hands of a sentinel up and down the main streets . . . wearing a placard reading 'See what stragglers come to. I stole a horse and a free Negro's shirt.' "

Morgan's troops "were almost all Kentuckians fighting a most personal war—often against their own brothers and frequently against neighbors and kinsmen," one Southerner recalled. This may have partially explained their devotion to an adopted Kentuckian who abandoned his thriving mercantile business in Union territory to form a cavalry company under the stars and bars.

Unquestionably, Morgan understood his men, as well as knowing how to get the utmost from them in times of danger. His coolness was an example all could see and emulate; if he knew the meaning of fear, he never let it be seen. He certainly, however, harbored no illusions about his troopers. One of his younger officers once introduced a clergyman to the General, and said he thought he would make a good chaplain. Morgan courteously acknowledged the introduction with a wan smile.

"Sir, my men don't pray very much," he said, "but I heartily welcome you, and you are at liberty to make them pray, if you can."

Adam Johnson may have been surprised to see his chief so calm, even after the harrowing dash through the ravine behind Pomeroy, but Morgan had a method for his behavior. Nothing could instill more confidence in the young raiders than the sight of their leader taking his ease while untold numbers of militia gathered close on his trail.

Why Morgan and most of his lieutenants felt so strongly that West Virginia represented a safe haven is not at all clear. It had separated from

157

Virginia because most of its citizens preferred the Union to the Confederate cause. The Union high command established the VIII Corps to serve as liaison between the strong forces in Maryland and Virginia in the east and Burnside's and Rosecrans' forces in the west. As a department it did little fighting, and its subordinate units busied themselves primarily with police duties. The rugged nature of the high Alleghenies made widespread military movement practically impossible.

The scattered battalions of the VIII Corps, however, held most of the main centers and mountain passes in the new state. With his 2,000 men Morgan could undoubtedly have cut his way through to Virginia— some survivors of the raid later crossed the state—but it was certainly no hotbed of Confederate strength. On the other hand, after the bitter opposition in Indiana and Ohio, north of the river, any less militant area must have looked as if it were the promised land.

After they had rested, the Southerners mounted and rode up a creek beyond the fairgrounds toward Chester. They entered the town at one o'clock in the afternoon. The sun was high, the heat enervating. Patrols were sent to guard against an attack that did not materialize, and the column, which had straggled, closed up as it occupied the town. Morgan wanted the men to rest their horses and he sent officers out to recruit guides.

During the excitement Joseph Giles, the Rutland blacksmith who had had enough of fighting after the running battle through the ravine, awaited his chance and hid under a pigsty. He was not the only civilian who was tired of war. The old farmer who had joined Morgan's division back on the Cumberland, in hope of getting a barrel of salt, was still very much "present and accounted for," having had no alternative once the Union forces started pursuit.

The old man walked up to Captain Calvin Morgan, the General's brother, and, with tears in his rheumy, tired eyes, voiced his complaint.

"I sw'ar if I wouldn't give all the salt in Kaintucky," he said, "to stand once more safe and sound on the banks of Calfkiller Creek."

Others, dejected and saddle-weary, felt the same way, but most of Morgan's raiders were looking forward eagerly to the morrow, when they hoped to stand across the broad Ohio on West Virginia soil.

Aware that Morgan was less than twenty-five miles from the river, Federal authorities made an all-out effort to prevent a crossing. Riverboats were converted into gunboats by the simple expedient of mounting a fieldpiece in the bow and moving cargo, sacks of coal and lumber forward as a substitute for armor.

158

A Captain Wood of the 18th Ohio Infantry, on recruiting duty in Marietta, was urged to lead a party of volunteers down to Buffington Island. He agreed, and marched 200 raw militia and home guards aboard a steamer which put him ashore below Long Bottom, Ohio, within a few hours of the time the raiders invested Chester.

A steamer loaded with flour and other produce was stuck fast on the bar at the lower end of Buffington Island. Fearing Morgan would make use of the craft, Captain Wood went into the stream, threw flour overboard until the boat was lightened, got up steam, and backed her off the bar. Then he busied his men building an earthen redoubt on the Ohio bank of the river.

In Cincinnati, Ambrose Burnside, sleepless for two nights and exhausted by his repeated failures to get regular cavalry in front of Morgan, was being bombarded with frantic messages for troops he could not supply.

Major General George L. Hartsuff wired that General Buckner was ready to move north through Big Creek Gap into eastern Kentucky. With Sanders gone, there was no cavalry to stop him.

Far to the west in Paducah, Brigadier General Alexander Asboth wired for help, saying Confederate General Gideon Pillow was marching north toward Paris, Tennessee, or Cairo, Illinois. Burnside could only telegraph his suppliants that he could spare no men.

"All my cavalry are after Morgan in Ohio, east of the Scioto River," he informed Asboth, and went on to add, a bit testily, "I have to hold the entire line of the Louisville & Nashville Railroad, the Cumberland River and East Kentucky, so that I really have not a man to spare. What kind of force do you need, and how much? Are there not plenty of gunboats on the river?"

While the Southerners were running the gauntlet inland from Pomeroy, Burnside sent an impatient order to Colonel Putnam at Camp Marietta:

"Dispatch engine immediately. Have boat fired up. Load your men on cars. Remain in office till I hear from Pomeroy. Have all means of transportation, except what you use, taken across the river. Enemy at Rutland, 12 miles from Pomeroy, and if turned back from there may possibly go to Buffington Island."

What Burnside feared was the thought that he might completely fail to capture Morgan. And the possibility of another failure was too terrible to contemplate. He had dallied at Antietam, holding back his men until Lee extricated his army, and McClellan had had to assume the major blame for not forcing Burnside to attack the Confederate right flank.

159

His generalship at Fredericksburg had been much worse. It was so bad that he publicly accepted the blame for feeding his Northern army into the Southern meat-grinder, regiment by regiment, division by division. All this, irrespective of the fact that he faced the ablest generals the South produced—Lee, Jackson and Longstreet.

He was now on the ragged edge of another catastrophe. He had put more than 10,000 regular Union cavalry on Morgan's trail, had helped Indiana muster 65,000 militia and Ohio 50,000 more, but Morgan had out-guessed and out-raced him and was within a few hours of his goal.

If he could have read the mesage Colonel Kautz sent to Hobson at 4:30 P.M. Saturday, from Rutland, it would have done his heart good. Kautz had done his utmost to catch the raiders, as Hobson had urged, but his horses had failed him. Someone or something else would have to stop Morgan. But his message had the germs of hope in it, for the first time since the raiders crossed the Cumberland.

"The Rebels tried to force an entrance into Pomeroy and have been repulsed," said Kautz, "Captain Higley, 7th Ohio Cavalry, left Morgan's rear an hour ago on the Chester road, 7-10 miles from here. They are supposed to be searching for Buffington Island, about 25 miles from here, where they will try to ford the river. It is too high, however, and the gunboats are on the alert. General Scammon commanded at Pomeroy. No serious damage done. I have stopped to feed and rest and shall push on tonight. An intelligent lady at whose house Morgan was this afternoon, thinks they consider their case hopeless unless they can cross at Buffington Island tonight."

Captain J. P. Higley was a Rutland man and was familiar with the roads of Meigs County. Kautz had sent him ahead with a few men to mark Morgan's track. That he could do, but neither his detachment nor Scammon's infantry, encountered the elusive foe. Hobson rode into Rutland five hours after the last Rebel had departed.

At Burnside's suggestion, General Scammon put most of his men on the boats that had brought them down the Kanawha and hastened up-river around the Great Bend and into the long reach that contained Buffington Island. He then put his men ashore on the West Virginia shore, and deployed them up and down the bank to prevent a Rebel crossing.

Judah was still several miles from Pomeroy, but, made eager by telegraph messages dispatched by Scammon before he left that town, was spurring his horses on the river road.

This was the Union situation as the Confederate column waited for

160

orders in the little town of Chester, which straddled Shade River less than fifteen miles from its confluence with the Ohio.

General Morgan called a council of war. It was attended by Duke, Johnson, the line officers commanding each regiment, Captain Byrnes, the artillerist, and several aides. The laughter was gone from the General's face. Scouts had brought word that the Ohio was running full and high in its banks. The horses were exhausted, the men weary and somewhat lackluster from loss of sleep. In the diary that nothing could make him forget, Leeland Hathaway jotted down his recollections of the atmosphere in which the officers met:

"The difficulties in our progress had increased greatly during the last few days and nights. The roads were obstructed by fallen timbers which had to be chopped away, and the home guards had thickened until we were in a continual and almost perpetual skirmish, and they were much emboldened by their own numbers and position. They could fire at us from behind the trees and retire before we could reach them. The advance guard suffered seriously, and the whole command was much worried and not a little hurt by the repeated stinging and buzzing of this horde of militia. Pursued in the rear by Hobson and Shackleford, our position was becoming critical. It was evident that even the elements were against us. Scouts brought word that the river was rising and was past fording at nearly every point. An old lady who had lived near the ford told us it had been that high with flash floods only twice before in her sixty years."

Morgan wanted a guide capable of leading him to the river by the best route. He waited until one was found, using the time to burn the grist mill and the bridge across Shade River. Then, an hour and a half after entering Chester, he left the town on the road that led through Bashan to Buffington Island.

Those ninety minutes spelled disaster for Morgan. Had he pushed on, he would have reached the Ohio before darkness, found the ford unguarded, and could have crossed to safety before his pursuers caught up with him and before Scammon deployed his men on the far shore.

This was Morgan's second mistake. The first one, the attack on the Union force at Tebb's Bend, had cost him a few score men, killed or wounded, but it did not imperil the division's future. This one was a thousand-fold more serious, it was the biggest single military mistake of the entire raid.

It has to be pointed out, in his defense, that the column had fought its way through the ravine, for the most part riding at a gallop. He had to

161

halt to breathe the horses, to enable his force to close up, and to restore order among 2,000 men who had ridden stirrup-to-stirrup with death for five terrible miles.

With the bushwhackers hanging about them like angry hornets and the smoke from the burning mill and bridge rising straight in the windless noonday air, the raiders climbed the slopes of the last hills between them and the river. The road was narrow and rough, the country about them generally wooded and broken.

Everywhere, when they found a clearing with a house, the owners had fled. The horses had been secreted—so many of them in one long grotto beneath the overhang of a cliff that the stream on which it fronted was known thereafter as Horse Cave Creek—and the cattle led into the woods, their bells removed to keep their whereabouts a secret.

A boy who lived near the creek sniped at the Rebel column as it marched toward the river. Scouts were sent to catch him, and he was punished by being made to walk in the midst of the spare horses. When he tried to climb on one of the animal's backs to escape the threshing hoofs, the angry soldiers fired over his head. He was forced to endure his sentence until twilight enabled him to escape.

Near Bashan the raiders came upon a funeral procession winding up a hill to a cemetery. The soldiers removed the coffin from the hearse, laid it reverently by the side of the road, and placed several of their wounded comrades in the vehicle. They then commandeered every horse in the procession and rode away with the hearse bouncing along the dirt road ahead of the four fieldpieces.

A skirmish with a company of militia occurred beyond the crossroads at Bashan, but the column fought through without dismounting. The shadows from the sinking sun then cloaked them and they rode on, hungry and dispirited, until the road wound out of the hills into a narrow stretch of open bottom land along the Ohio. It was good to be out of the woods, even though darkness had fallen. The men in the van could see the broad ribbon of water, faintly illumined by the light of a moon that was little more than a thin sickle of gold in a mist-splotched sky.

Dismayed, they could barely discern the entrenchments and redoubt that Wood and his Marietta volunteers had erected a few hours previously. They thought they saw the ugly shape of cannon above the earthen ramparts, but it was too dark for them to be certain.

Scouts filtered forward in the darkness and heard the sounds of a large number of men behind the ramparts. Others moved upstream to the

162

vicinity of Portland, the nearest hamlet, and found the home-owners had extinguished their coal oil lamps and either were sitting in the dark, terrified at the nearness of the raiders, or had fled into the woods.

Most of the troopers munched their iron rations, unwilling to light fires. Those not on picket duty promptly fell asleep. They would have been less serene had they known that Hobson's force, now resting in Chester, was being fed by Northern women who fired up their outdoor ovens and kitchen stoves to make biscuits and quick bread. From their root cellars and spring houses they brought fresh butter, milk and preserves. Boys and girls, who carried the food in hickory-chip baskets, passed among the weary Union soldiers and distributed the welcome fare.

In the river bottoms a fog crept in from the Ohio, shrouding men and horses. For a time, the moon seemed to be fighting for its existence against low-lying, scudding clouds, driven by a wind that did not reach into the valley to blow away the fog, but later the first-quarter crescent disappeared and was not seen again that night.

As the evening progressed, the chill of the fog penetrated the raiders' clothing, causing slight discomfort. This was nothing compared to the depression they felt at their enforced delay. Officers and men were aware of their cruel dilemma; they needed no maps or captured orders to sense their predicament. Hobson and Shackleford were only a few hours behind them and approaching fast. From the blue-coated uniforms they had seen near Pomeroy, they surmised that Judah was close at hand, unaware of Scammon's part in the mounting drama. Judah was, in fact, very near, having ridden into Pomeroy before nightfall. His men had rested in the streets for several hours while residents brought out fodder from barns and livery stables. The column had then marched off on the river road through Racine, Antiquity and Dorcas, driving hard for the ford at Buffington Island.

In addition, the raiders felt certain that somewhere in the mist swirling over the Ohio there were Union gunboats which, because of the very high water that prevented the raiders from fording the stream, had been able to cross shoals and sand spits that would have normally barred their progress.

"All were now on the *qui vive*," noted Major McCreary, "for the Ohio River is full of gunboats and transports, and an immense force of cavalry is hovering in our rear."

Morgan and his men had crossed the Ohio at Brandenburg nine days

163

before. Tonight they again stood upon its banks, having fought their way across two enemy states.

The time had now come for an accounting. The days lost chasing Northern cavalry in east Tennessee returned to haunt them. The time so lost had been sufficient for the unseasonal rising of the Ohio. Too, they now sensed the penalty of the hour and a half spent seeking a guide in Chester. Those had been daylight hours—a fatal loss now that darkness cloaked the ford. To John Hunt Morgan they represented "the most precious hour and a half since his horses' feet touched northern soil."

Morgan realized his predicament. Had he waited until morning, the foe would have him boxed between the hills and the river. He had to assume that some of the regulars who had skirmished with the column at Pomeroy were now in the earthworks guarding the ford.

He called a hurried council of war with his lieutenants. It was suggested that the heavier wagons be abandoned and a dash made to some point farther upriver, where fords might still be passable. It was even pointed out that if the two hundred wounded men were left behind with the wagon train and the four guns, the able-bodied men might swim the Ohio as they had swum the Cumberland. Without a minute's hesitation Morgan vetoed this proposal. He would save all—or run the risk of losing all. In his memoirs, Colonel Duke summarized the thinking of his leader at that eleventh-hour conference:

"General Morgan fully appreciated these reasons for getting across the river that night, as did those with whom he advised. There were also very strong reasons against attacking the work at night; without the capture of the work, which commanded the ford, it would be impossible to cross. The night . . . was intensely dark. Attacks in the dark are always hazardous experiments; in this case it would have been doubly so. We knew nothing of the ground and could not procure guides. Our choice of the direction in which to move to the attack would have been purely guesswork. The defenders of the work had only to lie still and fire with artillery and musketry directly in their front, but the assailants would have had a line to preserve and would have had to exercise great care lest they should fall foul of each other in the obscurity."

Morgan had to gamble. Faced with the situation existing at Buffington Island, there was nothing he could do but chance an early-morning attack on the breastworks in front of him and pray that the darkness which held him in such tight bondage might also deter his pursuers for a few hours at least. The Rebel chieftain requested Duke to move two regiments as close

164

to the redoubt as possible, and to attack it the instant daybreak afforded them sufficient light. The council then adjourned.

Colonel Duke asked Howard Smith and the 5th Kentucky, and Grigsby and the 6th Kentucky, to undertake this vital chore. The men stole forward in the darkness, trying to envelope the breastworks on the land side. He then sent Byrnes' two Parrotts to dig in on a knoll above the attackers' heads from which they could be fired. For a time, there was the rustle of feet in the grass, the creaking of gun axles, and the myriad noises of several hundred men trying to move stealthily over unfamiliar ground.

Leeland Hathaway took a patrol upstream, following the bank of the river, and looked for craft to use in ferrying the sick and wounded. He found two ancient flatboats, badly in need of repair, and put his men to work caulking the seams. There was neither oakum nor tar, but the men tore strips of cloth from the bolts of calico they still carried in their saddlebags and did the best they could in the darkness.

"Work went on all night in reliefs," noted Hathaway, "the men literally falling asleep at the boat side."

Down at the ford, men lay down in ranks, wondering what the next day would bring. The stamping and nickering of 2,000 weary horses was just loud enough to prevent the raiders from hearing the sounds of Captain Wood and his 200 Marietta militiamen tumbling their two fieldpieces off the bank into the murky Ohio and fleeing fearfully into the darkness.

This unforgivable failure to hold their ground would have caused General Burnside unmitigated anguish had he only known of it. So sure was the Union commander that at last all was well, he sent Governor Tod a summary of the situation as he believed it to be at that hour. It read:

"Judah and Hobson have no doubt made a junction in Morgan's rear by this time. Scammon has arrived at Pomeroy with a good force. Wallace [Colonel William Wallace, commanding the 15th Ohio Volunteer Infantry] has arrived at Parkersburg with the Camp Chase infantry and battery. Captain Conine holds Little Hocking Bridge, and all the roads are ordered to be obstructed, so I don't see how he can get well out if the gunboats do their duty."

Judah and Hobson had not yet joined forces, but they were within eight or ten miles of one another. Scammon was much nearer than Pomeroy, after having marched all afternoon on a road described as "crooked as a ram's horn" toward Buffington Island. The gunboats would do their duty. But none of these forces constituted the serious obstacle that the Ohio itself, swollen by heavy summer rains in the West Virginia mountains,

165

represented to the Southerners. They had eluded regulars as well as home-guards, and militia moved about the invasion chessboard by horse, train, and steamboat. But it was the Ohio in flood that finally brought them to a halt—and battle.

Some of the Confederate wounded, lifted from the motley train of carriages and wagons, were laid tenderly upon the softer earth. These men had gone to sleep before nightfall hid the view, gazing "upon the Virginia shore like the Promised Land by the doubtful light of the moon." To the others who had no duties and who could enjoy its benison, sleep came under a drifting blanket of river fog.

CHAPTER 13

Disaster at the River

ON OCTOBER, 29, 1770, George Washington took his diary from a saddle-bag, knelt by a campfire to get more light on the page, and wrote this entry:

"Opposite to the creek just below which we incamped is a pretty, long bottom, and I believe tolerable wide, but about eight or nine miles below the aforementioned creek and just below a pavement of rocks on the west side, comes in a creek with Fallen Timber at the Mouth on which the Indians say there is wide bottom and good Land."

The future General of the Continental Armies and first President of the United States was writing in his journal at a camp beside the junction of Shade Creek and the Ohio River. Although the grammar was bad and the spelling eccentric, he described with complete accuracy the level bottom on the western bank of the Ohio where Morgan's raiders had struck the river.

Upstream from where the tired Confederates slept beneath their gum ponchos, the hills approach the river in the form of weathered, eroded palisades, leaving scarcely sufficient room for a narrow road to pass between them and the Ohio. Below the town of Long Bottom, the hills begin to recede from the river, and form a narrow, triangular plain with the short base near the town of Portland and Buffington Island. Although the road from Hockingport on the north is little more than a treacherous defile, the one from Apple Grove and Antiquity to the south rises through a level stretch of farmland crisscrossed in places by low rolling ridges and occasional stands of timber. Into the bottom land from the west ran the road Morgan had followed through Bashan from Chester, a road that tumbles erratically down the ridge as if eager to leave the jumbled hills for the pleasant floor of the valley.

The fertile plain beside the Ohio was a peaceful place, not unlike a dozen other places along the river. This particular patch of earth, made

167

strategically important by the existence of the ford below the island, was the place toward which 2,000 Confederate soldiers, and four times that many Northern troops, had been drawn inexorably for more than seven days and nights.

Hungry crows, angered at the presence of so many men near the fields of ripening corn, ushered in the Sabbath on July 19, 1863, with raucous complaints. As they flew above the river bottom, the heavy mists that had cloaked the land all through the night began to disperse. Pickets roused the sleeping men to join those who had been unable to sleep. Smith and Grigsby formed the soldiers of the 5th and 6th Kentucky Regiments into ranks, whispered last-minute orders, and sent them to assault the earthworks. Instead of the crash of musketry they had anticipated, there was only silence. The first men over the rampart could not believe their eyes when they found it to be unoccupied. They could see the guns where they lay in the water under the sprawling branches of willow trees growing along the river bank.

Duke sent word to Morgan that the redoubt was empty, and immediately instructed Colonel Smith to take command of both the 5th and 6th Kentucky and move downstream astride the road to Pomeroy. Smith placed his own regiment under his next in command, Major William Bullitt, and led off to the south. Within a few hundred yards, they found themselves in a thick patch of fog that extended to where Joseph Buffington had built his grist mill in 1820, at the mouth of Groundhog Creek.

Suddenly, through the swirling mist, the raiders saw the figures of half-a-hundred men advancing toward them on foot and, less distinctly, a small body of mounted men to their rear. Smith's force had run head-on into Judah's advance. Both groups started firing within seconds. The Confederates recovered quickly, before the enemy could rally from their surprise, and poured a heavy fire into the Federal ranks.

One of his own officers said Judah had paid no attention to a warning brought him by a Negro farm hand and he blundered into the Southerners in the fog, little suspecting they was so close to the ford.

"On the instant the two parties discovered each other," wrote this officer, "our force received a rattling volley from a hundred carbines. The effect of this on a troop in a narrow line moving by the flank in fours, carbines carelessly dangling, may be imagined by those who have been there."

General Judah had sent the 8th Indiana, under Colonel Butler, forward with the 14th Illinois Cavalry in reserve to its rear. The 11th Kentucky had swung wide to form on Butler's right, and Lieutenant John O'Neil

168

with a detachment of the 5th Indiana, followed the river's edge, keeping pace with the Kentuckians.

Judah and his staff rode just ahead of a single gun belonging to Henshaw's Illinois Battery, and an escort of forty-five mounted men under Lieutenant Armstrong detailed from the 14th Illinois.

Had the Union soldiers realized how close they were to Buffington Island, they could have defended themselves better; but the fog hid everything ahead of them, and they had unquestionably absorbed some of their leader's feeling that danger was still several miles away. As it was, they were in serious trouble from the first fusillade. They recoiled under Smith's furious attack. The raiders, throwing their carbines aside, charged on the run, firing their pistols and yelling loudly. In minutes the recoil became a retreat and then a panic, brought on when the postilions on the lead horses of Henshaw's gun were killed, and the team pulling the gun and limber became hopelessly entangled in its traces.

A Union officer, describing the battle, said the overturned gun and frightened teams formed "an ugly barricade in the lane behind the staff, escort, and Armstrong's company."

Smith's men broke through the skirmish line, and Judah had great difficulty getting past the wildly threshing artillery horses. Despite the danger they all faced, some of his juniors could not help being amused at his plight.

"It was a comical panic . . . to those of the staff who had persisted in saying to the General that we were going into a trap," said his lieutenant. "We enjoyed seeing him 'getting out' as he lay on the opposite side of his horse's neck from the direction in which the leaden compliments were coming."

Most of the raiders fought on foot, but others were mounted. These men cut and slashed their way through the disorganized Union troops until Colonel Smith had to call them back to avoid having them cut off. The raiders made a quick check and found that they had killed or wounded twenty men, captured about fifty and seized Henshaw's gun. Among the prisoners were Judah's assistant adjutant general, several of his staff, including Captain John C. Grafton, and a wounded aide.

When he wrote his official report after the battle, General Judah did not stress his own narrow escape. That would never do. Although the report was very military and casual, his matter-of-fact words could not conceal how close he had come to being made a prisoner of the very troops he was trying to capture.

"Traveling all night," he said, "I reached the last descent to the river

169

bottom at Buffington Bar at 5:30 A.M. on the 19th. Here, halting my force and placing my artillery in a commanding position, I determined to make a reconnaissance in person. . . . A very dense fog enveloped everything, confining the view of surrounding objects to a radius of about fifty yards. I was accompanied by a small advance guard, my escort, and one piece of Henshaw's battery, a section of which, under Captain Henshaw, I had ordered to join my force. I advanced slowly and cautiously along a road leading toward the river . . . when my little force found itself enveloped on three sides—front and both flanks—by three regiments, dismounted and led by Colonel Basil Duke, just discernible through the fog at a distance of from fifty to a hundred yards."

Judah described how swiftly the Confederates responded with heavy fire and how they captured the fieldpiece and many prisoners. He then employed a very elegant circumlocution to tell how he had been forced to make a run for it:

"Searching in vain for an opening through which to charge and temporarily beat back the enemy, I was compelled to fall back upon the main body."

It must have been most embarrassing, but it was only a temporary setback. Judah had too many men with him for it to be anything less.

As soon as General Morgan heard the first burst of musketry, he ordered that the wounded to taken to the water's edge for their evacuation to the West Virginia shore, using the two flatboats Hathaway and his party had tried to repair during the night.

Among the Union wounded, carried back from that first skirmish in the battle of Buffington Island, was Daniel McCook, sixty-five years old. He had cajoled his way into the army as a paymaster and won the rank of major by the time he joined Judah in pursuit of the raiders. He fell from his horse, mortally wounded, but was helped to his own lines and died two days after the battle was ended.

Old Major McCook was the father of the "ten fighting McCooks of Ohio," and the uncle of five others. One of his sons, Daniel, a law partner of William T. Sherman, became a Union general. Three others, Robert, Alexander, and Edwin, also became general officers. Charles McCook, a private, was killed during the first battle of Bull Run, a few yards from where his father was serving as a surgeon's aide and stretcher-bearer.

When he talked his way into the army, the lionhearted Irishman had boasted of his ten boys, all in service, and said he also wished to be in uniform "to prove himslf worthy" of his sons.

170

After the first contact between Smith's force and Judah's advance, there was a lull, brought about partly by the thickening fog and partly by both sides seeking to improve their positions. Duke suggested that the men facing Judah fall back and dig in on a line just south of the ford. He wanted to take advantage of the level ground over which the Union forces would have to make their way without adequate cover.

Horse-holders took the animals to the rear and the 5th and 6th Kentucky waited for the enemy, guarding their ammunition which averaged less than ten rounds to a man. Some of the raiders took position behind Indian burial mounds that rose from the valley floor like miniature domes.

It was now nearly six A.M., and the sun occasionally broke through the mist, but for the most part the mile-long valley was shrouded in an eerie gloom. Duke conferred with Morgan, and left Smith's men spread across the southern end of the river bottom, holding a thin skirmish line about 800 yards from the Ohio to the ridge on his right flank. General Morgan told his staff he had decided their only chance lay in a retreat northward through the defile. A few wounded men had started across the river, but it was useless to hope that any sizable portion of the division could escape by this route.

As the officers talked, couriers brought word that Colonel Johnson's vedettes had been driven in by men from Hobson's force, attacking as they made their way down the bluff on the Chester Road. Duke hurried off to establish a holding force, and found Smith's regiments retreating in disorder. Three regiments of Judah's cavalry had struck from out of the fog. The detachment of the 5th Indiana under Lieutenant O'Neil had fought through them and to their rear. Men fired at their enemies whenever they could see them, but the weight of numbers was on Judah's side. Duke rallied the 6th Kentucky and established a new line. By then, however, the raiders had lost their two Parrott guns.

In the midst of the confusion, Captain Grafton of Judah's staff escaped from his guard and hid in the willows by the river bank. It did not seem important at the time, and no one went to hunt for him.

Also at about this time, with bullets whining through the air and shells from Judah's guns bursting erratically among the rear units of the Confederate force, a farmer approached Colonel Jacob in the Union lines. He was trembling with fear and could not speak. After a few minutes, he recovered enough to voice his distress at the battle being waged on his farm.

"Colonel," he said, "please save my corn as much as possible."

171

Laughing to himself, the Union officer saluted the terrified farmer and said, "Your request is granted, sir."

The 5th and 6th Kentucky, pinned down by Judah's murderous rifle fire, held their ground only by making each bullet count. Each man knew he would have to fight with the ammunition he had in his cartridge box. There was no reserve. At one time Grigsby pulled half his men out of the line and led them in a dash to where Byrne's Parrotts had been abandoned. Loaded with canister, a Parrott was similar to a giant shotgun, and the Confederates needed that kind of support. But it was of no avail. Grigsby and his party encountered an almost solid wall of lead from Union carbines. Federal soldiers were pouring onto the field as fast as marching columns could be wheeled into line from the Pomeroy road. Less than half of the suicide squad returned to the Rebel perimeter.

With less than 150 men, Colonel Smith extended his line to the right in an effort to get a few riflemen onto the ridge. Some of these raiders climbed so high they found themselves above the low lying fog. The battlefield was hidden from sight, but they saw the flashes when Judah's guns were fired, and could hear the shells screaming up the valley.

Down in the bottom land, Morgan was trying to restore order. He extricated his trains and started them for the defile at the apex of the triangle; and then he began withdrawing his regiments by columns of four from right of companies.

For a few minutes it appeared that he would succeed. He rode among the men, inspiring confidence, urging them to hurry but warning against panic. A semi-orderly movement to the rear got under way.

At that moment, disaster struck from two sides. Down the Chester road came Wolford and Kautz with Hobson's best units, stones rolling from under the hurrying hoofs, regimental flags waving in the breeze created by the downhill rush.

As Whitelaw Reid, the correspondent, saw it, this was the deciding moment of the battle.

"As Hobson's guidons fluttered out in the little valley by the river bank, every member of that little Rebel band that had defied a hundred thousand knew the contest was over," he said. "They were almost out of ammunition, exhausted, barely 2,000 strong. Against them were Hobson's 3,000 and Judah's still larger force."

Adam Johnson's men, reduced now to four or five rounds of ammunition and some of it worthless from friction in the cartridge boxes, held their ground for awhile, but more and more Union cavalry poured over the ridge. It was a torrent that could not be dammed. Kautz with the 2nd

172

Ohio rode north along the base of the ridge and struck the wagon train from the flank.

Wagons and ambulances locked wheels. Horses fell in their tracks and the vehicles behind became entangled with one another as the drivers tried to avoid running down their wounded companions. Injured horses galloped everywhere, plunging through the disordered ranks, upsetting wagons and trampling men.

The sun broke through the haze and the disheartened raiders, looking at the river, saw a gunboat and two steamers, from whose guns shells were being lobbed accurately into the ranks of the 5th and 6th Kentucky regiments.

"How in thunder are the Feds laying their fire so precisely?" Rebel soldiers asked one another.

What had happened was no mystery. Captain Grafton had waited in the willows until a break in the fog revealed the shapes of the steamer *Imperial,* towing the gunboat *Moose* over the bar at the foot of Buffington Island. Then he had swum out to the *Moose* and described to Lieutenant Commander Fitch just where the opposing forces lay. With this information, it was a simple matter for Fitch to open fire with his twenty-four-pounder Dahlgrens.

A few minutes later, another steamboat, the *Allegheny Belle,* churned her way into view and poured her fire into the bloody triangle between the ridges and the river.

Hobson unlimbered two guns as soon as they pounded over the last rise on the Chester road. Within minutes Morgan's men were being ripped with solid shot and exploding shells from three sides simultaneously. Yankee soldiers cheered, and Southern soldiers groaned and cursed, forgetting it was the Sabbath.

The raiders were cavalrymen, accustomed to fighting men on horseback or dismounted as infantry. They had cannons themselves, and were familiar with the difficulties the artillerists had in getting the field pieces into position and fighting them in a fluid action. Judah and Hobson had Parrotts and howitzers like their own; the sound of their shells, while unpleasant, was at least familiar. But with the heavy Dahlgrens on the *Moose,* it was another matter. The firing from the boats had a frightening psychological effect upon the rebel troopers.

"I heartily wished," Colonel Duke remembered, "that their fierce ardor, the result of a feeling of perfect security, could have been subjected to the test of two or three shots through their hulls."

If Captain Byrnes could have extricated his two howitzers from the

173

wrecked wagon train, he would have found a soft target in the *Allegheny Belle*. The *Belle* was an ordinary packet, built of wood, with a great stern paddle wheel. Under Burnside's prodding, many similar steamers had been fitted out as gunboats. This one had a single gun mounted on the main deck forward. Bales of cotton and heavy timbers had been erected as a sort of homemade turret to shield the gunners.

The raiders did not know it, but the gun captain on the *Allegheny Belle* was an eighteen-year-old boy named Nathaniel Pepper. He was the son of Captain Pepper of the *Alice Dean,* which had been burned to the waterline at Brandenburg. His face flushed with excitement and his eyes burning with an understandable hatred, he aimed his gun carefully and affectionately, and sent each three-inch shell ashore accompanied by a curse.

Duke's line, at right angles to the river, was also at rough right angles to Johnson's line, which was facing the ridge; but as the ridge bent toward the Ohio it meant that the two Confederate lines formed a "V," with the men fighting back to back. This was a most unhealthy situation, for the Rebels were thus exposed to a cross fire of musketry. Bullets fired at one line often felled men in the other, so that for much of the battle, the Southerners were being fired upon from front and rear. Most troops would have broken, but the men stood their ground under the galling punishment and hoped to give Morgan an opportunity to extricate the balance of the division.

Lieutenant O'Neil and the 5th Indiana took advantage of Duke's predicament and charged down a lane beside a cornfield into the battered ranks of the 5th Kentucky. Saber clashed with saber, dismounted raiders fought like demons with weapons they seldom used, but ammunition was nearly gone. Major Bullitt rallied a small detachment of the 6th Kentucky and attacked the Federals with such violence the Indianans broke and fled.

But wherever the outnumbered Confederates won a respite, it was only momentary. Within an hour of Kautz's descent into the valley, Hobson had 3,000 men on the field, most of whom were dismounted. To the south, Judah had at least an equal number. Because of the peculiar conformation of the river bottom, not all of Morgan's men could be employed. In the early hours of the conflict, the 2nd Kentucky and 9th Tennessee of Duke's brigade and the 8th and 11th Kentucky of Johnson's saw virtually no action. The men of these regiments, however, were exposed to the same artillery fire as those in the front lines. There was nothing they

174

could do but suffer as they hurried the rest of the column on its way through the defile.

Most of the regiments withdrew in good order, despite the exploding shells and heavy small arms fire. General Morgan sent aides to inform Duke and Johnson of his progress, and urged them to stand firm. Both men knew it was a hopeless assignment, but they also knew the safety of the balance of the division depended upon their ability to fight a stout rearguard action.

Behind them in the pandemonium that turned the Sabbath into a mockery, a few men sought escape on the river. Several soldiers of the 9th Tennessee under Captain Kirkpatrick, using one of the flatboats, made good their crossing, going north of the island while the gunboats were busy at the lower end. With them went "Little Bob" Walden, a boy of fourteen who had ridden with a Kentucky regiment for a year before the great raid. Older men, who sought to save the boy, got him to leave the battlefield. He swam his horse to the Virginia shore while the men of the 9th Tennessee cheered.

By midmorning the Southern situation was deteriorating badly. Judah sent a dismounted Michigan regiment onto the ridge where, early in the morning, Smith had tried to establish a link between his force and Johnson's. The Federal troops overwhelmed the thin Rebel skirmish line and drove a deep wedge into the southern section. At about the same time, Duke's left flank—under severe pounding from the gunboats—was turned by a powerful movement of Judah's dismounted cavalry. The brunt of this charge was taken by Major Bullitt and the badly depleted 6th Kentucky. Nearly surrounded, the regiment held firm and beat off the Federals. But Duke, who said the 6th "stood the heavy attack of the enemy like a bastion," knew the men could not again face such odds and win.

Colonel Duke rode off to confer with Adam Johnson. He was so badly pressed by the enemy that his line was falling back yard by yard, fighting Indian style from behind trees, fence rows, and even in the furrows between rows of corn. The two colonels, who knew that the bulk of the division had made good its escape from the field, agreed to fall back simultaneously. There was really no alternative.

Colonel Smith had done all he could to obey Morgan's early-morning order.

"General Morgan told me to hold the foe in check," he later wrote. "In less than an hour, it seemed the whole face of the earth was covered with them."

175

He had lost his Parrotts and was under fire from the gunboats on his left and the Michigan regiment on his right. When Duke brought him word to withdraw, his small force "was enfiladed from both flanks."

The men who had ridden with Morgan through two years of war were good soldiers. While shells screamed over their heads, and bullets flicked through the stalks of corn, they waited while the horse-holders brought up their horses and remounted without confusion. As if on a drill-ground they retreated in columns of fours from right of companies, horses trotting nervously as fragments of shells rained a deadly hail. Men fell and others closed the ranks. There was no longer time to care for the wounded. Three times the 6th Kentucky formed to the "rear into line" and charged the enemy cavalry, keeping it off balance. From the western side of the triangle came Johnson's battered remnants, and for a mile the stalwart raiders moved as if on parade.

But they had not counted on Fitch and his gunboats.

With the *Imperial* towing the *Moose,* and the *Allegheny Belle* churning along in the rear, the Union flotilla steamed up the chute between the island and the Ohio bank, and raked the dusty road and the shell-furrowed cornfields with grape. The noise of the case shot whistling around them was like the sound of heavy rain—it was almost more than human beings could endure. Horses and men fell under the storm of metal. Everywhere there was the terrible sound of wounded horses, neighing in agony.

"The scream of the shells drowned the hum of the bullets." Colonel Duke recalled. "The air seemed filled with metal, and the ground was torn and ploughed into furrows."

Past the Tunis Middleswart farmhouse, where some of the officers had dined the night before, moved the rear guard, beset on three sides. It held its ranks until the weary troopers beheld what was left of the wagon train. Near the entrance to the narrow defile, wagons and carriages were strewn about in a vast tangle, dead horses still in harness, living animals trapped in the traces. In a deep ravine, the rear guard saw the 2nd Brigade's two howitzers, which had been caught among runaway teams, up ended in the deep draw. Here and there, a few terrified stragglers were circling the field "in a delirium of fright," still clinging to bolts of calico and garments they had taken for their womenfolk back home. Each passing shell frightened them anew, and caused them to alter the direction of their flight.

"The upper end of the valley," said Duke in his memoirs, "was filled with wagons and ambulances. . . . The remaining section of artillery was

176

tumbled into a ravine during this mad swirl, as if the guns had been as light as feathers. . . . In a moment the panic was complete, and the disaster irretrievable."

Raiders who a moment before had behaved as if they were made of iron broke and ran for the one remaining escape route. Others headed for the river. Duke and Johnson became separated under the attack of men from Judah's force.

Into this melee charged Colonel Sanders and a regiment of Michigan cavalry. From his command post at the foot of the Chester road, General Hobson had ordered Sanders to deliver the *coup de grace* to the fleeing rear guard. As Sanders' own regiment—the 5th Ohio—was occupied, he took the Michigan regiment and dashed away. However, as they neared the northern end of the valley, they found themselves zeroed in by shellfire from the gunboats. Sanders led his men into a deep ravine for refuge from the shells. When Fitch's gunners switched to new targets, he ordered his men into ranks again, and they continued their charge. The Union regiment, fresher than most of the units because of their long boat ride, struck Duke's pitiful rear guard "like hail in a tobacco field." What had been a retreat became a rout.

To Leeland Hathaway, the scene was overpowering. Young and impressionable, he saw it as the tragic *Götterdämmerung* of the war, the end of the road for all his heroes. In the account he wrote for his daughter, that she might know what manner of man her father had been, he told of his last battle with Morgan:

"We faced front and rear and kept up the unequal fight for several hours. We were at bay and had the spirit of deathless resistance fully aroused. We were not used to being thus penned up like rats in a trap and were ready to take any chance, no matter how desperate or dangerous, if it only promised release from the toils around us. But 50,000 men [It must have seemed there were that many Federal soldiers to him although 8,000 would have been a more accurate estimate] well-armed and fully supplied with ammunition, many of them fresh, are more than a match for less than 2,000 worn and weary men.

"The enemy advanced his lines slowly, for there was not a commander who hadn't felt Morgan's blows. . . . Morgan with about 600 men escaped up a deep ravine . . . and went up the river. When this ruse was discovered, the Federals advanced in such force that our surrender was inevitable. Then Colonels Ward and Dick Morgan ordered us to go forward to the enemy's lines and surrender the two rear regiments. To reach the Yankee

177

lines, I had to go through a heavy undergrowth only traversed by an occasional path, one of them I followed, being startled by frequent firing from the front and hearing the balls passing unpleasantly near me. I give the enemy credit for suspending their fire as soon as they saw my improvised flag which, by the way, was a piece of cotton which one of the boys had taken from a store to have shirts made of, as he said. I rode forward as rapidly as the nature of the ground or timber would allow and soon reached a Michigan regiment commanded by a Major. He received me courteously, and I made my report, surrendering what was left of Ward's and Morgan's regiments."

Firing became sporadic, and after awhile the Sabbath calm again descended on the shell-torn, bloody triangle of farmland beside the river. Here and there men tried to escape or hide. Colonel Grigsby and Captain Byrnes rode their horses into the Ohio and made good their dash to freedom. But for about 700 raiders, it was ended.

Duke sent an aide with a white flag to Colonel Israel Garrard of the 7th Ohio Cavalry. A minute later Howard Smith sent in a flag. Federal cavalry rode in among the disorganized Rebels, accepting the surrender of small groups of men standing dejectedly by their horses. As the prisoners were moved toward the southern end of the field, Duke learned that Johnson had managed to reach the other end of the valley with enough men to form a rear guard for the 1100 raiders Morgan had saved from disaster.

Colonel Garrard observed the niceties of military protocol and sent Captain Theodore Allen of the 7th Ohio with a detachment of men to accept Colonel Duke's formal surrender. Allen and his men expressed surprise when they learned Morgan's lieutenant was a man of small stature. They commented upon the way he deported himself, calm and dignified in the face of a crushing misfortune. More than 120 Confederates were dead or wounded, 700 captured and the balance in full flight, with Hobson's cavalry eager to draw the net about them.

That John Morgan would continue to elude his foes for another week never entered the minds of Duke, Smith, Dick Morgan and the other captured raiders. Such a thought was just as fanciful to the Union commanders. With victory in their hands after so many days in pursuit, Judah and Hobson would not have given a spent cartridge for Morgan's chances.

CHAPTER 14

Back into the Saddle

WITH THE BATTLE over and the wily Morgan still uncaptured, the Federal high command took stock of their victory and turned to the next item on the agenda—a very familiar item—how to lay the fox by his heels. The Union forces had combined at the crucial moment, fought a good battle, and captured many prisoners, however, their main quarry with 1100 men was still to be caught. The dogged rear guard action fought by the regiments under Duke and Johnson had bought their commander many valuable hours.

Bickering broke out between Judah and Hobson before the surgeons started operating on the wounded. The friction that had existed on the banks of the Cumberland, and which had been responsible in large part for the success of the raiders in breaking through the Union perimeter, had not been dissipated by the long days of pursuit. West Pointer and volunteer argued as to which one should exercise command, now that the Northern forces were at last united. Judah outranked Hobson, but Burnside had put Hobson in command of the chase back in Kentucky when Judah was on the wrong side of the flooded Green River. Hobson had no intention of relinquishing that post now that ultimate success seemed within his grasp.

It is not clear from the records whether word of the dispute reached Burnside or whether he knew his lieutenants so well he could guess what the situation was, but within a few hours of the battle's termination he sent this telegram to Judah:

"Don't allow anything to stop the pursuit and capture of the enemy. Either Hobson or yourself have sufficient force to do this, and either one that retards this will assume a heavy responsibility, which will bring its retribution. Again I say the enemy must be pursued and captured. General Hobson has been in pursuit for many days, and he has done a good work, and he must not be balked. You understand my wishes, and I am sure you will carry them out. I thank you both for the work already done."

It reeked of honey and spice, but there was no disguising the tough threat of punishment. Fortunately for both generals, the condition of their men and horses provided the best solution. Neither would pursue Morgan. The task was delegated to Shackleford and Wolford, who would take the best men and stoutest animals, travel without supplies, guns or train, and drive on with no thought of quitting until the rest of the raiders were caught.

Shackleford called for 1,000 volunteers to pursue Morgan, men who would stay in the saddle with no food or sleep until he was caught. Only 500 stepped forward. This was not a sign of fear or laziness on the part of the Union troopers. Their horses were in worse shape than the raiders', since they had been forced to use those the Confederates had missed, or their castoffs. Finally, by switching mounts, detachments of the 1st Kentucky, 2nd Tennessee, 2nd Ohio and 45th Ohio Federal regiments and the 14th Illinois Volunteers, under Colonel Horace Capron, started after Morgan's men.

Behind them the battlefield began to take on some of the appearance of a picnic ground. Federal soldiers who had never been able to get close to the raiders gathered to stare at their prisoners. The Guthrie Greys of Cincinnati, who had boasted of what they would do to Morgan, disembarked from the *Allegheny Belle* to get a closer look at their foe and were impressed to act as guards. Several newspapermen—the only ones who had witnessed the battle—also left the *Belle* and strolled about the bottom, gathering impressions to forward to their readers.

One man from the Cincinnati *Gazette* wrote that "the Rebels were dressed in every possible manner peculiar to civilized man. . . . They wore, in many instances, large slouch hats peculiar to the slave States, and had their pantaloons stuck in their boots. A dirty gray-colored coat was most prevalent, although white dusters were to be seen."

Another reported that the battlefield was strewn with cloth, merchandise and knickknacks picked up in the stores in Indiana and Ohio. There were enough dry goods, he wrote, "to almost stock Shillito or Hopkins," two Cincinnati department stores.

Scammon's force, which had been guarding the West Virginia bank, was ferried to the Ohio side, a move Judah would regret within a few hours. Provost guards started listing the names of the prisoners and making arrangements to send them to prison camps.

180

By mid-afternoon the sun was a torture to victors and vanquished alike, and Colonel Garrard moved his captives to a grove of sycamores at the river's edge.

"As we sat on the river bank," said Captain Allen of the 7th Ohio, "first one man and then another asked permisison to go to the water's edge to wash his face, till pretty soon one-half the men, both Union and Confederate, were at the river's edge, washing their faces, and digging the dust out of their ears, eyes, and nostrils. This proved to be such a halfway sort of business, and so unsatisfactory, that the men asked permission to go in swimming."

Another Union soldier said, "Both Morgan's and Hobson's commands had been in the saddle for about three weeks, during all of which time we had ridden in the gray clouds of dust which our thousands of horses raised on the country roads in midsummer, and these clouds were so dense it was impossible for the riders to see their horses' ears."

Captain Allen, a kindhearted man, permitted the men to go swimming, half of the prisoners and half of the guards taking turns in the river so that sufficient Union men were armed to prevent escapes. A Confederate officer, seeing the men who shortly before had been intent on killing one another, now swimming naked in the Ohio, could not help commenting to the Federal officer:

"It's difficult to tell one from the other when they're like that," he said, and peeled off his own uniform.

The raiders had to surrender their arms and horses. Many thought losing their mounts was a worse blow than being shipped to a prison camp. Leeland Hathaway was one of these and he recorded his torment in his diary.

"He [a Union officer] was at once struck by my mare and began to ask questions about her," wrote Hathaway. "She was my pet and my pride, and I did not stint on telling of her merits. I realized that capture meant a parting from my speechless but gifted friend. On this long, weary march through four states and for three eventful weeks, she had never failed me, and no call had I ever made on her to which she had not responded. While most others were taking fresh horses, she never faltered, never seemed to tire, and when I rode her into the presence of the Federal major, he was ready with praise. She was a thing of beauty, standing fifteen hands, one inch high. She was the very picture of the war horse. For two years, her master had shared his crust and his corn with her . . . She was bred and reared on the sod of my home at Deer Park, and when the call of my

Southern brethren took me to the field, she was chosen out of two score good studs to carry me. No better horse carried a rider from the Bluegrass of Kentucky than my Mary. Now we were to part, and she was to go into a stranger's keeping. The officer promised to care for her and send her back to his home in Michigan, and this was the best I could do for my mare. I spoke no farewell, not trusting my voice. My daughter must realize a horse is more than a dumb brute to a soldier. It is a companion and friend. I never heard of Mary again."

Other Kentucky cavalrymen felt the same way.

Hathaway swam in the Ohio and thought it a luxury but was honest enough to admit that it was so swollen and muddy that it was more refreshing than cleansing.

Confederates and Yankees shared the contents of their haversacks, which worked to the distinct advantage of the Southerners. Some of the raiders had little to contribute except a few cold hoecakes purloined from Meigs County kitchens the previous day. A Yankee lieutenant heard Hathaway's name called and introduced himself, saying he had relatives of that name in Kentucky. The Yankee officer went out to one of the steamboats and came back with several bottles of Kentucky bourbon, which was downed in short order as former foes toasted one another. Men in blue were happy over the victory, and those in gray, while not happy, were at least glad they had come through the battle unharmed.

The Yankees could not agree on who was responsible for the victory at Buffington Island. General Judah laid great stress upon the overwhelming force he had mustered to throw against the weary raiders. General Hobson thought the relentless pursuit was primarily responsible for Morgan's discomfiture. Militia commanders proudly pointed to the work their volunteers had done in barricading roads and slowing down the enemy column. Nobody gave the rampaging Ohio the credit it deserved, although the Union Navy could never have operated across the shallow bars and fords if the stream had not been unseasonably high.

Captain T. J. Oakes, skipper of the *Imperial* which had towed the doughty *Moose* to Buffington Bar, had no doubt as to who played the dominant role in stopping the raiders.

"I think the credit belongs to the gunboats," he said "They were at all the fording places and kept him [Morgan] from crossing, checking him until troops could arrive and complete the work."

To Colonel G. S. Warner, of the 8th Michigan Cavalry, the Federals' better equipment made the difference.

182

"Our arms, the Spencer rifle, proved as before, a terror to the Rebels. They thought us stronger than we were, since each man could pour seven shots into them so rapidly."

Lieutenant Commander LeRoy Fitch was so elated with the results, he dispatched a telegram to Gideon Welles, the Union Secretary of the Navy. It was not a particularly modest message.

"After chasing Morgan nearly 500 miles, at last met him on the river at this point," said Fitch. "Engaged and drove him back, capturing two of his pieces of artillery. He abandoned the rest to General Judah. The enemy broke in confusion from the bank and left his wagon train, many horses and small arms in my possession . . . Several were killed, 25 or 30 wounded and 20 horses captured. Have but two men wounded slightly. Our shell and schrapnel (*sic*) created great confusion in the Rebel ranks, killing and wounding many."

Gideon Welles, an old newspaper editor, must have pondered over the message, wondering how a gunboat in midstream could have captured Morgan's guns and how the young naval officer handled the many horses left in his possession.

Far away from the battlefield, John Morgan's escape with more than a thousand men considerably reduced the luster of the Union victory beside the Ohio. The judge advocate of the Ohio Department sent Abraham Lincoln a message in cipher, urging him "to relieve Burnside from Command of the Department of Ohio immediately by telegraph."

The message continued:

"Send some thoroughly brave men to take his place. We are threatened with riots, mobs and bloodshed throughout our Western country . . . Burnside is foolishly and unwisely excited, and, if continued in command, will disgrace himself, you, and the country, as he did at Fredericksburg."

Poor W. P. Cutler, the Marietta and Cincinnati Railroad's vice-president, had hoped with all his heart and soul that Morgan would be caught at Buffington Island. Now he had to go back to blocking more roads in an effort to keep the Rebel raiders from crossing his mainline tracks. He sent a telegram to Mrs. Cutler at Harmar, confessing that he was utterly fatigued but adding that he could not walk out on the men who were chopping down trees and erecting more barricades. The work had to continue.

Within a few hours of the escape of 1100 raiders from the battlefield, Colonel Putnam published a general order addressed to the citizen soldiers at Camp Marietta. He praised them for their spirit, which he likened to that of the minutemen of 1775, and for patriotism, forbearance and love of freedom. Sending all men without guns back to their homes, Putnam ended his order with a short lecture on the evils of materialism and sloth.

"For the first time the war has reached our homes," said the Colonel. "Our easy, almost indolent security invited its appearance. The enemy has surprised us in the midst of the busiest season. He found us unorganized and unprepared and has thus been enabled to range through a vast region with apparent impunity."

In Richmond, Virginia, a faithful Rebel civil servant and diarist, Robert Garlick Hill Kean, was also aware of Morgan's ability to move about in the enemy heartland with considerable ease. On the day of the battle, of which he was totally ignorant, Kean jotted down an entry remarkable for its calm perspicacity:

"Morgan's raid into Indiana is one of the most remarkable smaller events of the war. He has been on the north side of the Ohio for several days, riding about very nearly at will. He will be captured."

For those Rebels already captured, there was nothing to do but wait. Long before the sun went down that hot July afternoon, the weary, dispirited raiders spread out the shocks of wheat in a field beside the river, threw themselves down on the rough pallets, and fell sound asleep. A few hours later Captain Wood and the Marietta volunteers who had fled at their approach the night before, leaving the ford unguarded, walked into the Federal camp. They were ordered to stand watch over the sleeping Confederates.

It was the final touch of irony at Buffington Island.

184

CHAPTER 15

Where a Goat Couldn't Climb

BETWEEN Long Bottom and Reedsville, John Morgan transformed the 1100 men who had escaped the battlefield from a disorganized, frightened crush of soldiery into a disciplined military column.

Only the chivalry and military genius that marked his earlier raids into Kentucky had saved his forces from a complete rout at Buffington Island. Circumstances had left his brother-in-law and Johnson the onerous task of guarding the column's rear as it broke through the defile along the river. Johnson's escape after the final charge of the Federals was a miracle. Duke and some of his best officers with at least 700 men were captured. Morgan would have to go on to the end with the few who remained.

An observer marveled at the way the commander restored order. "How the Rebel Raider ever reorganized his demoralized troops is a mystery," he said. "It was a splendid achievement, and easily the out-standing episode of that mad dash into Ohio."

Behind his success, obviously, was the deep esteem his men accorded him. Nothing endears a military leader to his men more than victories, and Morgan's men had achieved many. Once they realized that there was a possibility the Morgan legerdemain might continue, the troopers regained their spirits. Friends were gone, but so, too, were the wounded in the unwieldy wagon train, and the heavy guns that so often had delayed them. Eleven hundred men in the saddle, without impediments, were still a formidable force. Men laughed again, the old fire came into their eyes, and once more they gambled on escape.

At Reedsville the scouts found the ford unguarded. Morgan quickly decided the opportunity should be seized. He ordered his dragoons to swim their horses across, not bothering to look for boats. With a rush,

185

the forward units plunged into the Ohio. The river was not so high over the Reedsville bar as it had been at Buffington Island, but the current was just as swift.

Horses struck out gamely, their riders swimming beside them, trying to keep their weapons dry by holding them on the pommels of their saddles. Soon animals and men grew tired. Weary beasts became entangled in the reins. Threshing hoofs injured men struggling in the water.

Adam Johnson had been ordered to lead the first units into the water. As his mare swam sturdily across the muddy river, he saw that an aide, Lieutenant Woodson, was in serious danger.

"Lieutenant Woodson, who couldn't swim, was on a horse he had captured the day before—a big Norman common to Ohio farms," wrote Johnson in his memoirs. "Halfway across, the horse rolled over against my mare. I got off and swam along, holding to the cantle of my saddle, urging the mare to go on, and she somehow carried the dead weight of that big work horse and Woodson to the opposite bank."

Other men, with no one near enough to help, went under. But the crossing continued. Another hour would have seen all of Morgan's raiders in West Virginia. Scammon's men, who might have barred the crossing, were on the wrong side of the Ohio and more than a dozen miles downstream. Shackleford and Wolford were too far away to interfere. It appeared for awhile that all 1100 men would escape to the sparsely-settled hills of West Virginia.

Then, like the voice of doom, the raiders heard the heavy boom of cannon. Men on the shore waiting to enter the Ohio, and those on horseback in the water, looked downstream and saw the ugly, squat gunboat *Moose,* her Dahlgrens belching fire and smoke. Shells struck the water where the disorganized men and horses were struggling in the swift current. Fitch, the bulldog, had come to torment the raiders again. He sized up the situation quickly, dropped several shells into the ranks of the regiments waiting on the bank, and then lobbed 24-pound explosives into the water where the raiders were now swimming frantically for the eastern bank.

General Morgan, on Glencoe, was in midstream, calling encouragement to his men when the *Moose* started firing. The horse was swimming easily, and Morgan could have reached the far side without trouble, but he knew less than a fourth of his force had started to cross. Without hesitation he turned his mount around and swam back to stay with the bulk of his command.

186

As he neared the Ohio bank his servant, the Negro boy called "Box," started into the water. Fearing that he would be killed by the shells or drowned in the melee, Morgan urged him to return.

"Marse John," said Box, "if they catches you, they may parole you, but if this boy is cotched in a free state he ain't going to git away while the war lasts."

He kicked his big farm horse in the flanks and made his way across the river, unharmed by shell or the swift current.

Things were going badly on the West Virginia side just below Belleville. Many of the horses had become exhausted or frightened by the shelling, and their thrashing hoofs had injured several riders.

Others faltered, rolled over and drowned. Cunningham, the assistant adjutant general, was one whose horse gave out in midstream. He slid from the saddle and started swimming, weighted down with a rifle slung across his shoulder and a pouch containing division records. It was too much for him. Disheartened and exhausted, he started to sink. Fortunately, he heard a snorting and saw an unmounted horse swimming strongly for the shore. He seized the animal's tail and was pulled into the shallows.

Colonel Johnson turned around after carrying his aide to safety in the willows, and saw pandemonium.

"There were hats floating on the river as I looked back," he said, "and I knew each one meant a brave Confederate who had died. But one moved, and a voice cried for help. It was Captain Neil Helm, one of my truest friends, who had fought the Comanches with me in Texas. Seeing an old skiff on the bar, I rushed to it and somehow skimmed it over the sand to the water, by superhuman effort tore out a seat, and using it as an oar, paddled out to Helm. He had barely enough strength to hold on the side. Just then the gunboat bore down on us. We paddled, but they could have fired at us at close range. It was an act of humanity that they did not. We staggered up the bank and into the bushes, and there we finally rounded up 300 men."

Cunningham and Helm were among the last of the raiders to reach safety. Behind them, on the Ohio bank, Morgan and his 700 men fell back from the river to escape the plunging shells from the *Moose*.

"Just as daybreak was disappearing," Cunningham remembered, "the end of his command marched from our sight. We numbered 360 sad, dispirited men, many without arms, lost in the river."

The broad, muddy Ohio, much too high and swift for the last week of

July, flowed treacherously between the two segments of Morgan's stalwart band, having sliced it in two, as the battle had done earlier. The Sabbath had been an evil day for John Hunt Morgan.

Adam Johnson gathered his men, some mounted and some afoot, and started east for the safety of the high Alleghenies. Without stopping to rest, they followed unfrequented roads to Elizabethtown in Wirt County, and sought sleep. They marched along Steer Creek, over the mountains to Sutton and on the Gauley Bridge Road to Birch Creek. They crossed the Gauley at the mouth of the Cranberry and thence into Greenbrier County at Lewisburg. They lived on beef, shot in the pastures and cooked over hidden campfires, without salt, bread or coffee. Traveling as fast as they could on tired horses, with the men taking turns riding, they finally reached the Southern lines in east Tennessee.

Weeks later, Colonel Grigsby, Captain Byrnes, Lightning Ellsworth, still carrying his instrument, and several others reported at Johnson's temporary headquarters. It would be a long time before other raiders found their way back to the Confederacy.

In an effort to seek safety while attention was focused on the main action at Reedsville, a small party of Rebels rode hurriedly upriver to the vicinity of Hockingport. The residents had listened to the sound of cannonading during the battle at Buffington Island, and then noted, with growing fear, that the firing was getting closer as the *Moose* went into action at Belleville Ford. Later, scattered shots warned that the conflict was about to break out on their doorsteps.

The few men still at home took down their rifles and headed into the hills, leaving the women gathered in a group by the mouth of the Hocking River. One of these women was Miss Sophia Huntington, daughter of the village grocer. While waiting to see if the raiders were repulsed, she remembered her father had a sizable stock of ammunition in his store. She ran down the deserted street, unlocked the store, and made several trips to a woods back of town, hiding the powder and balls.

One of her neighbors wrote to the Athens *Messenger* several weeks later to praise the girl's foresight and bravery. In her letter to the editor, she explained just how the women felt as they waited:

"General Scammon put Federal troops ashore at Indian Run, and they headed into the woods. Then came the rattle of musketry; then the clear notes of a bugle. I am free to confess that some queer feelings ran along the nerves of us women congregated at this point, knowing that less than a mile away Morgan himself and some of his band were engaged in con-

188

flict with the brave boys to whom that afternoon we had been distributing apples, cakes, pies, bread, milk and vegetables. Ah, we thought then of our husbands, brothers, sons, and lovers in the army."

The skirmishing at Hockingport diminished as soon as the handful of raiders realized that escape across the river was out of the question. They filtered back through the woods and rejoined the main body.

As the sun went down behind the ridges to the west setting the sky afire and tinting the clouds with bright hues that were reflected by the river, it brought shadows to the deep ravines that string back into the hills from the Ohio. General Morgan called his men together for a council of war. He told the 700 that he wished to go on, but gave them the privilege of dropping out, if they preferred. He said that they could take their chances fording the river under cover of nightfall. No one voted to quit. They had horses and guns, and would follow where Morgan led, continuing to keep the Federal cavalry busy and away from Braxton Bragg's army.

Nothing the men said or wrote in later years indicated they faced the future with high confidence. The defeat at Buffington and the failure at the Reedsville ford had not bred a sanguine outlook. They had lost faith in their own capabilities. For the first time in the long, long ride up from Tennessee, the exhausted Rebels sensed that the road they were traveling would never turn back home. But they would not quit.

Morgan reorganized his brigades. Colonel Cluke, a cud of "mule harness" in his heavily tanned cheek, was given the 2nd Brigade. Duke's old command, the 1st, was taken over by Major Webber, who should have been in the hospital. For days Webber had suffered from dysentery so debilitating his aides often had to help him into the saddle. He had ridden in a carriage and regained a little strength just before the column had to fight its way through the gauntlet behind Pomeroy. He refused to follow a surgeon's suggestion that he drop out and surrender. It was small wonder the raiders called him the "Iron Man."

Morgan accepted his soldiers' loyalty and turned to the task of getting them away from immediate pursuit.

"He renewed the flight," wrote Whitelaw Reid, the correspondent. "His men were worn out and demoralized, discouraged by the loss of companions, but they rode on bravely. To the very last, the energy this daring cavalryman displayed was such as to extort our admiration."

The General pulled an old trick out of his war bag, one that had worked successfully in many wars and on many battlefields. He set the

189

men to cutting dry branches and collecting straw and had them pile it in a field as though for campfires. Then the soldiers mounted and rode stealthily away into the night as the rear guard set fire to the piles and raced to catch up. Shackleford's scouts came up the valley and saw the distant lights, blinking through the trees near the crest of the ridge back of Reedsville. Word was flashed back that Morgan had gone into camp and could be captured easily.

Couriers dashed about the countryside, riding madly on the dark roads, helping to the get the Federal regiments into position for an attack. The Union troopers gleefully circled the high pasture where the fires were beginning to burn low, and waited for the signal to grab the unsuspecting raiders. Before the time came, scouts crept forward and discovered there was no one left to capture. Again, the old ruse had worked.

The land north and west of Long Bottom and Reedsville was rough and hilly. Deep ravines sliced through ridges and valleys thick with honeysuckle, fox grapes, and snake briar. A few dirt roads meandered away from the Ohio, but most were little better than cowpaths. Horse chestnut, black walnut and beech trees grew thick on the hillsides. Their branches often arched across the narrow thoroughfares, making them dark and foreboding, even in the daytime. It was ideal terrain for John Morgan's purpose.

The raiders rode west and southwest, setting their course by stars that were glimpsed whenever the men crested the hills or passed between occasional tilled fields. A little after midnight, saddle-weary and dejected, they went into camp on a wooded hillside near the hamlet of Tuppers Plains.

Far off in Cincinnati the be-whiskered, befuddled Burnside had foreseen that his wily foe might escape defeat at Buffington Island. He made every effort to establish a new net with which to snare him if he escaped from the pincers Judah and Hobson had fashioned. So Old Granny had telegraphed Colonel Putnam at Marietta orders that, in the circumstances, turned out to be almost intuitive.

"If Morgan should be turned back from the Ohio, he will no doubt give up to cross at Blennerhassett or will try to seize the bridge at Marietta," said the commanding general. "You must not allow him to do this. The planking can be torn up, and rifle pits to protect infantry can be constructed at the bridgeheads of both the railroad and city bridge. The roads approaching your place, I hope, are all obstructed. I understand there is no bridge this side of Zanesville. Send up the river and have all means of crossing removed. I will try to get a battery to you before morning. How many armed men have you? Have you any artillery?"

Morgan's men had been in camp less than two hours when Shackleford's scattered outriders discovered them on the hill at Tuppers Plains. The Union general and Colonel Wolford galloped up to make a reconnaissance and found that the Rebels were posted in a dense woods at the head of a ravine. Even in the darkness Shackleford could see that his men could not reach the enemy without being exposed to murderous fire.

"I wanted Hobson on the river road to attack the flank, but it was dark, and the message I sent failed to reach him," reported the Union chief.

With only two hours of rest, the Confederates remounted and passed west of Tuppers Plains, moving in the direction of Cheshire and the ford at Eight Mile Island, six miles down the Ohio from Pomeroy. Grimly, the Union cavalry started pursuit.

As the railroad man Cutler had said, the work was all to be done again. Morgan had escaped through the wilderness between Coolville and Tuppers Plains, the only area left unguarded after the battle. Cutler wired his wife another message from his headquarters in the field.

"I now feel that the danger is over so far as the [rail] road and our house are concerned," said the vice-president. "You need have no fear of his coming to see you. I think he will be taken with his men, but just how or when I can't foresee. Our forces seem always to be a little too late. If they had closed up the gap from the Hocking River at Coolville west to Tuppers Plains, he would have been caught last night."

Shackleford urged Wolford and Jacob to press Morgan hard. The pursuit went on, over hill and dale, the van of the Union forces almost constantly skirmishing with the Rebel rear guard. Morgan then drew away and headed straight for the Ohio at the mouth of Kyger Creek. He hoped that the ford at Eight Mile Island would be unguarded, with most of the men and gunboats still far away around the Great Bend of the Ohio.

He overlooked the valiant militia of Meigs County. Pomeroy had put a company of infantry in the field under Captain Cyrus Grant. Its sister city, Middleport, had contributed an artillery company commanded by Captain John Schreiner. It was not much of an artillery company. Their only gun was an old relic usually fired at celebrations on the Fourth of July. During the mop up after the battle of Buffington Island, the militia had been busy capturing scattered groups of raiders who were trying to cross the Ohio. They had captured some at Racine and Syracuse, and a

191

few at Pomeroy and Middleport. The catch at Pomeroy had been accomplished with considerable military finesse, and the men were highly pleased with themselves.

A farm boy had told them that a group of Rebel stragglers was heading for the river above town. Captains Grant and Schreiner, with two scouts named George Womelsdorff and James Waddell, led their men to a spot where the road that the Rebels were following was flanked by a steep hill on one side and a creek with deep banks on the other. Schreiner loaded the gun with old nails, bits of iron and a healthy charge of powder and placed it in the middle of the dirt road. Grant placed his riflemen in the trees on the slope of the hill.

Scarcely had the dispositions been completed when the Rebels appeared. They took one look at the fearsome artillery piece, heard the sound of guns being cocked in the woods and surrendered. They were all marched to the Pomeroy jail and incarcerated to await the arrival of Federal troops.

The little town had just recovered from this excitement when scouts brought word that Morgan's main party was now headed for the shallows at Eight Mile Island. Grant and Schreiner knew they could not face hundreds of veteran cavalrymen, even if they could beat Morgan to Cheshire. Fitch and his gunboats would have been most welcome. They scanned the river but could see no tin-clad. These men had pioneer blood in their veins—they decided to make their own gunboat.

At the Pomeroy wharf was Valentine B. Horton's side-wheel towboat, the *Condor*—a low, fierce-looking, long-nosed craft, which had suggestive holes in her wheelhouse. Actually, however, she was very inoffensive. Horton, one of the founders of Pomeroy, used the boat to tow barges of coal and salt from the local mines to Pittsburgh, Wheeling and Cincinnati.

Grant and Schreiner directed their men to take the ancient cannon on board the *Condor*. Without proper tackle, but with plenty of brute strength, the militia manhandled the heavy fieldpiece across the wharfboat, up the gangplank of the towboat, and mounted it in the bow. Schreiner loaded the piece with bits of scrap iron and chain links as the *Condor* got up a head of steam and started downstream. As she reached the upper end of Eight Mile Island, the pilot and militia officers could see a gray-clad scout in midstream, testing the ford on horseback.

Morgan and his troopers saw the *Condor,* and assuming she was another Union gunboat, fled into the hills, wishing no more brushes with the doughty tin-clads. The *Condor* had saved the day for the North. While

192

she backed and filled in the channel between the island and the Ohio shore, the Confederate scout spurred his mount and made good his escape to the West Virginia bank. He would have a long, lonely ride to the Southern lines.

With the river blocked and Shackleford on his heels, Morgan climbed to a high hilltop on the bluff behind the town of Cheshire. At three P.M. the Federal cavalry came riding out of the woods and deployed at the base of the bluff. General Shackleford sent a flag of truce, demanding Morgan's immediate surrender. The flag was met by Lieutenant Colonel Cicero Coleman and other officers who conferred with the Union commander. They requested one hour to discuss the demand.

"I granted them forty minutes," reported Shackleford. "Within that time, all but Morgan and 600 men surrendered."

Most of the men who lay down their arms were the wounded who had hoped to go on but were too weak to do so, and a few who were dispirited by Shackleford's dogged pursuit. Typical of those who never thought of surrendering was a private named J. M. Lyons. Born in Morgansville, Kentucky, he had been captured earlier in the war and sent to Camp Morton at Indianapolis. He escaped, hiked 150 miles through enemy country to Kentucky, and joined Morgan's division, fighting with Company F of the 10th Kentucky Cavalry. He was wounded in the skirmish between Tuppers Plains and Cheshire, but continued with his companions to the end of the invasion.

Shackleford and Wolford were not the only Yankees angered by Morgan's break out at Cheshire. A local militiaman, Lieutenant Long, who determined to catch Morgan or kill his horse in the process, set out alone, paralleling the Rebels' erratic route. Five days later he rode into Bridgeport, Ohio, across the river from Wheeling. There he was captured by home guards who were certain he was a Confederate straggler. He was finally freed, but not in time to fire a shot at the enemy.

If, in retrospect, this dash of more than a hundred miles seems foolish, it must be remembered that large numbers of Ohio's citizens bordered on a state of hysteria. No one stopped to analyze facts. Morgan had escaped the biggest concentration of Union cavalry ever seen north of the Ohio. He had tricked his pursuers with one ruse after another. He was quick-witted and could not be caught. That his men were weary beyond belief, almost at the end of their endurance, and that attrition had cost him all but 600 hungry, dispirited soldiers did not seem to matter. Morgan's "terrible men" were still riding up the glen.

As a matter of fact, they were escaping through back country along

Kyger Creek. They then cut across hills and followed a path along the bank of Raccoon Creek. On the morning of July 21, the raiders halted to feed their horses in a cornfield not far from Vinton. As they waited, reins held loosely in tired hands, 250 Ohio militiamen under a Major Sonntag, marched over a rise of land from the direction of Gallipolis.

Because his men were dismounted and their steeds hungry and tired, the thought of battle was an abhorrent one to Morgan. He quickly sent five men under a flag of truce to enact a plan that he had devised as soon as he realized continued fighting would be too heavy a burden on his men. The five cantered off and told Major Sonntag that Morgan had 2,000 men, some with him and some just a few miles away. The Rebels were good actors, and they managed to keep straight faces as they demanded Sonntag's immediate surrender.

The major believed the story. He surrendered his entire company, was paroled, and marched away, leaving his guns with the elated raiders. The Rebels now each had twelve more rounds of ammunition than they had when they rode into the cornfield.

While the Confederate horsemen were still chortling over the bloodless victory, a band of Pike County home guards under Major Slain approached from the direction of Vinton. The trick that had worked so well was tried again—with the same results. Not a shot was fired, but victory was complete.

The Rebels soon crossed the route they had followed five days before, when the ford at Buffington Bar held all the lure of the Grail at the end of a long crusade. Most of them were young men, and they must have wondered if their own quest for safety would be as illusory.

For a considerable period of time they had outdistanced their pursuers. The rear guard no longer saw the telltale cloud of dust behind them that warned of Shackleford's approach. They had managed to cover their trail in the dash up Raccoon Creek, and the Federals were spread out on many roads, in search of the right one to follow. Glad of this small respite, the raiders rode around McArthur, the county seat of Vinton, and camped four miles north of the town on the McArthur-Logan pike.

Telegraph wires cut by Morgan on his way east were still not repaired. This, of course, contributed to the news vacuum in which the Southerners were moving. Almost as important was the land itself. Vinton County is one of Ohio's least productive. Its jumbled hills made agriculture rather unprofitable, so there were few centers of population. It is beautiful country, however—heavily forested and watered by many swift-moving

194

creeks. While the Rebels rode through it the next day, refreshed by the first real night's rest in many days, the countryside reminded them of the hill country in eastern Kentucky. They crossed the main line of the Marietta & Cincinnati Railroad, near Zaleski, and saved time by not stopping to tear up the tracks.

This neglect must have given comfort to Mr. Cutler. He was thankful by now for the smallest of blessings. His men had blocked roads all over eastern Ohio without deterring Morgan. If the raiders broke out to the north of the line, he could at least be happy that while doing so they caused no damage.

Morgan's virtual disappearance started reverberations from Cincinnati to Lake Erie.

Burnside spattered the Middle West with telegrams sending troops in all directions.

Governor Tod in Columbus wired a militia officer in far-away Cleveland, exhorting him to renewed vigilance.

"I announce to you," the Governor said pompously, "that Morgan may yet reach the lake shore."

Tod's militia chief, Colonel Runkle, urged Colonel Putnam at Marietta to send men up and down the river to cover the crossings.

Colonel Putnam, who had sent so many of his men home when all seemed secure, was told "to detain all steamboats until we know positively where John Morgan is."

"He may strike the river at any point," warned Runkle. "Send couriers ahead to press wagons into service to move infantry more quickly."

The trouble was that Putnam did not know where to send his couriers —or his infantry. The governor thought Morgan was heading for the state capital to plunder the treasury, and held men at Camp Chase who might better have served in the southern counties. Brigadier General Cox, commanding the District of Ohio, was certain that the raiders wanted nothing but to escape into West Virginia. He wired orders to Putnam:

"A battery has been shipped to you by rail. Please see that at all points between Marietta and Athens the people blockade the roads so that Morgan cannot dodge north between those places. This is very important. No gap must be left. There is abundant force around him, if this is done."

Colonel Putnam did his best. He sent four companies of militia down the river on the steamer, *Buck,* to open a channel at Blennerhassett Island for gunboats. "On the way," he told the commanding officer, "you will remove to the Virginia side or destroy all means of crossing the Ohio. Also send a detachment down as far as the mouth of the Little Hocking to remove all means of crossing."

Had the telegraph operators themselves not been a bit fearful, they would surely have laughed at how often they sent and received one particular message. It was repeated so frequently that it became the trademark of Morgan's raid. Militia officers asked it of subordinates. Regular army commanders asked it of home guards. State officials asked it of everyone. This was the message:

"How many men have you, and are they armed?"

By this time, Ohio had called 65,000 militia to arms. Many home guards, with no official military standing outside their own communities, had joined ranks in the hope of participating in the greatest manhunt in the Buckeye State's history. As the bright young correspondent, Whitelaw Reid, noted, however, "Most of them never came within three score miles of Morgan's little band."

The next accurate word of Morgan's whereabouts came from Nelsonville in Athens County. The morning stage from Athens to Columbus lumbered into town, bringing the good news that the Rebels had been captured at Hamden. The people in Nelsonville had exactly one hour during which to celebrate. John Riser then galloped into town, his horse in a lather, and shouted that the invaders were less than a mile away. Farmers and liverymen scurried to get their horses hidden. Unfortunately, most of them tied their animals near the Marietta Road, on Morgan's direct line of march, and they were captured.

Raiders came pouring into town from the south, crossed the Hocking canal, burned the bridge behind them, and then stopped at all the homes to ask for food.

"They behaved very civilly while we were handing out our provisions, which was more than we expected," wrote a resident. "They were the hardest-looking set of people we ever looked upon . . . After they had eaten all they could, they entered the stores and helped themselves to new clothes and other things that suited them. They paid for part of them. Then they visited the pastures and stables in town, searching for horses and took all they could that were able to travel."

The Confederates set ten or twelve canal boats on fire and then burned the bridge at the other end of town before riding out of Nelsonville.

Wesley Poston was one of the richest farmers in the Hocking Valley, but when the raiders departed he was left without a single horse. The

196

Rebels had taken seven of them from his barns. He told his son, Charles, to follow the invaders in the hope that he might be able to recover a few of the horses when they were abandoned.

The farmer's son, on a borrowed mount, trailed behind the raiders through Buchtel, up the Snow Fork of Monday Creek, to where Murray City and Corning now stand, and over the ridge to Sunday Creek Valley. Late that night Morgan's men camped near Millertown, and young Poston could see their campfires on top of a high ridge at the head of Island Run.

In the morning he saw them breaking camp and riding to the Muskingum River at Eagleport. The crossing seemed unguarded, and the Southerners were swimming their horses across when militia stationed on a dam 200 yards upstream opened fire. To the Poston boy, who stood on a small bridge over Island Run, it seemed that the Rebels paid little attention to the enemy. Then he noticed that cavalrymen were dismounting from their wet horses, and soon the militia came under heavy and accurate fire, which drove them away.

"I could see a lone man standing on a large rock on the south side of the river shooting toward Morgan's men," the farm boy later told his friends. "At this time, four men left the command and rode back to the river bank and dismounted, rested their guns on their knees and fired in the direction of the man across the river. The man threw up his arms and fell backwards off the rock."

When the Federal troops came through later that afternoon, the dead man was identified as James Kelly, superintendent of the charcoal furnace at Logan, who had never fired a gun until he went in pursuit of Morgan.

Scattered fighting continued for several hours. A small boy, who thought the raiders looked very formidable, ran home to warn his mother and seven brothers and sisters. Stopping long enough to get their dogs, the family hid in the woods until the excitement abated. When they returned home, they found their house undamaged, but every blanket and quilt had been stripped from the beds.

The Rebels rode past the farmhouse of Mrs. Daniel Meloy on the outskirts of Eagleport. Some of the men in the van asked ten-year-old Jim Crisman, her nephew, to guide them toward Rural Dale. The boy said he did not know the roads, so the raiders asked his aunt to show them the direction to follow. They lifted her onto a led horse, and she accompanied them for several miles until she put them upon the right route at a crossroads. The Southerners thanked her "and the woman and the boy started home, the troopers parting to each side of the road; and Jim and his aunt, as if on dress parade, marched between, with an escort that saw them safely home."

At a store in Eagleport one of the owners, William Price, heard the shooting, realized Morgan's men had entered town, and fled after emptying the cash drawer into a pocketbook. Some of the raiders called to him to return. He came back through a field of timothy and dropped the wallet in the tall hay. After the Confederates left town, Price recovered the money.

The last man to see the invaders in Eagleport was a farmer named Forgrave. He thought the firing was too close to him and tried to flee to the woods behind his home. In his unseemly haste, he stumbled and fell into the pigpen just as a party of Rebels cantered by. In the sty a sow was busily suckling several shoats.

"Do you think all those pigs are from the same litter?" asked one of the troopers. His friends roared with laughter, but no one offered to help the poor farmer out of his predicament.

Runkle's militia slowed the raiders and gave Frank Wolford's regulars an opportunity to get ahead of them in the open country beyond the Muskingum. In the afternoon, while the command was divided on parallel roads, Morgan lost about one hundred men to Runkle and Wolford. The respite was over; the pursuers were getting near.

Major Webber recorded that the enemy was guarding each road, making escape seem "utterly impossible." The telegraph wires were humming again. The head of the Athens County militia informed Colonel Putnam that "Morgan is six miles northeast of Nelsonville at six o'clock. Shackleford says he cannot overtake him unless checked in front. Two hundred infantry can check him at any ford."

He was wrong in his timing by almost twenty hours, but he was accurate in relaying Shackleford's thoughts. Everyone was having difficulty getting men in front of the hard-driving Southerners.

Runkle dispatched another order to Putnam, who was by now literally swamped with instructions from nearly every official in the state of Ohio. "Is there a steamboat at the landing?" asked Runkle. "We may have to go up the Ohio. Fill the country about Beverly and between Beverly and the Ohio with scouts. Arouse the people. Blockade the roads. The remnants of Morgan's men have gone that way."

Governor Tod ordered the 86th Ohio Infantry, which had been sent

198

from Cleveland to Zanesville, to take a steamboat down the Muskingum in pursuit of Morgan. If the 86th had moved immediately, the story at Eagleport might have been different, but civilians who act as weekend soldiers seldom understand the value of prompt obedience of orders. By the time the steamer reached the spot where Morgan had crossed the raiders were two hours away.

The Putnam Tigers of Marietta were sent by train to Belpre and then by the steamer, *Grey Eagle,* to guard the Ohio downstream from Parkersburg, West Virginia. Rumors bred rumors and the home guard destroyed a bridge at a stream outside Marietta "to prevent Morgan's return," although he had not been within twenty miles of it.

Burnside read the dispatches from the Muskingum and decided to use one last force which was scraped together from the ranks of men recovering from wounds and battle fatigue. The convalescents were stationed at Covington Barracks, just across from Cincinnati. Burnside summoned Major Rue to his headquarters and ordered him to muster every horse strong enough to see service, and to put his healthiest men in the saddles.

Rue went back to Covington, on the evening of July 23, and assembled an oversized regiment of 375 cavalrymen. There were seventy-five from Rue's own regiment, the 9th Kentucky; 120 from the 11th Kentucky; fifty from the 8th Michigan, small detachments from the 1st and 12th Kentucky, and three pieces of artillery from the 15th Indiana Battery, under Lieutenant Tarr.

The makeshift regiment crossed the Ohio and rode to the depot of the Little Miami Railroad. At that place they learned that Burnside had got together three trains: one for the men, one for the horses, and one for the artillery. The force went to Columbus, switched to the Ohio Central Railroad, and proceeded to Mingo Junction.

While this force was being rushed to eastern Ohio, Morgan's column was encountering strong resistance. Wolford's regulars reinforced Runkle's militia on his left flank, and Shackleford increased the pressure with skirmishers from behind. Morgan, in an effort to elude his enemies, decided to backtrack and strike for the Ohio at Blennerhassett Island. It was miles away, and thousands of enemy troops were scattered over the intervening countryside. But it was as close as any spot on the river except Marietta itself, and the Rebel chief had no intention of heading there, with all Putnam's militia gathered in camp, anxious to fight.

It is entirely possible that even with his difficulties, Morgan was drawn there by the island's romantic history. In a state where every foot of road was strange to him, the place where Aaron Burr had lived may have seemed familiar.

Harman and Mary Blennerhassett had built their home on the island after the Revolutionary War. The Irish aristocrat and his wife, a nineteen-year-old beauty, had conspired there with Burr to form a new nation in the Southwest. In those days, Blennerhassett had walked about his estate in blue broadcloth coat, scarlet knee breeches, and silver-buckled shoes, reciting the *Iliad* from memory. Mary had given Shakespearean plays in the drawing room of the big mansion. When the conspiracy was revealed, drunken militia destroyed the beautiful furnishings and on Christmas Eve of 1811 burned the house to the ground.

Morgan knew the story and may have thought he could rest there, had he been able to reach the river undetected. Whether his decision was based on this, or reasons of greater immediacy, is not clear, but he doubled back on his tracks to elude his pursuers and hurried as fast as the weary horses could go down the Muskingum. For a few hours, there was only the sound of hoofs on the hard-packed road, the sound of the animals' heavy breathing, and the rush of the cool evening air past the raiders' faces as the night of July 23 closed in about them.

Attrition had now reduced the column to 700 men. On the long road behind them that stretched to the banks of the Cumberland, more than 1700 of their comrades had fallen out. Some had drowned, some were wounded; the balance were killed or captured. Inexorably, fatigue, nature, and the enemy had diminished them until each man felt the end was near.

What had begun as a brave, gay challenge to all the Yankees above the Ohio was now a deadly race against an enemy aroused and angered at the invasion of their homeland.

The troopers thought of these things as they trotted through the evening quiet, but the quality of their courage was undiluted by adversity. Morgan, the peerless leader, was with them. They would go on with him as long as a single horse could walk.

Even as they pondered their chances, they were riding into a trap. Their backtracking had delayed the regulars, but before daylight had gone, Shackleford and Wolford noted the cloud of dust raised up by Morgan's horses. This dust betrayed the direction, and from three sides his pursuers closed in about him. Hobson, who had been slow to saddle up and leave the battlefield at Buffington, was now across the Muskingum. Runkle's men seemed everywhere. Shortly before ten o'clock, Rebel

200

scouts reported to their leader that the column was hemmed in. Wolford was just behind and Hobson so heavily armed on the opposite bank that retreat was unthinkable.

Morgan halted his column at a point where nature seemed to have conspired against him. The river was on his right, and across it the raiders could already see the flickering lights of Hobson's campfires. Before and behind him the valley opened into level bottom land skirting the eastern bank of the Muskingum. He knew Wolford was somewhere behind him, and Runkle's men were gathering. What Duke referred to as "a bold mountain" hemmed him in against the stream in his front. The campfires across the river were evidence that, so far as the Yankee regulars were concerned, they considered the chase over.

By the time the fires had died out, Morgan had determined on the one gamble that could save his force. He sent men up the side of the bluff to seek a way to the top. They returned with word that it might be possible, if raw courage could be substituted for a path.

It was enough for the General. Whispered commands were passed to the troopers to tighten saddle girths, wrap equipment so it would not bang against tree trunks and branches, and to shorten the reins, so that each man's hand was close to his mount's bit. Then, in Indian file, the 700 men started their climb, the men walking at the horses' heads, scrambling and clawing for footholds, their faces whipped by unseen branches and briers, their lungs aching from their exertions. They stumbled often but never fell, each rider leaving enough space between mounts so that if one did fall, it would not plunge on those below. Morgan led the way with Glencoe; the burly Cluke, whispering encouragement to a horse foaled on his own Bluegrass farm, brought up the rear.

The climb was difficult, even for boys of twenty and twenty-one. For the older troopers, it took all their determination to keep putting one foot above the other. For Tom Webber, the new acting Colonel, who was enfeebled by dysentery and intermittent fevers, it was hell. Yet no word of his own pain and discomfiture is reflected in the entry made in his diary for that terrible night. There was only the good soldier's admiration for a leader he loved and respected.

"Finding every road strongly guarded, and every hill covered with troops," he wrote, "it would have been impossible for anyone except Morgan to have led a column out of such a place, and he did it by what the citizens tell us is the only place where a horse can go; and that by a narrow pass leading up a spring branch hundreds of feet below the tops

201

of the hills, the perpendicular sides of which pressed closely on our horses as we passed in single file. And then we went up another hill, or rather mountain side, up which nobody but a Morgan man could have carried a horse. Up that·hill, for at least one thousand feet, we led our tired horses, where it seemed that a goat couldn't climb, until we reached the plain, and were soon in the rear of the enemy and on our road again."

By midnight, Morgan and his band were out of the trap, riding hard for the north. The Union troops beside the Muskingum slept until the dawn.

CHAPTER 16

Surrender at Scraggsville Church

ABRAHAM LINCOLN sent a telegram to General Burnside on the morning after Morgan escaped from the valley of the Muskingum:

"What, if anything, further do you hear from John Morgan?"

It seemed to indicate only a casual interest, but it was motivated by more than passing concern in the attempt to track down the remnants of one small Confederate cavalry division. The President had been corresponding with Rosecrans, urging him to attack Bragg. His messages contained none of the acidulous quality with which he had prodded George McClellan the year before, although he was eager to start his armies moving deeper into the South. Rosecrans explained his delays by citing bad roads, lack of supplies and—most serious of all—a critical lack of cavalry.

With so many of his cavalry units far away in Ohio chasing Morgan, Rosecrans had to move in a partial vacuum. He repeatedly spelled this out to Lincoln and to the general in chief, Halleck. This prompted the President to ask Burnside about the Rebel raider, hoping to get Rosecrans' cavalry back into Tennessee.

In Cincinnati Burnside did not have too clear an idea as to the whereabouts of the elusive Morgan. Even his commanders in the field had lost him when they almost had him in their hands; if they could not find him, how could he, who was miles away? But he scanned his morning dispatches and sent an immediate reply. Evan a general does not wait long before replying to the President of the United States.

"Just now we have conflicting reports as to Morgan's whereabouts," telegraphed Burnside. "One report places him within ten miles of Cadiz Junction, and the other between Antrim and Hendrysburg. Shackleford is

203

close after him, and we will try to have forces in his front, whichever report is correct."

July 24 was a day Burnside would not remember with particular relish. It was not, by any means, so horrendous as the one on which he showed such miserable generalship at Fredericksburg, nor even so disagreeable as that afternoon when McClellan could not get him to cross Antietam Creek and strike Lee's right. Neither was it one that afforded him any sense of well-being. His first indication the day would be unpleasant came when Rosecrans asked him when he could expect to get his cavalry back, so that he could find out what Bragg was doing.

"Your dispatch received," answered Old Granny. "I am sorry to say we have not yet got hold of John Morgan. He is still out with some 500 of his men, but our cavalry are after him in hot chase. I am confidently expecting to hear of his capture; the whole force is broken up and annihilated. The prisoners are now coming in, both men and officers."

Barely had this excuse been sent when another—and more insistent—query came from Halleck at Washington.

Halleck had none of Lincoln's forbearance. His inquiry showed he was almost out of patience with Burnside.

"You have not yet replied to my dispatch in regard to your movements toward east Tennessee," said the General in Chief. "You will immediately report the position and numbers of your troops organized for that object. There must be no further delay in this movement. It must be pushed forward immediately."

"Old Mutton Chops" thought Halleck was crowding him a bit too hard, so he shot back a reply he figured would stop criticism:

"Your dispatch received. All my available cavalry have been after Morgan. . . . Where is the Ninth Corps? Grant promised it to me after Vicksburg."

Halleck had not won his nickname of "Old Brains" without a reason. Instead of answering Burnside's petulant question about the Ninth Corps, he showed the telegram to Lincoln. The President wrote out a reply in his own handwriting—a reply that seemed tactful and understanding, but in which Burnside could not help reading a hidden reprimand:

"Let me explain. In General Grant's first dispatch after the fall of Vicksburg he said, among other things, he would send the Ninth Corps to you. Thinking it would be pleasant to you, I asked the Secretary of War to telegraph you the news. For some reasons never mentioned to us by General Grant, they have not been sent, though we have seen

204

outside intimations that they took part in an expedition against Jackson. General Grant is a very copious worker and fighter, but a very meager writer or telegrapher. No doubt he changed his purpose in regard to the Ninth Corps for some sufficient reason, but has forgotten to notify us of it.

A. Lincoln."

Burnside returned to his map and tried to determine how he could find more men to throw in Morgan's path.He wired the governor of Pennsylvania for troops, aware that the fleeing Rebels were headed toward that state. More militia were called up in the eastern Ohio counties. A few regiments that had failed to make their weight felt at crucial moments earlier in the pursuit were put onto the cars in a new attempt to make contact with the raiders. Among these was the 86th Ohio Infantry, which had been so slow in steaming down the Muskingum that Morgan had evaded them by more than two hours.

Then Burnside remembered Major Rue and the men from the Covington Barracks. Rue had made his way into Mingo Junction with his three trains and was awaiting orders. Governor Tod was instructed by Burnside to transfer Rue and his men to the Columbus & Pittsburgh Railroad for a fast run to Bellaire.

There was one more Yankee pawn to be moved on the chessboard. Major W. B. Way of the 9th Michigan Cavalry had been trying to get close enough to Morgan to try a clash of arms. Way believed in the old cut and slash tactics and boasted that once his regiment charged with sabers, Morgan's veterans would crumble. Burnside and Tod had done their best to provide him with the opportunity, shuttling him around the center of Ohio on one railroad after another. Now he, too, had reached Mingo Junction. Burnside wired him of the Confederates' approach and urged him to intercept them. Taking the first train available, Way and his dragoons, minus his artillery, steamed through Steubenville, looking for a good road on which to cut in ahead of Morgan.

While Burnside was shifting his forces, the Confederate government made a belated effort to aid Morgan. General Buckner ordered Colonel John S. Scott to push from east Tennessee into Kentucky to see if he could draw off any of the units pursuing the raiders north of the Ohio. Scott's brigade was composed of the 1st Louisiana, 2nd Tennessee, 5th Tennessee and 10th Confederate Cavalry regiments; the 5th North Carolina Battalion of mounted infantry, the Brown Horse Battery with four guns and the Louisiana Battery.

205

It was a last-ditch move, and what good it might have done was nullified by a slow start. Finally, Scott led his force through Big Creek Gap, driving a detachment of the 44th Ohio mounted infantry before it toward Loudon. There was a brisk fight there, and at Mount Vernon and Big Hill. This took many days, and by the time Scott defeated the Northern troops at Richmond, it was too late to help Morgan. He was too far away, and Burnside had no intention of diverting any of his forces to meet a new threat deep in Kentucky. Scott finally retreated under mounting pressure from local troops, and Morgan was abandoned to his fate.

Burnside's judgment in this matter was entirely correct. The Confederate column in Ohio was a greater menace than the one in the barren hill country of eastern Kentucky. It was a case of first things first. So, having shifted the militia units to where they could do the most good, and having urged the regular detachments to put on all possible speed, Burnside sat back in Cincinnati and waited for the outcome. It was all he could do; the rest was up to the forces in the field.

As a matter of fact, the outcome was up to the regulars. Militia and home guards had obstructed a few roads, done a little bushwhacking and slowed the raiders for a few hours. Considering the vast number of them under arms, however, they were not very effective.

In Indiana, Wallace and Love had failed to get their men in front of the raiders. Runkle's militia had been brushed aside near Jackson; Sonntag and Slain had surrendered in terror; and Wood with his Marietta home guards had fled from the redoubt at Buffington Bar without firing a gun. Only the Pomeroy and Middleport troops had put up a good fight, stinging the invaders badly as they raced for the ford near Portland.

There is no record of what Shackleford, Wolford and Hobson thought when they found Morgan had escaped up the mountain. They did not like the idea of putting down on paper a report of the way they had been deceived. They saddled up and rode in pursuit, leaving General Burnside to guess what had happened.

John Morgan led his 600 men into Guernsey County near the town of Cumberland late on the night of July 23, and took possession of that village without a shot being fired. The General found a pleasant inn, the Globe House, on the central square, and made it his headquarters for the few hours he stayed in town. The landlord protested valiantly, apparently motivated more by his cash drawer than by any strong anti-Southern feelings, but it was to no avail. He played host to more guests, and more unprofitable ones, than he had ever before entertained at one time.

206

Morgan enjoyed a hot meal with his staff, and then they all slept for a few hours before striking northeast toward the National Road.

The countryside around Cambridge is broken and hilly, cut by ravines and small streams. At the time of Morgan's raid it was still heavily wooded with beautiful stands of chestnut, beech and oak, through which a few dirt roads led from one small farming community to another. Despite the bad condition of the highways, the raiders kept up a steady pace and arrived at the village of Senecaville in the middle of the forenoon.

It was a quiet little town. Most of the men had gone off to war. The frightened women were all indoors behind locked and bolted shutters. An air of somnolence born of warm sunshine and pleasant breezes pervaded the entire village. Two by two, the raiders rode up the main street and dismounted, making no move to enter the homes. No one, without the power of clairvoyance, would have dreamed that in this hamlet John Morgan would come closer to death than at any other moment on his thousand-mile ride.

Early in the war between the states, a young man married to the village milliner had enlisted with the Ohio Volunteers. Before he left home, he gave his wife a pistol, citing the dangers that can confront a woman living alone, and advising her to take care of herself. The months went by and the pistol, laid away among the linens in a bureau drawer, was almost forgotten. Then, on this July morning, 600 Rebel troopers, about whom a thousand rumors had been whispered, rode boldly into town.

The milliner drew aside the blind in her parlor, looked out into the street, and saw a gray-uniformed man dismount from a beautiful black horse and start straight for her door. It was John Morgan. She recognized his well-built, powerful physique; the fresh, tanned complexion; the sandy hair and beard, and the clear, fearless eyes. The Northern papers had carried descriptions of the Rebel commander, and it is possible she had seen an ambrotype or crude photograph. There was no doubt in her mind as she stepped quickly to the chest of drawers and picked up the pistol.

She returned to the parlor window and aimed the sidearm at Morgan as he lifted his hand to knock at the door. The gun wavered; across her mind flashed the thought, "What anguish I would cause some woman of the South!" So she put the gun back in the drawer and opened the door to her visitor.

The General was most courteous and asked to be pardoned for his intrusion, which he said was necessitated by a desire to learn the best route to Campbell's Station. The milliner answered his question, and

207

they talked a few minutes before he turned to leave. Moved by an impulse she could not explain, she called him back and told him what she had done, and how close he had come to death. Morgan's face revealed the emotion aroused by her words.

"Do you know why you did not shoot?" he asked softly. "At that very moment Mrs. Morgan, at our home in Tennessee, was down on her knees praying for my safety. I know she was, because a year ago when I was in great danger and as near death then as I just was here, I learned on my return home that Mrs. Morgan was on her knees praying for me at that very moment."

The General bowed, walked from the house, and rode away with his cavalcade. Dust rose from under the horses' hoofs and settled gently on the milliner's dress and hair where she stood in the open doorway.

The raiders struck the main east-west pike a few miles east of Cambridge at the little crossroads hamlet of Old Washington. They rode into town and found it practically deserted by the men who had left to join the militia. The Rev. Mr. Ferguson, a Presbyterian minister, went out to meet the raiders, waving a white handkerchief. The younger Rebel soldiers laughed when they saw the faces of terrified women watching from the windows.

Morgan and his staff ordered a noonday dinner at the American Hotel. While the proprietor, James Smith, was calling for extra help, the raiders learned that the Guernsey County Bank had moved its money to Wheeling on the previous night and that all the horses in town had been hidden in a swamp beyond town. Among the village girls whom Smith persuaded to serve the raiders was sixteen-year-old Elizabeth McMullin, who later admitted that the General and his staff had few of the characteristics of the devil, but were polite and gentlemanly. The girl afterwards recalled how fatigued the invaders appeared.

"General Morgan seemed very tired and worried," she said, "and talked but little during the meal."

A century later, it is no more than proper to wonder if John Morgan was still thinking of his brush with death at the home of the Senecaville milliner.

With dinner out of the way, the raiders pushed on, veering east along the wider, better-paved National Road, heading once more toward the Ohio River, where they had learned a ford at Coxe's Riffle, downstream from Steubenville, might provide an escape route into West Virginia and Pennsylvania.

The rear guard had barely cleared the village when some of Shackleford's advance units came into town from the south. There was a minor clash which did little harm to either side. One Union soldier, carried away by the scene, left his impression:

"After traveling day and night we finally struck him [Morgan] at Washington, Ohio, on the 24th," wrote this inspired historian. "As we dashed through town the entire populace waved and cheered. One beautiful young woman stood on a knoll swinging her hat and cheering gleefully.

"We doubt if a cavalry charge was ever made before or since in the midst of so many brave, cultivated and charming women. Morgan made a stand a mile out of town and was driven to cover. He fell back two miles, burned a bridge over a rugged creek and took a strong position on a hill."

This lyrical description was in sharp contrast to the words Shackleford used in his own official report. The Union general contented himself with recording that the 14th Illinois Cavalry "under heavy fire" drove Morgan's men before them and continued the chase.

At this time, some men of the 2nd Kentucky were scouting ahead of the main Rebel column. While thus engaged, they were witnesses to and participants in a bit of comic-opera warfare.

It developed out of the hysteria which had gripped the inhabitants of Cambridge as the fleeing Rebels made their way northeast from Meigs County. At three A.M. on the morning of July 24, a detachment of the 86th Ohio Infantry arrived by rail from Zanesville. Although they were from different companies the men were from the same regiment as the lackluster soldiers who had been so slow boarding the steamer Grey Eagle on the Muskingum. They had two pieces of artillery with them, so the residents of Cambridge relaxed for the first time in many days. Then, at eight A.M., the militia again boarded the train and went steaming off for Campbell's Station.

The city fathers hurriedly called a meeting and ordered all citizens capable of bearing arms to form a company, using what weapons they could find in their homes. This untrained group of men marched out on the National Road, heading east for Old Washington. It was little better than a frightened mob, but its members boasted to the women they left behind that they would protect Cambridge against all foes. The company leader had heard enough about war to know the value of scouts, so he sent several mounted men ahead of the main body. This consisted of a few farmers mounted on their plow horses, a few-score foot soldiers, and still others who rode to battle in big farm wagons.

On a hill near a dip in the road called "Deep Cut," two miles from Old

Washington, the mounted scouts saw two of Morgan's outriders. The Rebels spurred their mounts and raced down the open road toward the enemy. The Cambridge men reined their horses around, and fled toward the city. When they reached the main body, the scouts yelled, "Morgan's men are coming," and kept riding at their mounts' best speed.

This was too much for the home guardsmen. The wagon drivers whipped their teams, not waiting for their passengers to climb in. The men who were on horseback galloped after the scouts, and the men on foot, threw away their guns and fled into the fields and woods. The two Rebel troopers rounded up six prisoners and started back toward Old Washington. Fortune favored the Ohio patriots, however, for within a few miles their captors saw Federal cavalrymen raising dust a few miles to the south. They abandoned their prisoners and rode off after Morgan's rearguard.

This bloodless engagement is known in Guernsey County annals as the Battle of Hyde's Hill.

Outside the town of Antrim, Samuel Knouff and his grandmother were picking blackberries when they heard the bells of Madison College begin to peal furiously. They hurried home and found the Presbyterian preacher, a man named Knox, engaged in calming the residents. He persuaded them to hide their horses and urged the women and children to remain calm and to stay in the street. The parson then went out to meet the invaders. Led by Colonel Cluke, the raiders moved through the town. At the rear of the column, where the greatest danger lay, Morgan was riding in a democrat drawn by two horses, his own Glencoe, saddled and ready, following behind.

Riding in a carriage may have given the Rebel leader a welcomed rest, but as he had been "eating dust" for miles, he asked a little boy to bring him a drink of water. The youngster brought the General a drink in a tin cup.

"Boy, I would give you a coin," said Morgan, thanking him, "but I have no money."

Little Anna Moss could not understand her old grandfather's behavior on that day. She saw him conceal a wad of paper money in a tin can and hide it under a ledge by a brook that coursed through his garden. This clearly indicated that he did not trust the soldiers who were approaching his village. The old man, however, noted the raiders were hot and thirsty, and handed out bottles of sarsaparilla from his store shelves. Little Anna thought this a strange turnabout. She was smart enough to watch and say

210

nothing. When the last of the Southern horsemen had left town, the old man had lost nothing but a few bottles of soda pop.

Only one inhabitant of Antrim suffered real damage as a result of the column's passing. Samuel B. Johnson, who rode into town on a well-knit horse found himself a captive and was ordered to guide the column toward the Ohio by the best route. After three or four hours, the raiders freed him but took his fresh mount. They gave him in its place a jaded old nag picked up the day before in some farmyard. Johnson started home, glad to be unharmed and free, but ran into a patrol from Shackleford's force. A Union soldier, mounted behind a companion, relieved the farmer of the worn-out horse—which was valuable only because it was better than no horse at all—and Johnson had to make the balance of his way home on shank's mare.

Through Londonderry, Smyrna and Moorefield moved the 600 raiders, drawn like homing pigeons toward the Ohio, hoping that despite its distance, and the nearness of Frank Wolford's "Wild Riders," that Morgan could still accomplish the improbable. They moved out of Guernsey into Harrison County, scattering occasional groups of home guards. As fast as they rode, panic raced faster ahead of them.

In the city of St. Clairsville men suspicioned that Morgan would go toward Wheeling, not noticing that the Confederates had studiously avoided passing through large communities. On Thursday night, couriers came in saying that the raiders were approaching on the National Road, and the Mayor had the courthouse bell rung. A local boy, still in his teens, wrote his father a long letter after the excitement was ended. In it he disclosed the "furore" that followed the alarm. His name was J. Eberle West.

Young West said the city fathers first appealed to Governor Tod for guns, and when told there were none close enough to help, they asked the governor of West Virginia for arms. He was also unable to provide them. The home guards then armed themselves with whatever guns they could find. Fear had gripped the town, with "men running to and fro, hunting firearms, molding bullets and girding on their armor." Horsedrawn omnibuses were hitched up and volunteers started for Morristown. They were joined there by companies from Lordsville, Belmont, Barnsville, and Flushing.

Numbers gave the militia courage, and they marched along the pike toward Fairview, where they learned of the skirmish at Old Washington and that Morgan and his men were heading for Cadiz. For the next five or

211

six hours there was a rash of marching and countermarching. They were interspersed by several breaks for meals which were provided by the womenfolk of every village they passed through. Night overtook them back where they had started in the morning—in Morristown. The home guards bivouacked near the infirmary, and for many of the young men it was not only their first night encampment of the war, but their first night away from their families. The West boy told his "Pa" his impressions:

"As this was my first experience at soldiering, it puzzled me somewhat to know how I was to put in the night. Presently Elb Kinnon came along and proposed that we go and hunt some place to sleep. Not fancying the idea of lying on the ground, we placed four sails on the ground and stretched ourselves lengthwise with our guns for our pillows. But finding this rather too hard a bed we began to look around for a softer one, when we found a haystack."

West and his companions were worn out from marching; when they fell asleep they were dead to the world.

"John Morgan may have come through our camp that night," admitted the boy, "but if he did I couldn't see him."

A big meal was prepared the next day by the women of Morristown, and it was served in the courthouse. Belmont County's defenders had gone to war, missed the enemy and come home without firing a shot, but they had done a lot of marching and an even greater amount of eating. It was a strenuous campaign.

While the militia of Eastern Ohio were ineptly playing at war, the main contenders, Confederate and Union alike, behaved like the veterans that they were. Morgan's raiders were giving one of the greatest exhibitions of courage ever shown by cavalrymen; the bluecoats, no less determined, kept up such pressure that the invaders seldom had more than a few hours' rest.

In Colonel Capron's 14th Illinois Cavalry there was a trooper named Connelly, who had joined a company called the Black Horse Cavalry. Every mount in the unit was a beautiful black horse. Two years of chase and battle in Tennessee and Kentucky, however, had seen the company broken up, men transferred, and the beloved black horses replaced with others of many colors. Connelly still had his black, and also a roan mare bred in Kentucky. When the Federals started in pursuit of Morgan on his great raid, Connelly took both of his mounts.

"I rode the horse in the daytime and the mare at night," the trooper later wrote for his state's historical journal. "She was sure-footed, never made a misstep and had the eye of an eagle."

Although he was better mounted than many of his companions, the torture of so many hours in the saddle was a memory Connelly could never forget.

"In the final chase after Morgan in Ohio," he said, "we pursued him six days and nights. Horses and men were exhausted. As we moved along, we slept on our horses, comrades side by side, taking the bridle reins of each to keep in column and avoid being dropped out. A brief halt would often find every man asleep. The officers would be compelled to pass along the line, and wake up the soldiers in order to be able to resume the march."

General Shackleford noted in his official report that on one occasion he had counted 600 of his men riding through the night, all fast asleep.

Morgan could have surrendered without any reflection upon his character at any time after the defeat at Buffington Island. His incursion into enemy territory had already reached deeper than any other during the war. With little more than 2,000 men he had withdrawn more than 14,000 regulars from the field in front of Bragg, and had caused the mustering of 115,000 militia and home guards. What drove him on?

In later years, when he wrote his memoirs during his term as congressman, Duke described the quality as one of raw courage. Some of his foes called it pure madness. His own men, according to the few who turned to the pen when they put down their carbines and sabers, never doubted that their commander was motivated by a strong belief that he could outwit his pursuers, get back across the Ohio and return to the Confederacy. As he rode along north of the National Road, always bending his course toward the river, he gave no sign that he had abandoned hope. His men later remembered how jaunty he was in the saddle, how he managed to keep his uniform free of the grime and sweat that soiled theirs, and how his voice remained calm and low in moments of greatest danger. Even the pretty milliner of Senecaville had remarked about his well-groomed appearance.

The William Penn Highway now follows the route Morgan and his men traversed after they crossed the National Road. In 1863 that turnpike was the best in Ohio. Fashioned after the manner in which the Romans built their roads, large rocks had been dumped in place for ballast and drainage and smaller ones packed around them. Finally, cobblestones were laid on top of these, providing a rough but reliable surface. Each stream and gully was crossed by arched stone bridges, some of which are still in use. Although it would have been a good road for the raiders, they chose the one to the north which was little more than a dirt track

213

through woodland and farms. It was much safer, however, than the well-traveled thoroughfare that connected Columbus and Pittsburgh.

Early on Saturday morning they passed through Cadiz without halting and went on to Wintersville. Some weeks later, a resident wrote in the local paper that the village was gripped by fear so great that women wept openly, convinced Morgan's column would kill the men and carry off the women and children. Yankee propagandists, like propagandists everywhere, had brushed the facts aside, and spread rumors. Instead of steadying the nerves of the populace it had the opposite effect.

Militia and "hundred-day men" spent that Saturday morning drilling in the streets and firing at a wooden fence, in preparation for the coming conflict.

During this martial activity, the Rebels marched through Hopedale and Bloomingdale and halted at the farm of John Hanna, a few miles from Wintersville. The night before Hanna had taken his gun and gone to help defend Steubenville, leaving his wife and two children alone. At the approach of the raiders, Mrs. Hanna and her children tried to run to a neighbor's but they were told they were in no danger. The woman finally agreed to prepare a meal for Morgan and his staff officers. Almost paralyzed with fear, she opened the drafts on her stove and sliced pieces from a flitch of bacon into a skillet. She then broke fresh eggs into the same pan and went to summon the intruders to the table. She found them all sound asleep on her beds and on the floor, not even having bothered to remove their boots.

Morgan and the others gathered at the table in the kitchen and were enjoying the meal when scouts brought word that a detachment of militia was marching in their direction. Morgan continued with his meal. He had by now gauged the fighting qualities of the home guards and was not going to let a few hundred of them interfere with his breakfast. Other vedettes then galloped in with the news that Shackleford was approaching from the south, since they had seen a cloud of dust along the road they had just traveled. The Confederates immediately mounted and hurried toward Wintersville.

When word that Morgan was approaching reached the village, the women and children fled to the Maxwell Tavern. The men seized their muskets and strode to the edge of town to sacrifice their lives to protect their homes. Fortunately, this was unnecessary. The arrival of a squad of militia from Steubenville, under Colonel James Collier, relieved the local guards. The instant that Morgan's van appeared over a rise, Collier's

214

men opened fire. The raiders charged the scouting party, drove it through the town, and the home guard fled. Some of the local men ran through a field of broomcorn, and the raiders could easily follow their progress by watching the swaying of the tassels.

The Southerners raided a store for groceries and clothing, then dashed on beyond the town, unaware of the fact that the women had fled the tavern and gathered at the home of the village physician, where the preacher's wife led them in prayer punctuated by the occasional whine of bullets.

Barely had the raiders left town before Colonel Collier's main body moved into sight from the east, formed into line on a hill dominating the town and wheeled into place an old six-pounder, loaded with scrap iron. At this critical moment, the van of Frank Wolford's cavalry trotted in from the southwest. The dust raised by Morgan's horses and the fleeing home guards hung over the village, and Collier mistook the Union troops for Southerners. His gunner opened fire with the six-pounder, and assorted bits of hardware smacked against the buildings in the center of town. One large piece of iron entered the taproom of Maxwell's Tavern which only a few minutes earlier had been filled with women and children. Wolford's cavalrymen dismounted, pulled their carbines from gunboots and prepared to fight for their lives. General Shackleford rode up to take command and at once saw that his men were exchanging fire with Ohio militia. He sent a courier forward under a white flag to Colonel Collier who was standing beside the cannon.

"What are you fools shooting at?" asked the regular officer. Abashed, Collier explained he thought he was engaging the enemy. His scouts then reported that Morgan's force was several miles away, making good their escape on the Richmond road.

It had been a narrow escape for the Confederates, much more so than they realized. If Collier's blunder had not detained Wolford's advance, the Union force might have caught the Rebels just outside town. As it turned out, Morgan gained a few hours time. But this was not all. Major Rue and his detachment of the 9th Kentucky Cavalry that morning had left the train that had carried him from Mingo Junction to north of Steubenville and had whipped their horses at top speed toward Wintersville. They heard the sound of Collier's six-pounder in the distance, as they rode along the road, climbing up the rise from the Ohio valley. By the time they arrived in Wintersville, the fighting was over.

Rue and his men went into camp, and Shackleford, who learned of

215

their presence, called on the Kentucky officer to join him in pursuit of the invaders. Major Rue was a proud man. He had traveled hundreds of miles to reach Morgan, and he was not happy at the prospect of losing his freedom of command when the end seemed in sight. He told Shackleford he was operating under Burnside's orders, and would join only if permitted to take the lead. Because Rue's horses were fresh, Shackleford grudgingly agreed.

John Morgan's success at Wintersville had its black side. Within five miles of the Ohio at the time, he had had to turn away from the river and head inland. The West Virginia bank had become a fading dream, an unattainable goal always just out of reach when it seemed to be the closest. No one complained as the raiders jogged along toward Richmond. The soldiers shared the groceries picked up in the store at Wintersville, and slaked their thirst at a creek that ran along the side of the road. They were tired; the July sun beat upon them relentlessly; their shirts and trousers clung to them with sweaty clamminess. Their feet were swollen and sore in their high leather boots. They were old campaigners, however, and the valley beyond the next hill was always worth waiting to see. At least, they did not have to excuse themselves to their womenfolk for their behavior, as did the home guards of Wintersville.

Those of the militia who had fled through the field of broomcorn returned home with stories that the Rebels had escaped through the swaying stalks. When the farmers came to harvest the corn, these imaginative fellows said, they would come upon the dead bodies of many a gray-clad trooper. For some strange reason, when the broomcorn was cut, there was not one dead raider in the field.

The afternoon sun on the Richmond-Wolf Run road cast shadows of the marching raiders that were ten to twelve feet long. Rabbits scampered across the fields at the sound of hundreds of hoofs. Redbirds flashed above their heads carrying weed seeds to their young in the nests hidden at the edge of the woods.

To the wounded soldier, Lyons, another tortured day in the saddle was nearing an end. To Ben Wathen, a private in Company K of the 8th Kentucky, the cardinals were a reminder of evenings in the fields beside his home in Lebanon. Elias Hardin Campbell, another boy from the Bluegrass, never forgot how his feet hurt, and that he was unable to remove his boots for three days and nights. Others suffered from dysentery, as did Major Tom Webber. They had eaten too much green corn and half-ripe apples.

216

The astounding thing was that they kept going. Throughout that long ride north, only a handful had straggled. Sick, bone-weary, and almost without hope, they never thought of surrender. In the final reckoning this was what made Morgan's cavalry the elite body that it was. Their uniforms were sweaty, torn and dirty; saddle leather was starting to rot from constant perspiration of horse and rider. Faces that were not lined and already tanned to a deep mahogany were now blistered and raw. It had been an excruciating ride, despite wide brimmed slouch hats and purloined veils. They now numbered only 600, on the final evening of their great adventure. Morgan and Cluke and Webber knew them for what they were—fine soldiers.

Beyond Wolf Run, nightfall overtook them. There were no farmhouses to grant the momentary cheer that comes from the light cast by a coal oil lamp. At first there was the music of an occasional whippoorwill, but soon they, too, became silent, leaving only the sounds of jingling harness and the sharp crack of shod hoofs against stone.

Many hours later the raiders came to Bergholz, where most of the villagers were retiring for the night. In obedience to orders, a few residents had hidden their horses. Few of them anticipated Morgan's appearance, having assumed that he was somewhere on the Ohio, attempting to cross.

Mrs. Sarah Allen was the first person to learn that the invaders had reached their village. She had blown out her lamps, except for the one in her hand, and was going upstairs to bed, when soldiers burst into her yard, pounded on the door and asked for food. Badly frightened, the woman went to the springhouse and returned with fresh bread, milk, buttermilk and honey. She watched in stricken amazement while the troopers ate fourteen loaves of bread and drank ten gallons of milk. The noise the hungry soldiers made awakened her children. They peered down the steps, saw the troopers, and promptly crept under a bed. Mrs. Allen thought of all the rumors she had heard about Morgan's "terrible men," and trembled as she served the food.

"Are you afraid?" asked one.

"Yes," said the woman, "I won't deny it."

"Well, you needn't be," said the soldier. "We never harm anyone who treats us right. But this is nothing to what we have to submit to in the South. Your Northern soldiers not only rob us, but they burn our houses and turn our wives and children out, homeless."

Down the road at the Dorrance home, a flax-pulling party was in progress when young Stuart McClave rushed in with word that Morgan was in town. "You'd better hurry and finish," he said, as if at this moment there was a great need for more good flax. Mary and Lizzie Dorrance ran to the barn and led two horses out into the woods beyond the pasture. By the time they returned, Major Webber and some of his men were in the village store, selecting clothing to replace their frayed habiliments and paying for it with greenbacks. Tom Webber paid a dime for a packet of smoking tobacco.

The major and his aides spread bolts of cloth on the store counters and lay down to spend the night. Before they fell asleep, they noticed the owner, James Wright, trying to hide some money from the cash drawer.

"Just leave your money where it is," said Webber, "and I pledge my honor it will not be disturbed." Wright did as he was ordered, and nothing was missing when the Confederates left town the next day.

General Morgan spent his last night as a free man in Ohio at the home of Herdman Taylor. He enjoyed a good chicken supper, saw that his horse was fed and curried, and then went to bed with his staff in half of the house, leaving the other half to the Taylor family. Some men slept in other homes, but most of them slept under the stars with only a few pickets to guard against surprise.

The morning of July 26 came to eastern Ohio in a sudden burst of light that climbed the sky long before the sun topped the horizon. There were no clouds. The fog that had formed in the low meadows disappeared before there was light enough to see it. Troopers going about their chores smelled the clean odor of oats growing behind the Taylor farmhouse. It was then lost in the pungent smell of scores of breakfast fires and boiling coffee.

Exhausted by her labors of the evening before, Mrs. Taylor called on her sister-in-law, Marion Taylor, to help prepare breakfast for the General and his officers. The women put coffee before their guests, and Morgan had barely tasted his when the vedettes galloped into town with word of approaching Federals. The Rebel leader clapped his hat on his head and stepped out to ride away, but Marion Taylor heard him remark to an aide: "We have never been run so hard before."

The Confederates trotted out of town toward Salineville. The minute the last of the rear guard disappeared, old Mr. Dorrance yelled for his horses. He would show the Rebels. He would trail them if he had to ride to Pennsylvania. But Mary and Lizzie had hidden the two horses so well in the dark that they could not find them the next morning. Dorrance had to sit on the front porch waiting for the Federals to come through. His

218

third daughter, Rachel, now fifteen years old, who had never seen a Rebel closer than the road that passed their house, heard that one had been left behind at John Allman's home. She visited the Allman's and found a very young raider, still in his teens, uninjured, but so exhausted that his captain had advised him to remain where he was until he was captured. The fifteen-year-old girl was surprised to see that he looked very much like any other boy who had worn himself out riding a thousand miles in three weeks. She could not see his feet, but there were no horns on his head.

One other soldier did not ride on with his regiment. He was found sound asleep in a sheep barn long after the Union cavalry had gone through in pursuit of his friends.

Some of the young soldiers in Bergholz realized that their time was running out. Not one of them hesitated to go with the column. They sensed that at long last capture might be close at hand and left some of their valuables, watches and rings with residents of the town who had been kind to them and fed them. With tears in their eyes, they asked the Ohio villagers to send the keepsakes to relatives in Kentucky. They then mounted and rode away.

By seven A.M. the Rebels were in Monroeville. On the way there they stopped at a gristmill owned by Edward Critser and helped themselves to grain for their horses. A few of them offered Critser a drink of whiskey. The miller who feared it might be poisoned, declined, saying "No thanks, I'm a temperance man." His hired man barely managed to smother a guffaw. He well knew that his employer would walk ten miles, under normal circumstances, for a stiff drink.

On this same stretch of road the column overtook a fat man riding in a heavy farm wagon. The native told General Morgan that he was a Vallandigham Democrat and boasted of his sentiments for the Confederacy. Morgan told him he hated Southern sympathizers who would not go south to fight, if they were young enough, or contribute money if they were not. The raider ordered the fat man out of the wagon and put two ill soldiers in the bed of the vehicle. Some of the soldiers forced the man to walk between their horses. When he complained that his boots hurt him, they made him remove them and walk in his socks. After awhile they tired of the sport and left him.

Mrs. James Twiss of Monroeville had finished baking bread. A Rebel soldier rode into the yard and permitted his horse's head to protrude inside the kitchen door.

"Don't ride into the house!" Mrs. Twiss shouted. "This is no stable."

The soldier asked for the bread and took the hot loaves to share with his companions.

Morgan decided to use the local blacksmith's services, as no enemy soldiers had appeared. One by one, the smith, Paddy Kerr, tightened loose shoes or nailed new ones on horses that had lost theirs. The last raider was alone in the smithy, and Paddy had the horse's left hind foot in his lap when the soldier saw the first of Shackleford's scouts coming over a hill. The Rebel leaped on his mount, spurred him, and was off toward Salineville. Paddy was left sprawled on the ground.

The General claimed that everything important usually happened to him on a Sunday. He had wed the pretty, vivacious Martha Ready on a Sabbath; the new division marched in front of the bride and groom in review just before it departed on the famous Christmas Raid of 1862 on a Sunday; and, much less pleasant to remember, he had lost the battle at Buffington Island the preceding Sunday.

But Morgan was too much of an extrovert to dwell upon such things as premonitions. He was in too much of a hurry, anyway, because Major Rue, with Shackleford's consent, was leading the van of the pursuit, his men and horses fresh. His eagerness to be in at the finish was so strong he could almost taste victory. If there had been such a thing as poetic justice on July 26, 1863, Colonel Frank Wolford, the unlettered soldier from eastern Kentucky, would have been the one who succeeded where so many had failed. He had been Morgan's prisoner and had that grudge to settle, and had driven himself and his men hard in order to stay in the forefront of Shackleford's column all the way from the Cumberland to Buffington Bar. But no one expects justice in war. Wolford was too good a soldier himself to do anything to hamper the pursuit. With his brigade almost exhausted, and his mounts in worse shape by far than Morgan's, all he could do was continue his efforts, leaving the glory to others.

Another Union force, the 1st Michigan Cavalry, under Major Way, would have an important role to play in turning Morgan back upon his pursuers, but it was Major Rue of the 9th Kentucky with a hastily-assembled regiment on whom the gods of war smiled on that beautiful Sabbath morning.

As the Confederates passed through Salineville, they learned from captured militia scouts that a Federal detachment was operating somewhere north of them.

Before they could act on this information, Major Way and his Michiganders swept out of a woods north of town, struck the Rebel column in the flank, and kept up a running fight. There were more than 350 Federals, all mounted on fresh horses. In such a battle, the man on the best horse is more apt to succeed. Those of Morgan's men who were on heavy, dispirited farm horses, were the first to suffer; they fell behind and were cut off or shot. Major Way was a driver. He continued pressure, and Morgan saw he would have to forfeit some of his men in order to save the balance. The man he called to lead this forlorn rear guard action was Captain Ralph Sheldon of Company C, 2nd Kentucky Cavalry. In his extremity it was altogether natural that the general would call upon a unit of regulars who had learned to fight under his bother-in-law, Basil Duke.

"This company," wrote Duke in his memoirs, "had maintained its organization and discipline without deterioration, although greatly reduced in numbers. In this last fight, it was ordered to charge a body of Federal cavalry, who were dismounted and lay behind a worm fence, firing upon the column with their Spencer rifles. Led by its gallant Captain Ralph Sheldon, one of the best of our best officers, the company descended on the enemy. The tired horses breasted the fence unable to clear it and knocked off the top rails. But with their deadly revolvers, our boys soon accomplished the mission upon which they were sent."

Seventy-five men were down, and more than two hundred were captured before Morgan led his dwindling band out of the reach of the men from Michigan. This maneuver was not easy, but the Southerners were good horsemen to the end, and those who escaped were the best-mounted. Those of Major Webber's men who were on plow horses showed their quick-wittedness when the escape route led past a rural church. Jumping from their mounts, they cut the reins by which the parishioners' horses were tied to the hitching rail and galloped off, elated to be on fresh animals again.

With Major Way's force rounding up prisoners, Morgan turned east for the last time, striking once more for the Ohio at Smith's Ford. He took the road toward Hanover and crossed the tracks of the Cleveland and Pittsburgh Railroad at Coon's Ford. Here he came upon the west fork of Beaver Creek, a stream that had its sources in Mahoning and Portage counties and meandered in three separate branches down across Columbiana County. They joined near the Pennsylvania border and turned south to empty into the Ohio. The raiders crossed the west fork and, with nothing to go on but his natural grasp of topography and terrain, Morgan led them toward Pennsylvania. He had once had a map, which was not

221

a very good one, that helped him on his way to Buffington Island, but in the attempt to ford the Ohio at Belleville, the map had become soaked and nearly illegible. He would have liked to pick up a guide, but the Federals were so close in pursuit he could not take time to find one. He decided to follow roads that followed along Beaver Creek, knowing they would eventually lead him to the Ohio River.

The troops who would prevent his reaching the river were now riding by a road that paralleled the one he was following.

Rue and his mixed regiment of Kentucky and Michigan cavalry had spent the night at Knoxville, four miles from the Ohio. At the break of day the command was in the saddle, heading through the Jefferson County hills for Hammondsville and the Columbiana County line. The horses were rested, and by nine o'clock Rue had rendezvoused with Shackleford at Salineville. There was delay, as there always seemed to be when different Yankee commands met in the field. On each occasion, highly individualistic commanders had to determine who was to give the orders. By the time Rue finished showing his telegraphed orders from Burnside and prepared to leave, Major Way's Michigan cavalry had bisected Morgan's force. On his way after the remnants, Rue passed the prisoners on their way to Salineville. He recognized several Rebels, who had gone to school with him in Kentucky.

At Salineville, Major Rue learned from the telegraph operator that the raiders had taken the West Beaver road. In his hour of ultimate danger, John Morgan found the telegraph, which he had often used to deceive his pursuers, used against him. Lightning Ellsworth was gone, fleeing through the mountains of West Virginia. It was Morgan now who was uninformed of his enemy's whereabouts.

As the little rural churches ended their services, the congregations of Columbiana County became aware that the war had come up from the South and was now going on all about them where, they believed, it should not be. They saw the gray-clad remnants of Morgan's band on one road, and the blue-clad men of Way's detachment not far behind. Other parishioners on a nearby road saw Rue and his men, all of them moving at a good pace in the direction of West Point. Other soldiers were also on the move. Home guards took their stand at crossroads, eager to try their hand at the martial art.

James Burbick, a native, had mustered a small company of volunteers in his home town of Lisbon and marched south in obedience to orders

222

broadcast by Brigadier General William Thomas Harbough Brooks, then commanding the Department of the Monongahela. Brooks was a crusty but amiable old West Pointer who had learned about guerilla warfare while fighting Seminole Indians in Florida and the Comanches in the West. He had also acquired considerable formal military lore while an aide to Robert E. Lee in the Mexican War. Brooks had moved toward the sound of guns, as a good soldier always does, and was guarding the eastern bank of the Ohio in the West Virginia panhandle. When Morgan moved in his direction, he disregarded the departmental boundaries and took temporary command of the Ohio militia just across the river. Burnside was in Cincinnati; someone who knew something about war had to give orders to the militia. Otherwise, John Morgan might reach Lake Erie.

Brooks had done his utmost with the green troops at his disposal. He had stationed the 57th Pennsylvania Infantry under Colonel James R. Porter at Warrenton; the 58th Pennsylvania Infantry under Colonel George H. Bemis at La Grange, and the 54th Pennsylvania Infantry under Colonel Thomas F. Gallagher at Rush Run, two miles above Porter's regiment. These troops were "90-day" men, untrained in the art of war, but they were armed and were numerous enough to bar the raiders from fording the river. Brooks had also deployed 1,000 West Virginia militia under Brigadier General James S. Wheat on the Ohio side of the river near Bridgeport, to bar the approaches to Wheeling. Before Morgan was out of Guernsey County, Brooks had barred virtually every ford in the Ohio south of East Liverpool.

It was more than coincidence that the fortunes of war brought into juxtaposition these two men, both good soldiers, each unknown to the other. A believer in astrology would have had his beliefs challenged and possibly strengthened had he known that John Hunt Morgan was born in Huntsville, Alabama, and William T. H. Brooks, a Yankee beloved for his genial disposition and good judgment who helped capture him by alerting James Burbick, would end his days farming in the Alabama town of Morgan's birth.

While Burbick and his tatterdemalion volunteers walked south from the middle branch of Beaver Creek, toward the southern fork of the same stream, which for some unknown reason was called the west branch, Rue and his men crossed the C. & P. Railroad tracks and held their horses to a fast trot, moving rapidly toward the same small stream. Along the way, the Federal officer met a country doctor riding home from church. He

223

asked him to lead the detachment to a position where he could enter the road ahead of Morgan. The physician fell in beside Rue, and the regiment struck off on a small side road.

It was now past one P.M. The sky was cloudless, the air clear and still, without even enough breeze to stir the willows that grew along the stream. It would have been better for Morgan's raiders had there been a high wind. As it was, they could not move without stirring a telltale cloud of dust. But the Union cavalry was leaving its own trail, and within a few minutes each column knew exactly where the other was.

On to the stage thus set for the final act stumbled Burbick, unwittingly cast as the comedian. His squad debouched on to the West Beaver road just as Morgan's van cantered up. For a short time it appeared as if there would be a fight. The one thing, however, that Morgan did not want just then was a delay. It would take time to drive the home guardsmen out of the way, and the cloud of dust to his right was coming much too close.

The Confederate leader sent a flag of truce forward with instructions to the bearer to conduct himself in such a manner that the militia captain would assume that the raiders would annhilate his squad if he showed signs of fight. The ruse succeeded. Burbick, on foot, was at a disadvantage, as foot soldiers always are in the presence of mounted men. He had no way of knowing that the invaders were each down to a few rounds of ammunition.

Morgan promised the home guardsman that he would do no damage to any person or home in the vicinity providing Burbick's men let his column pass unmolested. It was about as strange an agreement as any made during the war, but Morgan won an informal laissez-passer, which was the most he could expect—or wish for—in the circumstances. In addition, Burbick agreed to act as guide and lead the Southerners by the most direct route to Smith's Ford.

The raiders found a horse for Burbick to ride, and he and John Morgan started off on the road side by side, discussing an arrangement for the surrender of the sick and wounded. The Lisbon militiaman, a country man unaccustomed to the ways of the world, was charmed by the soft voice and pleasant manners of the Kentucky cavalier and never once interposed an objection. Stirrup to stirrup, the Rebel general and the Buckeye captain jogged along the west branch of the Beaver, chatting amiably, and looking as if they were exercising their saddle horses or enjoying a class in horsemanship.

224

According to his official report, Major Rue and his 300 troopers, were closing the distance between himself and Morgan's force at seven miles an hour. Shortly before two P.M. he crested a rise that gave him a clear view of the entire valley of the west branch. On the far side of the creek, he spotted a cloud of dust coming from the West Beaver Road, which followed the stream down the north side for several miles until it left the creek and cut straight across country for the Ohio.

"When I first saw the cloud of dust, it was rising slowly," said Rue in his formal report. "Soon it began to move faster. The doctor told me the road we were on crossed the other about two miles away. Morgan was traveling toward the intersection. I had the greater distance to travel, so I ordered a brisk trot. About this time my troop started to throw some dust. Morgan evidently saw it, and his guides must have informed him the road we were on led into the one he was following, trying to hit the Ohio River. Morgan ordered his horses spurred into a faster gait and passed the crossroads ahead of me. I just missed the rearmost men. I didn't want a stern chase. I wanted a head-on fight."

The country physician who was guiding Rue was familiar with the roads. He had probably traveled every one of them many times, ministering to the ill of southern Columbiana County. He told the Federal commander that they could use a private road, little more than a path, which the horses could follow and which would, in effect, be the chord of the arc Morgan was following. In one mile, said the doctor, the Union troop could reach an intersection that the Rebels would have to ride two miles to reach. Rue waved his arm, the trumpeter signaled for a gallop, and the detachment raced down the creek.

The dust they stirred rolled above the willows, and Morgan saw it as he rode along with Burbick. He knew the horses that were creating the cloud were fresh and moving faster than his own. With that knowledge came the realization that he had finally come to the end of the trail. Way and Shackleford were but a few hours behind him. The unidentified but obviously fresh force on his right had all the advantage of fresh mounts. Worst of all he was nearly out of ammunition. There were not enough powder and balls to sustain his men in a five-minute fight. A charge with naked sabers and clubbed carbines might have been a heroic finale to the long ride north, but Morgan dismissed the thought immediately. After all, the agreement that provided for exchange of prisoners was still in effect, and men who fell in a fruitless battle could never again fight for

225

the Confederacy. He had done the best he could—now he would save his men.

Turning quickly to Captain Burbick, the Rebel leader asked if he would like to accept his surrender. Burbick muttered something indicating that it would please him greatly.

"But," said Morgan, "perhaps you would not give me such terms as I wish."

"General Morgan," answered the militiaman, "you may write your own terms, and I will grant them."

"Very well, then," agreed the raider, "it is a bargain. I will surrender to you."

Morgan proposed that the officers and men be paroled and allowed to keep their horses, and the officers their sidearms as well. Burbick nodded in agreement and Morgan formally surrendered.

Throughout this discussion, the raiders had been trotting leisurely along, dispirited by the thoughts racing through their minds. Most of them could not visualize their place in history or realize that they had already served their country. The Ohio River was only a few miles away, but now forever out of reach. They were suffering physical and mental fatigue. It now was finished. They would soon be prisoners of war.

The column had advanced less than half a mile after the formality of surrender when the troopers in the lead saw a line of Union soldiers strung across the Beaver Creek road. Rue had placed his men to his right in a bit of timberland and to his left across the road in an orchard. The Rebel scouts turned back, conferred with Morgan and appeared again with a white flag of truce. Morgan had given one of his aides a white handkerchief which the man impaled on the point of his saber. Rue called it a bit of muslin, but it was linen, hand-rolled and stitched by a devoted Southern woman.

What happened next depends on whose version is accepted. Rue claimed that Morgan demanded the surrender of the Federal force but that he sent back word for the Rebels to give up or face battle with the 9th Kentucky Union Cavalry. Duke and Webber remembered, or heard from comrades, that Morgan simply stated he had already surrendered to Captain Burbick and the Lisbon militia. Rue's version is the more melodramatic; the latter, more in keeping with the true condition of the raiders. Morgan knew that the two forces were about equal in numbers, but that every other factor was weighted in the Yankees' favor. Having

226

decided to surrender to Burbick before he even knew the identity of the Union detachment, it appears unlikely he would then have thought he could overcome a regiment of regulars.

There was no fight in any event. Major Rue immediately went with an escort to where Morgan stood with his staff under a great tree a few feet from the road in a pasture belonging to David Crubaugh.

"His men," reported Rue, "were lying on both sides of the road, almost all of them asleep. It was a hot July day, and they were the tiredest lot of fellows I ever saw in my life. I went on to meet Morgan, seated on a fine sorrel mare, a thoroughbred from Kentucky, which he said had made the trip all the way for twenty-seven consecutive days. He was loath to part with her but gave her to me. Somehow she was given to Shackleford."

The way the sorrel mare changed hands was indicative of the rivalry that marked the Union leaders and their efforts to grab for themselves the honor of being Morgan's captor.

Major Way had taken time out after his running battle with the raiders to send a courier back to Salineville with a dispatch for Burnside. He could not claim actual surrender, but by getting his message in first he saw to it that his name reached the newspapers ahead of that of anyone else.

"After a forced march yesterday and last night," said Way, "with almost continuous skirmishing, we succeeded this morning in pressing Morgan to an engagement about one-and-a-half miles from this place. After more than an hour of severe fighting, we scattered his force in all directions. The following is the result of our engagement: 20 or 30 killed, about 50 wounded, 200 prisoners, 150 stands of arms and horses. Our loss is light. Our horses are very much jaded, but I shall follow as rapidly as possible. My force was 200 to 250 strong."

It would certainly look good in the papers, even if he had exaggerated about scattering the enemy.

Rue made his report in person to General Shackleford, who reached the scene within an hour. He claimed the capture in no uncertain terms, but that did not impress Shackleford. Rank has always had its privilege, since the first cave man took command of his fellow tribesmen by virtue of owning the largest club. Shackleford penned a stirring dispatch to Burnside and sent it before he bothered to talk with his prisoners. It follows:

227

"Scraggsville Church—3 miles south
from New Lisbon, Ohio
July 26, 1863
"By the blessings of Almighty God, I have succeeded in capturing
General John H. Morgan, Colonel Cluke, and the balance of his com-
mand, amounting to 400 prisoners.

J. H. Shackleford,
Brig. Gen. Commanding."

Then the General, with Colonel Wolford at his side, rode to where
Morgan was talking with Major Rue. Shackleford was most discourteous
and refused to acknowledge Morgan's statement that he had surrendered
to Burbick and the Lisbon militia. Wolford, on the other hand, seemed
genuinely pleased to see his old enemy, although he was worn out from
the pursuit.

Basil Duke later said that Wolford concerned himself in seeing that the
parole was honored. Having been Morgan's prisoner the year before, he
remembered that the Rebel cavalryman had shown him every courtesy.
But there was no budging the monolithic Shackleford. He was disdainful
of his prisoner and showed it in every gesture. When the Confederate
leader proposed that if the Union general was unable to honor the parole, the raiders should be allowed to fight it out with their enemy,
Shackleford lost his temper.

"General Shackleford's passion got the upper hand of his judgment,
and he began to bestow some caustic epithets upon the conquered chieftain," one of Wolford's soldiers said later. "Colonel Wolford interrupted
and rebuked the irate general, and told him that it was wrong to speak
harshly to one whose hands were figuratively confined. Morgan, as a
token of appreciation of his kindness, presented Wolford with his fine
silver spurs."

Badly outranked, Major Rue took little part in the negotiations, although had he dallied on the way from Mingo Junction, Morgan might
have reached Smith's Ford, crossed the river, and there would have been
no surrender. Perhaps to show his contribution, Rue finally decided to
stake his claim and sent a dispatch himself to Burnside. It read: "I captured John Morgan today at 2 o'clock, P.M., taking 300 and 36 prisoners,
400 horses and arms."

Old Mutton Chops must have found it very perplexing to determine

228

just who had caught the great raider. Not stopping to settle the issue, he sent numerous messages of his own. His relief at finally having engineered the raiders' round-up was apparent in every word.

With the exception of Rue's dragoons, every soldier in the valley of Beaver Creek, Blue and Gray alike, was at the point of exhaustion. Union and Confederate troopers fell asleep while their superiors haggled under the big tree.

Connally, the Illinois soldier who had gone to war with the Black Horse troop, tried to find forage for his remaining black, now only skin and bones. The previous day, he had had to abandon the gallant little mare with the sure step and eagle-eye. He did what he could for the other steed and later that week shipped him back to Glasgow, Kentucky, and had him turned out to pasture. The black recovered, went back into service and was captured the next year when Morgan, after escaping from prison, staged his last raid into the Bluegrass.

Most of the soldiers on both sides displayed no hard feelings toward their enemies. They were too tired even to jibe at one another, and since they were all regulars, they appreciated each other's proved qualities. There was one maverick, though, in the Union force, who did not share his companions' respect for the defeated raiders.

He was riding in Shackleford's column just prior to the surrender, and mistaking a chaplain, W. H. Hennell, for the general, since each was wearing a linen duster to protect his uniform, he rode alongside.

"General," he said, "I have a request to make. I have a brother-in-law in Morgan's gang. I wish you to allow me to shoot him when they are captured."

"Shoot a prisoner, you coward?" replied the shocked chaplain. "Begone at once, or I'll put you under guard to be tried by a court-martial at our next camp."

By mid-afternoon the Union provost guards had finished their head-counts, collected the prisoners' arms, and completed the other housekeeping chores prescribed in the War Department manuals for such a situation. But the weighing of the effect of the great raid was something else. Men on both sides debated that point in the hours immediately following the surrender, in the remaining months of the war between the states, and for long years after Appomattox.

The majority of Union officials believed that the loss of Morgan's fine division hurt the Confederacy to a greater extent than the damage it inflicted hurt the North. Orlando B. Willcox, Indiana's adjutant-general, declared that Morgan's absence contributed to Bragg's defeat.

The South saw it differently. Morgan's adjutant, S. P. Cunningham, later summed it up in a report in which he cited the paroling of 6,000 Northern troops, the destruction of thirty-four important bridges, the demolition of railroad tracks in sixty different places, the burning of warehouses and army depots, and the enforced spending of huge sums to put better than 120,000 militiamen in the field.

"Our loss was by no means slight," he admitted, "with 28 commissioned officers killed, 35 wounded, 250 men killed, wounded or captured [before the surrender]. But the damage to railroads, steamboats, bridges, added to destruction of public stores and depots, cannot fall far short of ten million dollars."

Basil Duke's appraisal was fair and accurate.

"The objects of the raid were accomplished," he wrote. "General Bragg's retreat was unmolested by any flanking forces of the enemy, and I think that military men, who will review all the facts, will pronounce that this expedition delayed for weeks the fall of East Tennessee and prevented the timely reinforcement of Rosecrans by troops that would otherwise have participated in the battle of Chickamauga. It destroyed Morgan's division, however, and left but a remnant of Morgan's cavalry."

Statistics tell only part of the story. With the loss of less than 2,000 men, Morgan kept a large portion of the Middle West off balance for weeks. More men than that were lost in bloody battles that did not change the positions of opposing armies by more than a few hundred feet. If it was unsuccessful, it still rekindled a hope in Southern hearts, and instilled fear in the minds of hundreds of thousands in the three states through which the raid was carried out.

Seldom in warfare have so few men ridden so far and so fast within enemy lines. And never in any war had 2,000 men fought their way against such odds, damaging but few private homes and without harming a single woman or child. It may well have been chivalry's last appearance on war's sordid stage.

It is unknown whether such thoughts as these passed through the minds of the Rebel raiders as they marched away from the pasture beside the west fork of Beaver Creek. Cavalrymen riding through enemy country cannot mail letters home, even if they have time to write them; Morgan's troopers, with but few exceptions, were not confirmed diarists.

230

The raid was over for the weary Rebels. They were alive, and that was a benison no man overlooked, even with prison camp a few days away. Some hoped for exchange, others for escape; but every one of Morgan's "terrible men" looked forward eagerly to one thing—a chance to rest and sleep.

Shackleford placed Colonel Wolford in charge of the prisoners, and by four o'clock in the afternoon the column of mounted men, Blue and Gray together, were on the road marching toward the Ohio at Wellsville, where trains would take them to Northern prisons. Farmers and their families gathered by the side of the road to watch the raiders go by.

John Hunt Morgan rode at the head of the column, Shackleford on his right and Colonels Wolford and Capron just behind. If he was dejected, he gave no sign of it. A few miles along the route toward the river, the column crossed a small stream on a timber bridge. Morgan turned in his saddle, a smile on his face, and said:

"Adjutant, see that that bridge is burned."

CHAPTER 17

Over the Wall
Lay Freedom

AFTER THE BATTLE of Buffington Island the Confederate prisoners who were captured there were put aboard the steamboats Judah had used to transport his troops, and taken down the Ohio to Cincinnati.

Exhausted beyond belief, the raiders had slept soundly wherever evening found them. Leeland Hathaway said "the worn body and weary brain gave way." When he awoke on the morning of July 20 he was soaking wet from a heavy rain that had fallen during the night.

Basil Duke, Dick, Calvin and Charlton Morgan, the General's brothers, and about thirty other officers and nearly 650 men were guarded by the 12th Ohio Infantry. Sergeant Henry L. Stone regaled his guards with stories of the long ride. The Buckeye foot soldiers found it difficult to believe, but Stone was telling the truth when he said that he wore out eight horses himself and that the Rebels had used 15,000 horses in all.

Sergeant Stone, who later became general counsel for the Louisville & Nashville Railroad, the line he had helped cut during the invasion, and who was at one time a judge of the Kentucky Court of Appeals, said that Hobson's troopers had had to make out with 10,000 mounts, most of them castoffs left by the Southerners.

The prisoners found their guards to be courteous and understanding. Because they were regular soldiers, the Ohioans knew how the vagaries of war can turn a fighting man into a prisoner within minutes, and they showed respect for men who had faced such great odds for so long. Along the river banks civilians were not so understanding. The raiders could hear insults and threats shouted from nearly every town's wharf boat.

Some of the men who had to sleep on the weather decks of the steamboats slipped over the side during the night and swam for the West Virginia shore, not relishing the prospect of months in a prison camp. One who escaped was Captain Tom Berry, who had secreted a civilian suit in his blanket roll. On the first night of the trip, while the steamer *Tariscon* was making its slow way downstream over the shoals between Gallipolis and Portsmouth, Berry shaved off his flowing beard leaving only a small goatee and mustache, asked a companion to cut his hair, which had grown to shoulder length, and then changed into the store suit. When the guards were busy elsewhere, he moved forward to that section of the deck reserved for the few civilian passengers on board. When the *Tariscon* slowed up near the small town where some of these passengers lived, Captain Berry went ashore with them in a small boat. He later rejoined the Confederate army near Dalton, Georgia.

When his companions arrived in Cincinnati, they found the wharf boats and levees swarming with curious people who wanted to see Morgan's men at close range. First the officers were taken ashore. Then the boats moved nearer the railroad station where trains were waiting to take the enlisted men to Camp Morton, the prison camp Governor Tod had feared would be taken over by Morgan.

During the transfer another Rebel officer escaped. The records fail to identify him, but Colonel McGowan described him as a small, dapper man, "with a firm mouth, kept resolutely closed, and a pair of keen black eyes." He had a full head of hair and a long beard, black and curly. As the boats tied up, a patrol was sent to clear the main deck of prisoners. He avoided the Federal soldiers, walked down the gangplank, and explained to a group of Yankee officers that he was an officer from the steamboat. Then he walked to the railroad office at Front and Broadway, rounded the corner and stepped inside a barber shop. He had his hair cut short and his beard trimmed and shaped into the then popular burnsides, named after the general who first affected that style. He later bought a wide-brimmed straw hat and a linen duster and walked to the Spencer House, secure in his disguise. He ate and drank with several Union officers until it was time to board the Louisville mail packet.

He spent several days in Louisville eating well, drinking with new-found friends and enjoying himself after the long weeks in the saddle. He addressed a letter to a Louisville newspaper and then rode into the back country. The next day the paper published the note in which the Rebel officer thanked Captain D. W. H. Day, one of Judah's aides who had been in charge on the boat trip down from Buffington, and his staff for their kind treatment.

He ended the letter, said McGowan, by saying "he regretted that he had to leave us in unceremonious style; was sorry we could not have made the "grand round" of Louisville with him; but, really, his engagements called him South, and we must excuse him."

Other Confederate officers marched off the steamers and walked two-by-two between heavy files of soldiers from the river to the city prison on Ninth Street. Duke, who was lame, and Dick Morgan, who had an infected leg wound, rode in an open victoria.

"Great crowds thronged the wharfs," wrote Hathaway, "and as we were marching through the streets we were greeted with curses and pelted with questionable missiles until the guard, growing indignant, threatened to turn us loose on our persecutors. We were marched to the Ninth Street station house and turned in among thugs, thieves, and that ilk."

Describing the scene for their readers, newspaper reporters said Colonel Morgan had "the outward seeming of a gentleman" and that "Colonel Duke looks like a Spanish bandit on a small scale," but they sprinkled their copy with many less pleasant words like "assassin," "cutthroats," "horsethieves," "robbers" and "arsonists." The authorities permitted reporters to talk with the captive officers, and the newspapermen could not help remarking about the way the men jumped up from the pallets on which they were resting and how "they courteously greeted us, evincing in their manner good birth and education." It was almost as if the Northern reporters had expected to see a gang of murderous bandits—some, at least, with horns, tails and cloven hoofs.

Colonel Duke had many friends in Cincinnati, and some of the others were not strange to the city. They were visited by residents who, under the pretense of seeking kinsmen, brought the prisoners food, soap and other gifts.

The Rebels stayed in Cincinnati only a short time and then were transferred to Johnson's Island.

A week later trains rolled in to the Little Miami Railroad station bearing General Morgan, Colonels Cluke and Webber, and the other men captured on Beaver Creek. It was night, and the darkness gave some of the more evil members of the crowd of 5,000 false courage. They milled about the station, some brandishing firearms, and shouted vile epithets at the prisoners. Some even called out for them to be hanged. But as is the way with most crowds, they subsided before the bayonets affixed to rifles carried by the regulars of the 111th Ohio Infantry, and nothing happened.

234

Reporters were eager to interview the famous guerilla leader, and one described him as "in good spirits and quite unconcerned at his ill luck." Another described the General as dressed in a linen coat, white coat, black trousers and a light felt hat; "a well-built man, of fresh complexion and sandy hair and beard."

Morgan conferred with Burnside in the prison and voiced a plea for his captors to honor the letter of the surrender and parole agreement arranged with Captain Burbick. Old Mutton Chops, elated at having the whip hand, denied the request.

General Halleck had already decided that Morgan and his chief lieutenants would spend their time in a common penitentiary rather than in a prison camp. This decision was based on the belief that the Confederates were subjecting Colonel Abel Streight, a Union officer captured by Nathan Bedford Forrest during an attempt to blow up the arsenal in Rome, Georgia, to imprisonment with common felons. It was not true, as Streight himself reported when freed, but Halleck hated Morgan and one excuse for the indignity was as good as the next.

Therefore, on the morning of July 30, General Morgan and his officers, with Ohio regulars guarding them, marched to the railroad station and boarded the train for Columbus, where they were locked up in the state prison. A keeper who locked them in their cells laughed sadistically and told them they were "here to stay." The horror of the thought chilled them to the marrow of their bones.

Duke recalled that most Confederate soldiers at that time believed the Civil War would continue for many years and might "outlast the generation." With no hope of exchange, the younger officers in particular were grievously depressed. Turnkeys ordered the prisoners to strip and bathe in wooden tubs with disinfectants prepared for the purpose. Convicts scrubbed them with horse brushes as if to compound the insult. Even this was not as bad as the next event. Each man with a beard, mustache or long hair was seated in a barber chair and shaven until he looked like a convict.

Most of the Kentuckians were proud of their beards, especially the younger men who had cultivated them with considerable difficulty because of their tender years. In an era when most men wore beards, to be shorn of them was akin to public degradation and humiliation. None suffered so deeply, however, as Colonel Smith, whose beard was a leonine adornment that swept almost to his waist.

After this experience, the thought of being locked up in a double-tiered cell block, each man in a narrow cubicle measuring seven by three-and-a-half feet, was not so bad as it would otherwise have been.

They were in a section of the penitentiary separate from the ordinary felons. All they knew of the other inmates was the noise made by the clanging of iron gates and the releasing of great locks on cell block doors. After a few days in the prison, the lack of exercise came to be the most burdensome aspect of their existence. They had lived outdoors for years, been active as only cavalrymen can be, and suddenly were denied almost all movement. In the daytime they could walk in the corridor past the double tier of cells. With the coming of evening, they had to return to their individual cells. Gas lights were turned out early, and candlelight was permitted for an additional hour only.

Prison officials have seldom been noted for their charitable or warm-hearted feelings, and the warden at Columbus, a man named Merion, must have had a heart of stone. Infractions of discipline were dealt with brutally. Conditions at first were bearable, but Merion soon began to deal harshly. Men were not allowed to talk in the mess hall, or after the lights went out, and their mail was censored in such a way that any comment was interpreted as an attack on the prison personnel.

When the new, more stringent rules were put into effect, Colonel Duke, Dick Morgan and a few other officers who had been at Johnson's Island were transferred to Columbus. At the prison camp they could swim in the lake, and conditions were rather pleasant. Duke and the others were shocked when they saw their brother officers.

While Duke was waiting to be assigned to a cell, a man whom he thought was a convict spoke to him. He turned to a companion to comment about how friendly the inmates were on such short acquaintance. The "convict," shaven and with almost no hair on his head, broke into laughter. Only then did Duke recognize his brother-in-law, General Morgan.

Merion, the jailer, became more and more sadistic. He began sentencing prisoners to a dungeon cell deep in the cellar. Major Tom Webber was one of the first to be incarcerated in the damp chamber. There was no furniture except a single toilet bucket, and it was infested with vermin. He was given two slices of bread and one cup of water for the twenty-four hours he was kept there. When he emerged, he looked like a ghost. He was still suffering from dysentery and other illnesses, and the punishment was almost more than his weakened body could stand. General Morgan was never forced to serve a term in the dungeon, but Duke, Calvin Morgan, Major McCreary and several others were. Calvin Morgan said he was covered with green mold when he emerged; McCreary, who had to suffer the inhuman torture for five days and nights, called it "a hell on earth."

Morgan complained to the governor, and Tod visited the raiders' wing of the prison. He professed amazement at the manner in which they were treated and that the Southerners had been shaved and shorn, not by any military order, but because of the warden's cruelty. This, unfortunately, did not restore the officers' hair or beards.

Tod apologized for "an outrageous and disgraceful act," Charlton Morgan noted in his prison diary, and ordered a change in their routine. Things became better at once. The governor was a man of his word, and Merion was frightened at the chief executive's anger. Webber and other men who were ill were permitted to have beer and ale. Military rations were substituted for prison food, and the raiders were allowed to make outside purchases.

McCreary was the last man to have to suffer in the slimy dungeon cell. It was well for his sanity that he was not again put in solitary.

"When I was taken out I was scarcely able to stand up," he said, "and some of my comrades had to be helped to their cells, with their feet swollen and blood oozing out of their fingernails and toenails."

The Confederate officers were deeply religious, but were denied participation in church services and were not permitted to leave their cells on Sundays. They read psalms to one another and recited prayers through the iron bars, but Charlton Morgan noted in his diary that he had never known "a people who possessed so little pity and respect for religion as the Yankees." This was a blanket indictment that was unfair to most Northerners, but it applied with singular truth to those in charge of the Southern soldiers.

The days dragged by. Younger men found a ladder propped against a wall and used it as a gymnasium, running up and down the rungs, hanging from it and chinning themselves until they dropped with fatigue. It was good to be tired again.

Routine was a repulsive thing to men who had served with Morgan. At seven A.M. the turnkey knocked on the potbellied stove in the corridor and the men arose, washed and then marched into the mess hall for a breakfast that usually consisted of bread and molasses. Other meals were little better. At seven P.M. the turnkey rapped on the stove again, and the men went to their cells for the night. The lights were turned out, soon afterward.

237

As a result of Governor Tod's intercession, the prisoners were permitted to receive packages from relatives, and for some time they feasted on delicacies from home. Then, as Duke said, the trap fell. Merion waited until there was a huge pile of mail and packages to be distributed and then revoked the permission. He confiscated the provisions and served them at his own table.

After this occurrence, Charlton Morgan wrote in his diary: "If a single man of us here ever survives the war, Merion will be held to strict responsibility for his unkindness to us. One who can forget these wrongs has none of the instincts of a man."

Throughout August and September, the men suffered from the heat, poor ventilation, and the privations of enforced idleness. General Morgan, however, seemed to endure imprisonment better than any of his men. It may have been good acting on his part, practiced in order to keep up his men's spirits. He never seemed to despair of eventual exchange and did not permit his fear to color his letters to his wife. Limited to one page at a time, he wrote as often as the officials allowed, urging Mattie to bear up under the separation "like a soldier's wife." In one letter he said, "You can little imagine my darling, my great anxiety in regard to yourself. If I only knew that you were in good health I would be much better reconciled."

One of the reasons he did not know about his wife's health was the sadistic, inhuman practice of the jailers in censoring incoming mail. They quite often refused to pass a letter from the soldiers' relatives, forwarding only the empty envelopes. This was a torture that nearly broke the spirit of several officers. Morgan told Mattie that he realized the difficulties of getting mail through the lines and told her how many letters he had written to her, so that she could keep track of his efforts.

Once he wrote about a long letter he had received from his mother in which she had devoted a large part of her missive to the praise of Mattie.

"I wrote her today," said Morgan in his next letter, "that by your example and advice, I was a much better man, that the little prayer book that you presented me upon our marriage had been my constant companion ever since, & that a night has not passed but that I have read it . . . Your daguerreotype I open often during the day & pray that the time may soon come when I may again see you . . . May God's blessing rest upon your head is the earnest & constant prayer of your devoted husband."

Late in August he received several packages from both his wife and mother and shared the contents, so that several in the group had what he called "a feast spread out on a plank." In a note to his wife he described how much he had enjoyed "some black Hamburgh grapes" purchased for him by a guard from a market outside the prison walls.

". . . eating each grape," he said, "I thought of you, but when do I not?"

When one of the General's numerous female relatives sent him a bunch of fresh violets, he pressed several of the flowers into his next letter to Mattie, and the prison officials, perhaps in a good mood that day, let them pass.

It would have surprised many Northerners who thought of Morgan as a horsethief and despoiler of peaceful towns, if they could have seen the General's letters and read how deeply sincere he was in trying to live up to his Christian beliefs.

On many occasions he ended his letters to Mattie with the phrase, "My light will be extinguished in a few moments and I must read a psalm."

Mrs. Morgan and her sister Alice had spent many weeks in Augusta, Georgia, but had returned during the great Union raid on Knoxville. A few weeks after ordering Morgan and his officers to be thrown into a felon's prison, Burnside had finally done what Lincoln, Halleck and Stanton had been urging, and invaded east Tennessee. Mrs. Morgan, Alice Ready and the General's young brother, Key, fled before the Yankees arrival to Danville, Virginia. It was an arduous trip for the General's wife, who was expecting a child.

Because of these frequent moves, Morgan received only scattered letters from his wife, and he became quite concerned. He wrote her whom to see to get money, naming men who held funds in his name, and urged her to return to Augusta if she thought that wiser.

"If you think best to go to Augusta, do not hesitate," he wrote. "At this distance, I cannot give you advice. Take a good deal of exercise in the open air and keep the rose upon your cheeks as when I left you."

Mattie chose to remain in Danville, closer to the seat of government in Richmond, so that she could exert whatever pressure she could in an effort to work for an exchange of prisoners. But the cartel of exchange had broken down after Vicksburg and Gettysburg. General Grant, in particular, had opposed the exchanges, not for any inhumane reason, but because he realized that a lack of manpower in the South would help bring an earlier peace. Confederate officials wrote kind letters to Mrs. Morgan, explaining the North's refusal to renew the practice of exchanging prisoners. Colonel Robert Ould, the Confederate agent of exchange, felt impelled to tell her the odds against her husband's returning to her in the foreseeable future:

"The Yankees themselves seem to be indisposed to make such exchanges, and I am very confident they would never agree to exchange your noble husband for any general of theirs we now have or may hereafter capture. They think him too great a prize and dread him too much in his liberated future. General Morgan's only hope is our refusal to make special exchanges, thus forcing, by pressure from the North itself, the Lincoln government to resume the cartel and release all officers. I hope we will stand firmly by that policy. I think we will win on it, and your husband be restored to you."

This crushing thought was too much for Mattie Morgan. It came just after news that her brother, Horace, had been wounded during Bragg's great victory at Chickamauga and Alice's departure for Augusta to nurse him. With no relative near at hand, and in the home of friends of only short duration, Mrs. Morgan became gravely ill, and her child was stillborn.

General Morgan knew nothing of this tragedy, locked in the grim penitentiary in Columbus, Ohio. He sensed something was wrong because he received no more letters from his wife, but he blamed it on the disorganization caused by the movement of the enemy forces in Tennessee or on the vindictiveness of his jailers.

The one thing that cheered him, as it did the other raiders, was the news of the victory at Chickamauga. It reached their cell block in whispered words from friendly guards or in the columns of smuggled newspapers. They believed that their invasion of the North and the forced detachment of so many cavalry regiments from Rosecrans' army had been a major contribution to Bragg's victory, and it went far to assuage the anguish of their almost hopeless outlook. When they obtained copies of papers that carried a full, accurate account of the battle, they took turns reading it aloud, while the others stood guard. Newspapers had been banned by Merion; no one wanted to be caught with one in his possession.

As one privilege after another was taken away from the imprisoned raiders, and as the usual time-killing pursuits of reading, letter writing, checkers and the devising of secret codes for communication grew tiresome, some of the men turned to poetry. Basil Duke composed some of the best, although no anthologist would have rated them highly. He smuggled one out to relatives, a satirical verse called "The Rebel's Dream," which revealed how earnestly each man was praying for the day when the dungeon doors would open. Morgan wrote a few, according to friends, but they are not to be found among his papers.

The General spent more of his time writing to authorities, demanding better treatment for his men and transfer to regular military prisons. It did no good; the old spirit of friendliness between men on both sides in the war seemed to be dying as the conflict dragged on and battle casualties mounted.

A Northern general, Neal Dow, was captured by the Confederates at Port Hudson; and Alabama newspapers, charging him with having helped slaves to escape, demanded he be tried in civil courts. The government at Richmond, adhering strictly to the law, refused this request and General Dow was held in a military prison and treated with dignity. The North assumed the Alabama request had been granted and cried out for steps to be taken to insure the Maine officer's safety. Abraham Lincoln told Stanton to do what he could, and Stanton shrugged the matter off on General Halleck. "Old Brains" decided that Morgan should be held as a hostage for Dow's safety and directed the Rebel raider to be kept in maximum security, not allowed to fraternize with his fellow prisoners, and that he have no visitors except by special permission of the Union War Department.

In a fit of pique Burnside had already established the last rule before going off to east Tennessee. General Morgan's mother, who was neither strong nor well, endured great hardships to make a trip from Lexington, Kentucky, to Columbus in order to visit her sons in prison. With obscene cruelty, the Morgan brothers were forbidden to talk to her.

"My mother and Mrs. Hoch Gibson arrived here today," Charlton Morgan wrote in his diary. "They were not permitted to talk with us; but we were marched out in the hall where Mother and Mrs. Gibson were permitted, as an especial favor, to peer through the grating at us."

It was just what they would have expected from Merion, but it seemed inordinately brutal for a man of Burnside's rank. Charlton made this clear when he added this note about the warden in his diary:

"May God some day smite him with His wrath and make him realize in the torturing of his mind his own inhumanity."

The tightening of restrictions, the lack of letters from home, and news that Rosecrans had recovered from defeat at Chickamauga and was driving Bragg back through northern Georgia all conspired to depress the prisoners. More than anything else, the incident of Mrs. Morgan's visit to the penitentiary made it evident that they could expect no help from outside the grim, gray walls.

Before this time, there was no evidence in their letters or entries in their journals that the Rebels had given serious thought to escape. Hopes of transfer or exchange had encouraged them. Now, however, their minds became obsessed with thoughts of getting out of the prison.

At least two of Morgan's lieutenants thought it would be possible to tunnel out beneath the walls. They were Captain Tom Hines, the scout, and Captain L. D. Hockersmith of the 10th Kentucky. Other plans based upon a sudden rush of the guards were considered but dropped in favor of the tunneling.

Colonel Duke later gave the major portion of credit to Hines. He said Hines found the impetus for the scheme while reading Hugo's *Les Misérables*. Hines noticed one salient feature of their prison that made the whole attempt feasible. This was the fact that regardless of the weather or temperature, the floor of his cell, which was on the ground tier of the block, always remained dry. He figured that if the cement floor had been laid upon the earth, moisture would seep upward and cause condensation on hot days. This made it apparent to him that there had to be an air space beneath it. To test his theory he entered into conversation with an old prison turnkey, named Hevay, who had been as kind to the prisoners as his superiors would permit, and who had a peculiar pride in the impregnable nature of the fortress in which he worked. Hines cleverly led the conversation around to the architectural design of the structure and learned his theory was correct. An air chamber extended beneath the lower range of cells.

Hines told his findings to General Morgan, who immediately held a secret conference with nearby officers and gave his approval to an attempt to escape by tunneling.

The men's depression changed to high hopes overnight. With almost boyish enthusiasm, they tackled the gigantic chore of cutting a way out of the cell block. The beginning was made in Tom Hines' cell on November 4. The iron bed was lifted up, and the 18-inch-thick cement floor was attacked with knives stolen from the mess hall. During the period when the men could circulate in the hall, different ones dug and chiseled at the hard cement while other prisoners took stations to serve as pickets and guard against detection.

November 4 was a good day to begin the work, because it was on that day that the authorities had decided to use military guards in the daytime and let Merion assume responsibility for the men at night. This change in routine led to a dispute as to which group of guards should be responsible for inspecting and cleaning the cells. Neither group liked the job, and finally each side left it to the other.

242

"Let the goddamn Rebels clean their own cells," said one official.

This was ideal for the raiders' plans. Captain Hines kept his cell scrupulously clean, so even a casual glance through the grated door would arouse no suspicion; he used an old carpetbag to hide the hole. Small bits of cement and dust were carefully secreted in the men's handkerchiefs and dumped into the stove's ash pan. Larger chunks were hidden in Hines' mattress. Under the cement was a three-tiered arch of brick masonry; once it was reached the work went faster, for the prisoners had only to pry the mortar out between a few bricks before the could knock others out of place with their boot heels. Finally, a hole large enough for a man to get through was opened up, and Captain Hockersmith jumped down to inspect the air chamber beneath. He found the four-foot-high passage extended under the entire range of ground floor cells. It came to an end under a stone foundation wall. Within a few days some of the large stones were cut loose and moved aside, revealing nothing more difficult than earth on the outer side.

Men took turns working in the dark tunnel. They had hoarded candles given them for reading after the gas lights in the corridor were turned off; some had been stolen from a supply room. They could see to work with these. Hines devised a signal code by which the men in the cells could warn the diggers of danger and tell them when to come out.

On several occasions the plotters were nearly detected. The narrowest escape occurred one day when Hockersmith was working in the tunnel, prying out the stones in the foundation wall. He failed to hear the signal and did not emerge for the line-up at dinner time. Morgan quickly noted his absence and dallied to repeat the signals. Hockersmith emerged, dusted himself off to remove telltale dust and was about to go to dinner when a guard came by, making a check of the cells.

"Where is Captain Hockersmith?" asked the turnkey.

"I left him lying on my bed a few minutes ago, complaining of not feeling well," General Morgan said with quick wit. "I had come back to look him up. Let's go to my cell and see if he is there."

Duped by Morgan's superior thinking, the guard climbed up to the second tier, and, in the interim, Hockersmith ducked into his own cell and covered himself with a blanket. The turnkey found him there and forgot the incident. To impress the authorities with Hockersmith's presence, Morgan had him stay in bed for two days, feigning illness.

More men were told the secret in order to divide the backbreaking work. This led to another close shave. A guard, Milo H. Scott, noted a man was missing and asked where he was. Again General Morgan out-witted the "enemy." He drew Scott aside, and gave Hines a chance to signal the missing man. Morgan pulled from his pocket a letter he had written to Secretary Stanton, and asked the guard for an opinion as to the appeal for better treatment. This fed Scott's ego, and he took time to read the message and to comment upon it at some length. By the time the duped turnkey had discussed it to his own satisfaction, the man in the tunnel had emerged. The danger was past.

The men were locked in their individual cells when each day drew to a close and they could no longer work in the tunnel. The evening hours were used to figure out problems and to lay plans for each detailed step in the ultimate break for freedom. One of the problems to be solved was the direction the tunnel should take after it penetrated the outer wall of the cell block. The prison yard was still to be considered; the outer wall of the institution would obviously have to be passed by climbing, since its foundation went down too deep, or rested on rock. Therefore, careful measurements had to be taken. Since such things could not be done openly, many schemes were hatched in the eager, fertile brains of the raiders.

Hines deliberately promoted a dispute with one of the guards with regards to the dimensions of the cells and the cell block. The gullible keeper fell into the trap, got a string and helped Hines measure the distances. The scout was such a good actor that he even retained the string after the argument was ended. Of course, this was invaluable since one of the major problems of the escape involved the method by which those who would make the attempt would enter the tunnel. The attempted escape would have to take place after dark, or the men would be seen climbing the wall; by then each man should have been locked in his cell. Therefore, it was decided that the floor of each cell would have to have the masonry removed from underneath it in advance. By use of the string the plotters could tell exactly where to start digging the floor supports from under each cubicle. This was done clandestinely until only a thin layer of cement remained between the cell and the air chamber beneath.

Another problem arose—how far under the yard should the tunnel go before it turned upward to the surface? If the prisoners had been able to see the yard, they could have answered their own question. All the cells, however, had blank walls at the rear, and the men could see only into the inner court, toward the women's wing of the prison. At one time, the raiders made an exploratory opening toward the surface and discovered they had come up beneath a mammoth pile of coal. Not knowing of the

244

coal pile's existence, or its size, they had no idea how far or in what direction to continue the tunnel.

Faced with this contretemps, General Morgan devised a way of learning what the yard looked like without arousing suspicion. He had once before been successful in deceiving Scott; he would try again. After warning Captain Sam Taylor, the most wiry, athletic man in the division, Morgan became embroiled in a heated argument with Scott. It dealt with the manner by which several convicts had escaped years before. They had climbed straight up the face of the iron balconies in front of the cell tiers and then made their way out of the block through the skylights. Scott fell for the lure. He stoutly maintained that there were not two men alive in North America who could duplicate this athletic feat. This gave Morgan his opening.

"Why," he said, "Captain Taylor, small as he is, can do it."

Finally Scott said Taylor could try it, and the Kentuckian, taking no chance of Scott's changing his mind, swung onto the first balcony. Duke said Taylor was "as active as a squirrel" when he later described it. The raider behaved like one, swinging himself from one level to another until he reached the topmost section of the iron cage. On the way down he took his time and seized the opportunity of peering out of a row of windows near the roof, from which place he could see the yard. Scott was so discomfited by losing his argument that he never dreamed Taylor had a clear picture as to the lay of the land between the cell block and the outer wall.

With this information, the raiders shifted the direction of the tunnel and began excavating. At first, they worked with stolen knives and bare hands, using an old wooden box to transport the earth back into the air chamber. But this was an extremely slow process. A bigger implement was needed. Each day increased the chances of discovery, and nerves were already wearing thin. Almost as if in answer to their prayers, someone noticed an old, rusty shovel lying in the yard through which the prisoners had to walk to reach the mess hall. The Rebels again talked it over, made their plans, and assigned roles for each participant who was to help steal the shovel. Captain Jake Bennett, who had been wearing a long, loose duster he had acquired on the raid, was the key figure in this scheme—or, rather, his coat was.

When all was ready, the men started for breakfast and got into a noisy argument which developed into a scuffle. Bennett was thrown to the ground when the conspirators reached the spot where the shovel lay. While his companions continued the horseplay, shoving one another around as a

245

screen for his actions, Bennett slipped the spade under his linen duster. He had a difficult time eating and sat like a ramrod to keep the shovel from protruding, but all went smoothly. and the Southerners had a tool to expedite the tunneling.

During the weeks while the underground work was going on, Morgan and his men discussed who should make the escape attempt. All the raiders were agreed on one point—the General himself had to be one, because they all hoped he could get away safely, find his way back to the Confederacy, and form a new cavalry division. One of his brigades had been left with Bragg when the raid started, and the prisoners felt certain that many men had escaped from Northern soil after the battle of Buffington Island.

Morgan was the most valuable of the raiders; everyone wanted him to escape. Some preferred not to make the attempt, and many, like Major Webber, were too ill or weak from disease or wounds to undertake such a strenuous adventure. There was no bickering and no disputing over who should go and who should stay. The scattered memoirs of those raiders who wrote of their wartime service mentioned no friction. When the war was long over, those who spoke of the great raid at veterans' encampments and services never indicated that there had been bad feelings. It was an eloquent tribute to their patriotism and to their affection for and faith in John Morgan.

When the discussions were ended, all agreed on the six men who with their chief would try for freedom. They were Hines, who had thought up the plan; Ralph Sheldon, who had led the last charge against the Union soldiers at Salineville; Sam Taylor, Hockersmith, Bennett and J. S. Magee.

Men who did not expect to escape helped those who did by working in the tunnel in shifts. Morgan's brother Calvin took upon himself the task of making a rope with which to scale the twenty-five-foot outer wall. The plotters tore some of their bed coverings into strips for this purpose, and Calvin braided them into a stout rope. A poker, filched from the stove in the corridor, was bent into the shape of a hook and fastened to one end of the rope as a grappling iron.

Morgan and the six who would accompany him had purchased civilian suits. Warden Merion forbade the wearing of uniforms, but had permitted the men to buy ordinary black suits when their prison garb wore out. By careful hoarding, each of the seven had kept one change of clothing in good condition. Morgan bribed a prison employee into getting him a timetable on the Little Miami Railroad. It was risky business, in that

246

the man might have taken the money and then betrayed the Rebel leader, but Morgan knew that the employee was greedy for extra money, and had promised him more in the future. There was some debate as to where the men should go when they had escaped from the penitentiary. Some thought it would be safer to head for Canada, since the authorities would be expecting them to go south. Morgan, however, was afraid it would take too long to reach the border, and that the alarm would be out for them long before they had reached Canadian soil. It was decided that the seven men should separate immediately after escaping and move in different directions. Morgan and Hines planned to travel together to Cincinnati and then try to get across the Ohio into Kentucky.

Men who had secreted money or who had received some surreptitiously in food, contributed it to a central fund for the seven who would leave. Finally, each one of the seven was provided with a knife fashioned from stolen table hardware, with which to defend himself from the dogs which roamed the prison yard at night as an added precaution against breakouts.

As the preparations went on with feverish, yet quiet, precision, the tunnel was completed to a point just inside the main wall. A thin crust of frozen earth was left intact and shored up from inside to prevent anyone from breaking through, falling into the opening and disclosing the tunnel.

Everything was ready, and the Confederates waited for a rainy night. They wanted this for two purposes; one to make the night's blackness even darker, the other to keep the dogs in their kennels, which were situated at the other end of the yard from the tunnel. Worst of all was the waiting. It seemed as though their luck could not hold forever, and nature, as if out of contrariness, sent one clear night after another. By now it was late November, and to all the other hazards was added the fear that it might snow. Then, their tracks would help pursuers to catch them before they got out of Columbus.

Then came bad news. The raiders learned, on November 26, that the Federal government had ordered a change in military commandants to take place at Columbus. They were experienced enough as soldiers to know what that meant. The new commandant would immediately call for an inspection of all facilities under his control, and the plans for the escape would be disclosed by even a casual search of the prison. Morgan told his men that they could not afford to wait, and so they decided to break out the next night, November 27.

The last day seemed never to end. The raiders tried to behave as usual in order to avert suspicion, but it was not easy to be nonchalant. Those who were leaving and those who were not were having a hard time to keep from showing their impatience. The General was the only one whose cell was on the top tier. He made arrangements with his bother Dick to swap places at the moment the signal came for prisoners to go to their cells at seven P.M.

During the late afternoon the prisoners on the ground floor scattered small bits of broken coal along the corridor, knowing that it would crackle under the boots of their guards. At the evening meal the seven men cleaned their plates and even ate portions slipped to them by their friends, who knew that it might be a long time before they would dare seek food on the outside.

Finally, when the meal was over, the men returned to the cell block. Scott tapped on the stove with his key and Dick Morgan hurried to the General's cell and threw himself on the cot, face to the wall. John Morgan darted into his brother's cubicle and sat down, with his back to the door. There was a strong resemblance between the two, and in the half-darkness the guards noticed nothing suspicious.

The escape had been planned for ten minutes after midnight. This would give all the men sufficient time to get a considerable distance away from the penitentiary before dawn. It would also give Morgan and Hines an opportunity to reach the railroad station and yet not subject them to a long wait during which they might be recognized. Captain Taylor's cell was considered the most advantageously located, so he was given General Morgan's watch. It would be his responsibility to make the initial descent into the air chamber and at the right moment signal his fellows.

Between seven o'clock, when they were locked in their cells, and ten minutes after midnight the raiders waited, and hoped that nothing would go wrong at the last minute.

"Sixty-odd men lay awake, silent and excited, with hearts beating louder and blood rushing faster through their veins than the approach of battle had ever occasioned," said Basil Duke in his memoirs. "Perhaps the coolest of all that number were the seven who were about to incur the risk."

Eight o'clock . . . nine o'clock . . . ten o'clock . . . eleven o'clock. . . . The hours seemed to crawl by. Each time the bell sounded for the hour, the guard made his rounds as the men held their breaths. He carried a lantern, and they could see the shadows move as he passed by each door. The sound of the coal crackling under his feet sounded extremely loud to

248

the raiders. They welcomed it, knowing that they could detect his approach if he decided to backtrack without his lantern. This night, however, the turnkey had no suspicions.

The prison bell clanged for midnight.

Morgan and his men heard the sound of footsteps on the brittle coal dust, saw the faint glow of the kerosene lantern approach and then disappear. For a few minutes they did not move. Captain Taylor then arose from his bunk, rolled some clothing into a dummy that he slipped under the top blanket, and stepped over to the spot where an opening had been cut under the floor. Stomping carefully with his boot heel, he broke through the thin cement and let himself down into the air chamber. He quickly tapped on the under sides of the thin sections of cement floor in the other six cells. Each man rolled a blanket into a crude dummy, placed it under the coverlet of the bed, broke through the floor, and joined Taylor in the chamber below.

Tom Hines delayed long enough to pin a note to his bed blanket—a note he had composed with great glee earlier that day. It was addressed to Warden Merion and bore this short message:

"Castle Merion, Cell No. 20. November 27, 1863—"Commencement, November 4, 1863; conclusion, November 24, 1863; number of hours for labor per day, five; tools, two small knives. *La patience est amère, mais son fruit est doux.* By order of my six honorable Confederates.

THOMAS H. HINES, CAPTAIN, C.S.A."

With Hockersmith, who had once been a stonemason and who had made most of the decisions about how to dig the tunnel, in the lead, the seven started for the far end of the escape route. Each wondered if the night would be bright and, also, if they would find the dogs prowling about the yard when they reached the surface.

Hockersmith felt his way to the end of the tunnel and then brought out a straightedge razor he had kept hidden through a dozen inspections, and cut through the sod above the wooden shoring. The raider behind him made a step with his hands, and Hockersmith vaulted easily out into the yard. The others followed, and to their great satisfaction at once noticed that it was raining—a cold drizzle that would hide most noises and which had kept the dogs inside their dry kennels. In the daytime, sentries patroled the walls, but by prison grapevine the raiders had learned that they were left unguarded at night. Even so, they felt certain that sentries must be within earshot. They waited apprehensively while Captain Taylor, the man who moved like a squirrel, tossed the hooked rope over the brick coping of the outer wall. It thudded against the bricks, and, involuntarily, the men started, since the noise seemed thunderous. Nothing happened and Taylor went up the rope, hand over hand. He secured the hook more carefully and the larger, heavier men followed him to the parapet.

They peered carefully over the edge. Almost underneath them stood three or four guards who were warming themselves beside a small fire. Only the patter of the rain and the crackling of the fire had prevented their hearing the bent poker strike the brick masonry. Morgan and his men crept stealthily along the wall, turned a corner, and breathed deeply for the first time since climbing the rope. As he prepared to help Taylor change the position of the grappling iron, General Morgan's fingers touched a thin rope stretched along the outer edge of the wall. His mind flicked back to boyhood days when he used to set snares for rabbits, and he realized it was a tripping device obviously connected with a bell in the warden's headquarters. Gently, the general cut the rope, released the tension slowly, and no sound was heard in the prison office. The raiders then removed the dirty outer garments which had protected their new suits, using a vacant sentry box as a dressing room. Taylor switched the grappling hook so that it caught under the lip of the inner brick coping, and the fugitives went down the rope, burning their hands on the rough, plaited strips of cloth.

Morgan only then remembered that he had left a valise on top of the wall. The agile Sam Taylor climbed the rope and retrieved it, while the others waited, with drawn knives, to see if any of the men at the fire intended to patrol in their direction. Taylor tried to shake the rope and hook loose, but it would not budge and they had to leave it. In the morning it was spotted, and an alarm was sounded two hours before their escape would have been detected otherwise, but it did not matter; by then they all had disappeared.

Morgan and his men shook hands and whispered words of cheer and good hope to one another. The General and Hines then walked toward the railroad station. Bennett and Hockersmith paired off and went one way; Taylor and Sheldon teamed up and went in the opposite direction; and Magee, whose home was in West Virginia, nearest of all, walked alone into the night. Morgan did not know Columbus, but he knew that the tracks of the Little Miami line passed near the penitentiary walls and, walking along the ties, he followed them to the station.

There were only a few people in the station. Hines bought the tickets

250

while Morgan kept his back to the waiting passengers, because his countenance was better known that his companion's. W. H. Eckert, the conductor, was on the platform suprintending the making up of the night express to Cincinnati. As he later described it, two men in dark clothing stepped up shortly after one o'clock and asked about the schedule. He thought they looked like cattle drovers.

"When will the Cincinnati train leave?" one of them asked.

"It is due to leave at one-twenty," the conductor answered, "but . . . other trains from which we make up have not arrived."

"Are you going to wait for them?"

"I am not," Eckert said firmly. "I shall leave just as soon as I can get my train ready."

Later, during an investigation of the escape, the conductor said that one of the men carried a fine gold watch, which a railroad man would be sure to notice. He believed that man was Morgan. Sam Taylor had returned his chief's watch after they had fled the prison.

Eckert was as good as his word. The train pulled out of the Columbus station only ten minutes late. As he entered the coach, Morgan wondered if provost guards would check the passengers for credentials, of which he had none.

He spotted a Union officer of field rank and sat beside him, thinking he would be less open to suspicion, and started a conversation with him to heighten the impression that they were friends. Fortunately, the authorities did not care who was riding the train. The General reached into his valise and brought out a flask of brandy which he offered to his seat companion. The Union officer's throat was dry, and he gladly accepted.

As he sipped the brandy, the train rolled past the dark walls of the penitentiary.

"That is the hotel at which Morgan stops, I believe," said the Yankee officer.

"Yes," answered the General, and tipped the flask to hide the smile on his face. "He has given us his fair share of trouble, and he will not be released. I drink to him. May he ever be as closely kept as he is now."

The train stopped at Xenia, and Hines jumped off to chat with the telegraph operator. He learned that no alarm for their apprehension had been sent as the telegrapher was not in the least excited. This reassured both fugitives. Near Dayton the train ground to a halt, and Morgan and Hines moved toward the vestibule, ready to flee into the night if it appeared that the cars had been stopped for searching. It was only an ob-

251

Corridor and cells in the Ohio State
Penitentiary, Columbus, Ohio. *A* —
Captain Hine's cell, No. 20.

From Century Magazine,
January 1891

The exterior of the penitentiary. *B*—Exit from
escape tunnel.

*Drawing by W. H. Shel-
ton from* Century Maga-
zine, *January 1891*

251A

Drawing by W. H. Shelton from Century Magazine, *January 1891*

The escape from the penitentiary.

struction on the track, and the two Southerners went forward and helped with the work of removal. They were delayed an hour, however, and the sky began to turn lighter.

Remembering the rope left dangling on the prison wall, Morgan and Hines realized that if they stayed on the train, due in the Cincinnati station at 7:05 A.M., word of their escape might have reached the city, and they would be caught. Therefore, when they reached the suburbs, Morgan stood up and pulled the bell cord, signaling the engineer to stop the train.

Since engineers of trains of the Civil War era had no control over the brakes of the coaches and could only apply those on the locomotive, trainmen had the duty of applying those on the platform of each coach, but only when the engineer signaled. On this morning the trainmen heard no whistle from the engine, but General Morgan moved to one platform and Hines to another and tightened the brakes with all their strength. This slackened the train's speed, and the two men jumped off. Morgan landed almost beside two or three Northern soldiers sitting on a pile of lumber near a small fire.

"Why in the hell are you jumping off the train?" asked one soldier.

"What in the devil is the use of a man going on to town when he lives out here," replied Morgan testily. "Besides, what matter is it to you?"

"Oh, nothing," admitted the soldier, turning back to the fire.

Morgan and Hines strode off together toward the Ohio, which the tracks paralleled for several miles. They finally found a boy who agreed for two dollars, to take them across to Kentucky in his skiff. Daylight had come when the skiff grounded on a sand bar at Newport. With only one of his raiders at his side, John Morgan had finally made his way back across the Ohio.

252

CHAPTER 18

End of the Ride

GOVERNOR TOD telegraphed Secretary Stanton that his prize prisoner had escaped.

"I regret to announce the escape of John Morgan and five others from the penitentiary last night," he said, even before the head count showed that the number was six and not five. "They dug out under the walls. I cannot charge anyone in the military service with negligence. The warden and his guard are alone to blame. Shall take all measures to recapture him. Have instructed the commander of this place to offer a reward of $1,000 which I hope you will approve."

Someone had seen the rope hanging from the wall, and shouted an alarm. A search had been initiated. Merion and his men were so excited that for a long time they did not notice that dummies were in beds where prisoners should have been. And it was more than an hour before they realized that it was the General, not his brother, who had left through the tunnel.

Guards, soldiers, officials and newspapermen swarmed through the cell block, prying into the air chamber, the cell exits, and the tunnel. In view of later charges of collusion, bribery and clandestine aid from Copperheads, a story carried by the Columbus *Dispatch* is perhaps the most important single evidence that the Southerners got out of prison by their own labor and that alone. The reporter told exactly what he saw—the holes in the cement floors, the tunnel, and the opening from the tunnel in the prison yard.

Many official inquires were ordered. Four went on within a few days of one another. When Governor Tod's investigation was completed, forty-eight hours after the escape, he admitted in a telegram to the War Department that the raiders had escaped prison with no outside assistance. Tod told Stanton:

"I cannot learn that any person had been permitted to see or correspond with Morgan, save only the necessary guards and attendants. Neither do I find any evidence that he received aid or assistance without or within in making his escape. A failure to examine and inspect the cells is the sole trouble. The civil authorities connected with the prison insist that was the duty of the military authorities, and the military authorities claim that it was the duty of the warden and his assistants. Both were certainly to blame, for between the two, no inspection was had for the last twenty days."

The prison official had said, "Let the goddamn Rebels clean out their own cells." They had taken him at his word and had cleaned Morgan and his men out of the penitentiary.

Following another inquiry, Tod expressed the feelings of all the authorities at the time. "I am glad to know," he wrote, ". . . that there is not the slightest evidence to be found of fraud or corruption on the part of the officers, either civil or military . . . nor on the part of any individual citizen without or within the prison."

In the years that followed, a few publicity-hungry old soldiers and former officials made charges that Morgan gained freedom only as a part of a vast mysterious conspiracy. The Copperheads and Knights of the Golden Circle were named as probable accomplices.

To a few doubting Thomases it just did not seem possible that seven men could want to fight again for the Confederacy so badly that they would be willing to work a month digging their way out of prison.

Now that he was back in Kentucky, John Morgan felt the worst was over. Although under Union domination, the state had almost as many Southern sympathizers as Northern, and the Rebel raider had friends in scores of towns. He found one of them in a house near the boat landing in Newport and sent a note upstairs by a servant, announcing who he was. He was then given a guide to the home of Dr. William Robinson Thomas, four miles from the river in Boone County. In the physician's home the fugitives had a good meal for the first time since riding through Ohio's small towns. It was also the first food of any kind since supper in the penitentiary the previous night. Dr. Thomas had several small daughters who stood in the doorway of the dining room, shifting from one foot to another, and watched their guests eat. They noticed the General's hands were chafed and raw and asked him the reason. He explained that he had burned his hands sliding down the rope to freedom, and they

254

could hardly contain themselves at the thought of such daring adventures. One of the older girls asked for locks of hair, and the two officers granted her wish, telling her she was a better barber than the last one who had cut their hair and beards.

Dr. Thomas' twelve-year-old son, proud as punch, guided the two fugitives along back roads until they reached the home of Henry Corwin in Union. It was Saturday night and the two men had had no sleep since Thursday night. The strain of the last few hours had exhausted their reserves. They fell into bed and slept until Sunday afternoon.

Corwin, a devoted Confederate, was too old to go to war but was eager to contribute all possible aid. He supplied Morgan and Hines with money, fresh horses, and his son to guide them along their way. The boy noticed that the General had no coat and that his civilian suit was no shield against the chilly night air. The best he could do was to offer a pair of blue jeans which the General pulled over his black trousers.

Riding by night, sleeping by day, Morgan and Hines traveled from Boone County through eastern Gallatin and into Owen County, thence into Henry and Shelby Counties. The General had friends in each of them.

"Everybody vied with each other as to who should show him the most attention—even to the negroes," said Duke of his brother-in-law, "and young ladies of refinement begged the honor of cooking his meals."

The two Confederate officers posed as drovers, at times as quartermaster department inspectors, and as government contractors buying beef for the Union armies. But their main reliance was placed upon the darkness, and the willingness of friends to run any risk to hide and feed them. On several occasions they barely escaped running into Federal patrols, but Morgan and Hines were no tyros at the art of scouting.

December 1, 1863, was a raw, blustery day. Their guide at the time did not know the roads or of any Southern sympathizers beyond the Kentucky River. The two men watched him turn back at the ferry and proceeded alone. Growing hungry and suffering from the bitter cold, they decided to risk seeking quarters in a house near the river. It was two A.M., not the best time to knock on a stranger's door, but they were desperate and decided to risk it. The house was far from any town, and they told themselves that if things went wrong they could fight their way out and get away before enemy patrols could be notified. They were not without trepidation, however, as they rapped on the door.

The owner, named Pollard, admitted them. Morgan said he was a hog

255

dealer and had been delayed on his way home. While he was talking to the farmer, his companion noticed a copy of the Cincinnati *Enquirer* on the Table. The *Enquirer* had strong Democratic leanings and Hines surmised this meant that Pollard was pro-Southern.

Bold headlines for that era announced that General Morgan and six other raiders had escaped from the Ohio penitentiary.

"I see that General Morgan, Hines and other officers have escaped the penitentiary," Hines remarked, trying to sound casual.

Their host turned up the wick in the kerosene lamp he was holding and peered more closely at the scout.

"Yes," he said, "and you are Captain Hines, are you not?"

Hines bowed courteously and turned to his friend.

"Permit me to introduce General Morgan."

Captain Hines' deduction, based on the editorial convictions of the newspaper, proved accurate. Pollard made them at home, let them sleep late, fed them and sent them on their way, after presenting them with cattle whips to abet their pose as drovers and beef buyers.

Two days later the two reached Bardstown, through which they had passed five months before when they rode at the head of a column of more than 2,000 raiders. Backtracking on their route from there, they finally reached the bank of the Cumberland River, nine miles downstream from Burkesville, where the raid had started.

Brigadier General Jeremiah Tilford Boyle, in command of the District of Western Kentucky, learned from Burnside that Morgan had escaped. Acting on his own initiative, and with no more information to support his actions than a strong belief that the Rebel leader would strike for the Confederate lines by the shortest route, Jerry Boyle broke up his mounted units and scattered them in small patrols guarding every pike and road.

Morgan and Hines could never have passed through this screen by day, but darkness gave them their chance. They repeatedly heard the sound of hoofbeats or the nickering of horses and pulled off the road into the woods or underbrush seconds before Union riders pounded by.

They emerged once from a cowpath into the back yard of a cabin. As they prepared to dismount and ask for food, a woman stepped out of the door and motioned them away. They rode back into the forest, unsure of their next move. While they talked it over, the woman came out again, beckoned them to come in, and when they did, told them a Federal cavalry patrol had just stopped at her cabin for water and had informed her they were looking for General Morgan.

256

After eating, the two men went on, crossing Obey's River near the mouth of Wolf Creek, and started climbing into the foothills of Overton County. Many of the residents were pro-Southern, and from them they learned of a group of thirty or forty Rebel soldiers who were also trying to make their way back to the Confederacy. To Morgan's surprise he found that some of the men were members of his own division, and together they struck out for the Tennessee River.

Fifteen miles below Kingston, at Bridge's Ferry, the little company of Southerners, only five of them mounted, reached the river. It was running full and angry, more than 150 yards from bank to bank. With an ax borrowed from a farmer, they started building a rough log raft, hurrying their labors when they learned that a Federal cavalry patrol was bivouacked only a couple of miles downstream. With so strong a current, it required three hours for the party to cross to the southern bank of the Tennessee. As the last men stepped from the flimsy raft, Federal pickets on the other side opened fire on them. Morgan wanted to stay with the dismounted men and share their chances, but Hines persuaded him to ride on and let the others scatter in the hills.

They went on—Morgan, Hines and the five enlisted men on horseback, climbing as they headed for the mountains. Later that day, Captain Hines persuaded a mountain woman to allow her ten-year-old son to ride with them as a guide. The boy had barely mounted behind Hines when Federal horsemen appeared. Hines pushed the boy off and galloped away from where Morgan and the others had waited. Then, allowing the enemy to draw near, he shouted, "Hurry up, Major, or the Rebels will escape."

For several miles they rode in silence, spurring their mounts on the steep hill road. Unfortunately for Hines, it had been raining that day, and a dry run that bisected the dirt road had been turned into a patch of mud. The Yankee Major noticed that there were no hoof marks in the silt and realized he had been duped. Drawing his pistol, the Major demanded Hines' name, and the Rebel officer admitted he had been traveling with Morgan.

Livid with rage, the Union officer ordered one of his troopers to remove the halter from his horse in order to make a noose and hang Hines from a tree limb by the side of the road. But Tom Hines pushed the noose away and asked the Major just one question:

"Suppose that was General Morgan, as you insist, and I have led you astray, as you insist, wouldn't I, being a member of his command, deserve to be hanged if I had not done what you charge me with?"

257

The Major looked at Hines for a long time. He then said, "Boys, he is right. Let him alone."

The Federal patrol took Hines to camp in Loudon, but before the night was over he escaped into the hills. Eventually he reached Virginia.

When his lieutenant led the Northern horsemen away from the mountain cabin, Morgan wasted no time in putting as many miles between his small party and the place of ambush as he could. Each hour found him deeper in the mountains, and as he neared the North Carolina line he was recognized by more and more friendly Southerners. On one occasion, a woman in a small crowd of people on the main street of a village spotted the tall figure, recognized the General, and started clapping her hands. "I know who it is," she cried out. Then realizing what she had done, she bit her tongue and turned away.

Following the Little Tennessee, Morgan and his five men rode east into the Great Smokies. Snow lay deep in the high passes, but while it bothered them it also prevented the movement of Northern patrols. When the Rebel leader crossed the divide, high up among the whitecapped domes, he knew he was safe. It had taken him almost a month from the time he slid down the rope at the penitentiary in Columbus, Ohio.

A few days later two small parties of mounted men rode out of the hills and into the little town of Franklin, North Carolina. One of them, led by Morgan, went straight to the only hotel, where the General registered. The other was led by Lieutenant Josiah Gathright, who had led forty-two men to safety from Twelve Mile Island on the Ohio. Lieutenant Gathright had joined a new brigade under Colonel Adam Johnson, after he, too, had made his way back to the Confederacy.

Gathright was en route to Decatur, Georgia, after a tour of picket duty in the mountains. With night coming on, the lieutenant decided to break his march in Franklin. Once his men were cared for, Gathright dropped into a cobbler's shop to have his boots repaired. He was lolling in a chair, soaking up the welcome heat thrown off by a big potbellied cannon stove when a resident of the town burst in and shouted: "General Morgan is in the hotel!"

"What General Morgan?" asked Gathright, who had every reason to wonder.

"Why General John Morgan, the great cavalryman."

Pausing only long enough to pull on his boots, Gathright hurried out of the cobbler's and into the hotel. In the lobby, surrounded by a bevy of excited ladies and a few employees, was John Morgan, "as chipper," said

258

Gathright later, "as if he had never been in a penitentiary in his life."

The next day the General went to Columbia, South Carolina, where he was lionized by thousands who thought he was still behind gray stone walls in Ohio. The reception pleased him but he was anxious to join his wife. He wired Mattie in Danville: "Just arrived. Will make no stop until I reach you."

But at each stop on the trip to Virginia, Morgan was forced to make an appearance before madly excited throngs of Southerners. News from the battlefields had been bad, and Confederate armies everywhere were retreating. Morgan's escape was like an antidote for the gloom that had settled over Dixie. People saw in the famous raider's exploit a small, but brilliant, ray of light gladdening their winter of discontent. Bragg was discredited, Knoxville had fallen to Burnside, pressure against Lee was mounting in Virginia and the war in the "West" had somehow reached deep into Georgia. The Southerners had every reason to welcome John Morgan.

The General went on to Danville, where he learned from Mattie that his child had been stillborn. He tried to console her, telling her he would go to Richmond to see the President and ask for a new command. The great raid had proved the value of operations behind enemy lines, and he told his wife he would again ride at the head of a column of horsemen, deep in enemy territory. As he spoke of the future, his nearness did what he had urged by letter from prison. The "roses" returned to Mattie Morgan's cheeks.

They would remain in Danville for only eight months, but they did not know this, and were happy together. John Hunt Morgan and his wife enjoyed Christmas dinner there with friends. With a bottle of wine that had escaped the exigencies of civil war they toasted the more than 2,000 men who had marched and fought with him on the long ride North.

Bibliography

Original Manuscripts

W. P. Cutler papers, Marietta College Library, Marietta, O.

Duke-Morgan papers, personal papers of the Morgan and Duke families, Southern Historical Collection, University of North Carolina, Chapel Hill, N. C.

Leeland Hathaway Recollections, Southern Historical Collection, University of North Carolina, Chapel Hill, N. C.

James McCreary papers, Duke University, Durham, N. C.

John Hunt Morgan papers, 1840-70, Southern Historical Collection, University of North Carolina, Chapel Hill, N. C.

James L. Norris papers, Southern Historical Collection, University of North Carolina, Chapel Hill, N. C.

Random papers, Ross County Museum, Chillicothe, O.

R. M. Stimson papers, Marietta College, Marietta, O.

C. A. Withers Reminiscences, Southern Historical Collection, University of North Carolina, Chapel Hill, N. C.

Other Original Sources

Official Records of the War of the Rebellion, Washington, D. C.

War Department Collection of Confederate Records, the National Archives, Washington, D. C.

Newspapers

Athens [O.] *Messenger*
Chillicothe [O.] *Scioto-Gazette*
Cincinnati *Gazette*
Lexington [Ky.] *Herald*
New Orleans *Picayune*
New York *Herald*

Pomeroy [O.] *Sentinel*
Pomeroy [O.] *Telegraph*
Richmond [Va.] *Sentinel*

PERIODICALS

Century Magazine
Confederate Veteran
Filson Club Historical Society Quarterly
Harpers Monthly
Harpers Weekly
Indiana Historical Society Publications
Indiana Magazine of History
Journal of the Illinois State Historical Society
Literary Digest
Ohio Archaeological and Historical Quarterly
Register of the Kentucky State Historical Society
Southern Bivouac
Random copies of the Vidette, published occasionally by Morgan's Brigade.

BOOKS

Annals of the War, Philadelphia Weekly Times, 1879
Appleton's Railway and Steam Navigation Guide, issues for 1863
Basso, Hamilton, *Beauregard, the Great Creole.* New York, 1933
Battles and Leaders of the Civil War, 4 vols. Ed. by R. U. Johnson and C. C. Buel, New York, 1887
von Bernhardi, Friedrich, *On War of Today.* 2 vols. New York, 1914
Berry, Thomas F., *Four Years with Morgan and Forrest.* Oklahoma City, 1914
Bowman, Heath, *Hoosier.* Indianapolis, 1941
Brockett, L. P., *The Camp, the Battlefield and the Hospital.* Philadelphia, 1866
Brown, Dee Alexander, *The Bold Cavaliers.* Philadelphia, 1959
Cable, George W., Ed. *Famous Adventures and Prison Escapes of the Civil War.* London
Carter, Howell, *A Cavalryman's Reminiscences of the Civil War.* New Orleans. n. d.
de Chambrun, Clara Longworth, *Cincinnati, Story of the Queen City.* New York, 1939
Chesnut, Mary Boykin, *A Diary from Dixie.* New York, 1905
Cleland, Hugh, *George Washington in the Ohio Valley.* Pittsburgh, 1955

Cox, Jacob Dolson, *Military Reminiscences of the Civil War*. 2 vols. New York, 1900

Crafts, W. A., *The Southern Rebellion*. Boston, 1867

Dictionary of American Biography. New York, 1934

Dowdey, Clifford, *The Land they Fought For*. Garden City, 1955

Duke, Basil, *Morgan's Cavalry*. New York, 1906

Evans, Clement A., Ed. *Confederate Military History*. Atlanta, 1899

Ford, Sally Rochester, *Raids and Romances of Morgan and his Men*. Mobile, 1864

Galbreath, Charles B., *History of Ohio*. Chicago, 1925

Hardesty's Historical and Geographical Encyclopedia. Chicago, 1883

Harlow, Alvin F., *The Serene Cincinnatians*. New York, 1950

Harris, Charles H., *The Harris History*. Athens, O., 1957

Henry, Ralph Selph, *The Story of the Confederacy*. Indianapolis, 1931

Herr, John K., and Wallace, Edward S., *The Story of the U.S. Cavalry*. Boston, 1953

Holland, Cecil Fletcher, *Morgan and his Raiders*. New York, 1942

Hopkins, Charles Edwin, *Ohio, the Beautiful and Historic*. Boston, 1931

Howe, Henry, *Historical Collections of Ohio*. Cincinnati, 1900

Illustrated Historical and Business Review of Meigs and Gallia Counties, Ohio. Private printing. Coshocton, O., 1891

Johnson, Adam R., *The Partisan Rangers of the Confederate States Army*. Louisville, 1904

Jones, Katharine M., *Heroines of Dixie*. Indianapolis, 1955

Kimmel, Stanley, *Mr. Davis's Richmond*. New York, 1958

Kirwan, A. D., *Johnny Green of the Orphan Brigade*. Lexington, Ky., 1956

Logan, India W. P., *Kelion Franklin Peddicord of Quirk's Scouts*. New York, 1908

Lonn, Ella, *Foreigners in the Confederacy*. Chapel Hill, 1940

Mathews, Joseph J., Ed. *The Capture and Wonderful Escape of General John Hunt Morgan*. Atlanta, 1947

McGiffin, Lee, *Swords, Stars and Bars*. New York, 1958

Moore, Frank, Ed. *Anecdotes, Poetry and Incidents of the War*. New York, 1882

————, Ed. *The Rebellion Record*. 12 vols. New York, 1862-71

Mosgrove, George Dallas, *Kentucky Cavaliers in Dixie*. Ed. by Bell Irvin Wiley. Jackson, Tenn., 1957

Ohio Adjutant General's Report for 1863

de Paris, Compte, *History of the Civil War in America*. 4 vols. Philadelphia, 1888

Plum, William R., *Military Telegraph of the Civil War*. 2 vols. Chicago, 1882

Pollard, Edward A., *The Lost Cause*. New York, 1868

262

Poore, B. P., *Life and Public Services of Ambrose E. Burnside.* Providence, 1882

Post, Lydia Minturn, Ed. *Soldiers' Letters, from Camp, Battlefield and Prison.* New York, 1865

Reid, Whitelaw, *Ohio in the War.* Columbus, O., 1893

Report of the Ohio Commission on Morgan Raid Claims. Dec. 15, 1864

Ridley, Bromfield L., *Battles and Sketches of the Army of Tennessee.* Mexico, Mo., 1906

Roberts, Carl H., and Cummins, Paul R., *Ohio, the Geography, History and Government.* Columbus, O., 1956

Robertson, Charles, *History of Morgan County, Ohio.* Chicago, 1886

Robertson, John, Ed. *Michigan in the War.* Lansing, 1882

Senour, Fauntleroy, *Morgan and his Captors.* Cincinnati, 1865

Shaler, N. S., *Kentucky, a Pioneer Commonwealth.* Boston, 1884

Simmons, Flora E., *A Complete Account of the John Hunt Morgan Raid.* Louisville, 1863

Simms, J. H., *Last Night and Last Day of John Morgan's Raid.* East Liverpool, O., 1917

Sketches of War History. (Papers prepared for the Ohio Commandery, Military Order of the Loyal Legion of the U.S.) Cincinnati, 1903

Smith, Sydney K., *Life, Army Record and Public Service of D. Howard Smith.* Louisville, 1890

Snow, William Parker. *Southern Generals.* New York, 1866

Stern, Philip Van Doren, *Secret Missions of the Civil War.* Chicago, 1959

Stone, Henry Lane, *Morgan's Men; a Narrative of Personal Experience.* Louisville, 1919

Storke, Elliot G., and Brockett, L. P., *Complete History of the Great American Rebellion.* Auburn, N. Y., 1865

Surby, Richard W., *Two Great Raids.* Washington, 1897

Swiggett, Howard, *The Rebel Raider.* Indianapolis, 1934

Tarrant, Eastham, *Wild Riders of the First Kentucky Cavalry.* Louisville, 1894

Terrell, W. H. H., *Report of the Adjutant General of the State of Indiana.* Indianapolis, 1869

Van Horne, Thomas B., *History of the Army of the Cumberland.* Cincinnati, 1885

Victor, Orville J., *History of the Southern Rebellion.* 4 vols. New York, 1861-8

Lew Wallace; an Autobiography. 2 vols. New York, 1906

Wolff, William G., *Stories of Guernsey County, Ohio.* Cambridge, O., 1943

Wood, C. J., *Reminiscences of the War.* n. p. 1880

Woodbury, Augustus, *General Burnside and the Ninth Army Corps.* Providence, 1867

WPA Guide to Ohio.

WPA Guide to West Virginia.
Yeary, Mamie, *Reminiscences of the Boys in Gray.* Dallas, 1912
Young, Bennett H., *Confederate Wizards of the Saddle.* Boston, 1914
Younger, Edward, Ed. *Inside the Confederate Government—the Diary of Robert Garlick Hill Kean.* New York, 1957

Index

Because of the very nature of this book, no attempt is made to index the activities of John Hunt Morgan. For the same reason, the Ohio River is not included.

Little Hocking River, 196
Little Miami Railroad, 131, 199, 234, 246, 250
Little Tennessee River, 258
Lockland, O., 130
Locust Grove, O., 137-138, 141
Logan, O., 116, 127, 197
Londonderry, O., 211
Long Bottom, O., 159, 167, 185, 190
Lordsville, O., 211
Loudon, Ky., 206, 257
Louisville, Ky., 46-48, 50, 53, 56-57, 61, 68, 75, 80, 100-101, 110, 121-122, 125
Louisville and Nashville Railroad, 159
Love, John, 88-91, 206
Lyman, George, 72
Lyon, G. W., 66, 67
Lyons, J. M., 193, 216

McArthur, O., 194
McCaslin, C. H., 96
McClain, John, 119, 126
McClove, Stuart, 218
McCreary, James, 34, 119, 150, 163, 236-237
McDowell, Malcolm, 121
McMullen, Elizabeth, 208
Madison, Ind., 85-87, 90, 93, 106
Magee, J. S., 246, 250
Manchester Ridge, 112
Manson, Mahlon D., 86
Marietta, O., 143, 149, 162, 165, 190, 195
Marietta and Cincinnati Railroad, 139, 143, 145, 183, 195
Marrowbone, Ky., 25, 27-28
Marrowbone Creek, 26-27
Mauckport, Ind., 63, 66-67
Mayfield, F. F., 94
Meloy, Mrs. Daniel, 197
Merriwether, Clay, 48, 53, 61-62, 66
Miami River, 117, 124, 126
Miamitown, O., 122-123, 128
Middleport, O., 151, 153-154, 191-192, 206

Milan, Ind., 108, 110, 112
Milhaus, Victor, 100
Miller, James, 142
Millertown, O., 197
Mingo Junction, O., 199, 205, 215, 228
Mitchell, Ind., 80, 88, 91
Monday Creek, 197
Monroeville, O., 219
Moody, Granville, 121
Moore, D. H., 152
Moore, Orlando H., 32-35, 39
Moore, T. D., 23
Moorefield, O., 211
Moose, the, 173, 176, 182, 186-187
Montgomery, O., 131-132
Morgan, Calvin, 42, 158, 232, 236, 246
Morgan, Charlton, 232, 237-238, 241
Morgan, Key, 239
Morgan, Martha Ready, 114-115, 208, 220, 239-240, 259
Morgan, Richard C., 29-31, 38, 71, 137-138, 177-178, 232, 234, 236, 248
Morgan, Tom, 38, 42
Morgansville, Ky., 193
Morristown, O., 211-212
Morton, Oliver P., 74-77, 87-88, 91, 98, 108, 111, 118, 120
Mosgrove, George Dallas, 27, 156
Moss, Anna, 210
Mount Auburn, O., 124
Munfordville, Ky., 56
Muskingum River, 144, 197-198, 200-202, 205
Murphy, Tom, 140

Nance, George, 67
Nashville, Tenn., 50
Neff, George Washington, 121, 132
Nelsonville, O., 196, 198
New Albany, Ind., 63, 85
New Alsace, 115-116, 127
New Baltimore, O., 123-124, 126
New Burlington, O., 124, 126
New Haven, O., 123

270

271